Short Stories from Dickens (annotated)

by Charles Dickens

CW01426461

Contents:

A Message from the Sea

by Charles Dickens

CHAPTER I

THE VILLAGE

"And a mighty sing'lar and pretty place it is, as ever I saw in all the days of my life!" said Captain Jorgan, looking up at it.

Captain Jorgan had to look high to look at it, for the village was built sheer up the face of a steep and lofty cliff. There was no road in it, there was no wheeled vehicle in it, there was not a level yard in it. From the sea-beach to the cliff-top two irregular rows of white houses, placed opposite to one another, and twisting here and there, and there and here, rose, like the sides of a long succession of stages of crooked ladders, and you climbed up the village or climbed down the village by the staves between, some six feet wide or so, and made of sharp irregular stones. The old pack- saddle, long laid aside in most parts of England as one of the appendages of its infancy, flourished here intact. Strings of pack- horses and pack-donkeys toiled slowly up the staves of the ladders, bearing fish, and coal, and such other cargo as was unshipping at the pier from the dancing fleet of village boats, and from two or three little coasting traders. As the beasts of burden ascended laden, or descended light, they got so lost at intervals in the floating clouds of village smoke, that they seemed to dive down some of the village chimneys, and come to the surface again far off, high above others. No two houses in the village were alike, in chimney, size, shape, door, window, gable, roof-tree, anything. The sides of the ladders were musical with water, running clear and bright. The staves were musical with the clattering feet of the pack-horses and pack-donkeys, and the voices of the fishermen urging them up, mingled with the voices of the fishermen's wives and their many children. The pier was musical with the wash of the sea, the creaking of capstans and windlasses, and the airy fluttering of little vanes and sails. The rough, sea-bleached boulders of which the pier was made, and the whiter boulders of the shore, were brown with drying nets. The red-brown cliffs, richly wooded to their extremest verge, had their softened and beautiful forms reflected in the bluest water, under the clear North Devonshire sky of a November day without a cloud. The village itself was so steeped in autumnal foliage, from the houses lying on the pier to the topmost round of the topmost ladder, that one might have fancied it was out a bird's- nesting, and was (as indeed it was) a wonderful climber. And mentioning birds, the place was not without some music from them too; for the rook was very busy on the higher levels, and the gull with his flapping wings was fishing in the bay, and the lusty little robin was hopping among the great stone blocks and iron rings of the breakwater, fearless in the faith of his ancestors, and the Children in the Wood.

Thus it came to pass that Captain Jorgan, sitting balancing himself on the pier-wall, struck his leg with his open hand, as some men do when they are pleased--and as he always did when he was pleased--and said, -

"A mighty sing'lar and pretty place it is, as ever I saw in all the days of my life!"

Captain Jorgan had not been through the village, but had come down to the pier by a winding side-road, to have a preliminary look at it from the level of his own natural element. He had seen many things and places, and had stowed them all away in a shrewd intellect and a vigorous memory. He was an American born, was Captain Jorgan,--a New-Englander,--but he was a citizen of the world, and a combination of most of the best qualities of most of its best countries.

For Captain Jorgan to sit anywhere in his long-skirted blue coat and blue trousers, without holding converse with everybody within speaking distance, was a sheer impossibility. So the captain fell to talking with the fishermen, and to asking them knowing questions about the fishery, and the tides, and the currents, and the race of water off that point yonder, and what you kept in your eye, and got into a line with what else when you ran into the little harbour; and other nautical profundities. Among the men who exchanged ideas with the captain was a young fellow, who exactly hit his fancy,--a young fisherman of two or three and twenty, in the rough sea-dress of his craft, with a brown face, dark curling hair, and bright, modest eyes under his Sou'wester hat, and with a frank, but simple and retiring manner, which the captain found uncommonly taking. "I'd bet a thousand dollars," said the captain to himself, "that your father was an honest man!"

"Might you be married now?" asked the captain, when he had had some talk with this new acquaintance.

"Not yet."

"Going to be?" said the captain.

"I hope so."

The captain's keen glance followed the slightest possible turn of the dark eye, and the slightest possible tilt of the Sou'wester hat. The captain then slapped both his legs, and said to himself, -

"Never knew such a good thing in all my life! There's his sweetheart looking over the wall!"

There was a very pretty girl looking over the wall, from a little platform of cottage, vine, and fuchsia; and she certainly dig not look as if the presence of this young fisherman in the landscape made it any the less sunny and hopeful for her.

Captain Jorgan, having doubled himself up to laugh with that hearty good-nature which is quite exultant in the innocent happiness of other people, had undoubted himself, and was going to start a new subject, when there appeared coming down the lower ladders of stones, a man whom he hailed as "Tom Pettifer, Ho!" Tom Pettifer, Ho, responded with alacrity, and in speedy course descended on the pier.

"Afraid of a sun-stroke in England in November, Tom, that you wear your tropical hat, strongly paid outside and paper-lined inside, here?" said the captain, eyeing it.

"It's as well to be on the safe side, sir," replied Tom.

"Safe side!" repeated the captain, laughing. "You'd guard against a sun-stroke, with that old hat, in an Ice Pack. Wa'al! What have you made out at the Post-office?"

"It is the Post-office, sir."

"What's the Post-office?" said the captain.

"The name, sir. The name keeps the Post-office."

"A coincidence!" said the captain. "A lucky bit! Show me where it is. Good-bye, shipmates, for the present! I shall come and have another look at you, afore I leave, this afternoon."

This was addressed to all there, but especially the young fisherman; so all there acknowledged it, but especially the young fisherman. "He's a sailor!" said one to another, as they looked after the captain moving away. That he was; and so outspeaking was the sailor in him, that although his dress had nothing nautical about it, with the single exception of its colour, but was a suit of a shore-going shape and form, too long in the sleeves and too short in the legs, and too unaccommodating everywhere, terminating earthward in a pair of Wellington boots, and surmounted by a tall, stiff hat, which no mortal could have worn at sea in any wind under heaven; nevertheless, a glimpse of his sagacious, weather-beaten face, or his strong, brown hand, would have established the captain's calling. Whereas Mr. Pettifer--a man of a certain plump neatness, with a curly whisker, and elaborately nautical in a jacket, and shoes, and all things correspondent--looked no more like a seaman, beside Captain Jorgan, than he looked like a sea-serpent.

The two climbed high up the village,--which had the most arbitrary turns and twists in it, so that the cobbler's house came dead across the ladder, and to have held a reasonable course, you must have gone through his house, and through him too, as he sat at his work between two little windows,--with one eye microscopically on the geological formation of that part of Devonshire, and the other telescopically on the open sea,--the two climbed high up the village, and stopped before a quaint little house, on which was painted, "MRS. RAYBROCK, DRAPER;" and also "POST-OFFICE." Before it, ran a rill of murmuring water, and access to it was gained by a little plank-bridge.

"Here's the name," said Captain Jorgan, "sure enough. You can come in if you like, Tom."

The captain opened the door, and passed into an odd little shop, about six feet high, with a great variety of beams and bumps in the ceiling, and, besides the principal window giving on the ladder of stones, a purblind little window of a single pane of glass, peeping out of an abutting corner at the sun-lighted ocean, and winking at its brightness.

"How do you do, ma'am?" said the captain. "I am very glad to see you. I have come a long way to see you."

"Have you, sir? Then I am sure I am very glad to see you, though I don't know you from Adam."

Thus a comely elderly woman, short of stature, plump of form, sparkling and dark of eye, who, perfectly clean and neat herself, stood in the midst of her perfectly clean and neat arrangements, and surveyed Captain Jorgan with smiling curiosity. "Ah! but you are a sailor, sir," she added, almost immediately, and with a slight movement of her hands, that was not very unlike wringing them; "then you are heartily welcome."

"Thank'ee, ma'am," said the captain, "I don't know what it is, I am sure; that brings out the salt in me, but everybody seems to see it on the crown of my hat and the collar of my coat. Yes, ma'am, I am in that way of life."

"And the other gentleman, too," said Mrs. Raybrock.

"Well now, ma'am," said the captain, glancing shrewdly at the other gentleman, "you are that nigh right, that he goes to sea,--if that makes him a sailor. This is my steward, ma'am, Tom Pettifer; he's been a'most all trades you could name, in the course of his life,-- would have bought all your chairs and tables once, if you had wished to sell 'em,--but now he's my steward. My name's Jorgan, and I'm a ship-owner, and I sail my own and my partners' ships, and have done so this five-and-twenty year. According to custom I am called Captain Jorgan, but I am no more a captain, bless your heart, than you are."

"Perhaps you'll come into my parlour, sir, and take a chair?" said Mrs. Raybrock.

"Ex-actly what I was going to propose myself, ma'am. After you."

Thus replying, and enjoining Tom to give an eye to the shop, Captain Jorgan followed Mrs. Raybrock into the little, low back-room,-- decorated with divers plants in pots, tea-trays, old china teapots, and punch-bowls,--which was at once the private sitting-room of the Raybrock family and the inner cabinet of the post-office of the village of Steepways.

"Now, ma'am," said the captain, "it don't signify a cent to you where I was born, except--" But here the shadow of some one entering fell upon the captain's figure, and he broke off to double himself up, slap both his legs, and ejaculate, "Never knew such a thing in all my life! Here he is again! How are you?"

These words referred to the young fellow who had so taken Captain Jorgan's fancy down at the pier. To make it all quite complete he came in accompanied by the sweetheart whom the captain had detected looking over the wall. A prettier sweetheart the sun could not have shone upon that shining day. As she stood before the captain, with her rosy lips just parted in surprise, her brown eyes a little wider open than was usual from the same cause, and her breathing a little quickened by the ascent (and possibly by some mysterious hurry and flurry at the parlour door, in which the captain had observed her face to be for a moment totally eclipsed by the Sou'wester hat), she looked so charming, that the captain felt himself under a moral obligation to slap both his legs again. She was very simply dressed, with no other ornament than an autumnal flower in her bosom. She wore neither hat nor bonnet, but merely a scarf or kerchief, folded squarely back over the head, to keep the sun off,-- according to a fashion that may be sometimes seen in the more genial parts of England as well as of Italy, and which is probably the first fashion of head-dress that came into the world when grasses and leaves went out.

"In my country," said the captain, rising to give her his chair, and dexterously sliding it close to another chair on which the young fisherman must necessarily establish himself,--"in my country we should call Devonshire beauty first-rate!"

Whenever a frank manner is offensive, it is because it is strained or feigned;

for there may be quite as much intolerable affectation in plainness as in mincing nicety. All that the captain said and did was honestly according to his nature; and his nature was open nature and good nature; therefore, when he paid this little compliment, and expressed with a sparkle or two of his knowing eye, "I see how it is, and nothing could be better," he had established a delicate confidence on that subject with the family.

"I was saying to your worthy mother," said the captain to the young man, after again introducing himself by name and occupation,--"I was saying to your mother (and you're very like her) that it didn't signify where I was born, except that I was raised on question- asking ground, where the babies as soon as ever they come into the world, inquire of their mothers, 'Neow, how old may you be, and wa'at air you a goin' to name me?'--which is a fact." Here he slapped his leg. "Such being the case, I may be excused for asking you if your name's Alfred?"

"Yes, sir, my name is Alfred," returned the young man.

"I am not a conjurer," pursued the captain, "and don't think me so, or I shall right soon undeceive you. Likewise don't think, if you please, though I do come from that country of the babies, that I am asking questions for question-asking's sake, for I am not. Somebody belonging to you went to sea?"

"My elder brother, Hugh," returned the young man. He said it in an altered and lower voice, and glanced at his mother, who raised her hands hurriedly, and put them together across her black gown, and looked eagerly at the visitor.

"No! For God's sake, don't think that!" said the captain, in a solemn way; "I bring no good tidings of him."

There was a silence, and the mother turned her face to the fire and put her hand between it and her eyes. The young fisherman slightly motioned toward the window, and the captain, looking in that direction, saw a young widow, sitting at a neighbouring window across a little garden, engaged in needlework, with a young child sleeping on her bosom. The silence continued until the captain asked of Alfred, -

"How long is it since it happened?"

"He shipped for his last voyage better than three years ago."

"Ship struck upon some reef or rock, as I take it," said the captain, "and all hands lost?"

"Yes."

"Wa'al!" said the captain, after a shorter silence, "Here I sit who may come to the same end, like enough. He holds the seas in the hollow of His hand. We must all strike somewhere and go down. Our comfort, then, for ourselves and one another is to have done our duty. I'd wager your brother did his!"

"He did!" answered the young fisherman. "If ever man strove faithfully on all occasions to do his duty, my brother did. My brother was not a quick man (anything but that), but he was a faithful, true, and just man. We were the sons of only a small tradesman in this county, sir; yet our father was as watchful of his good name as if he had been a king."

"A precious sight more so, I hope--bearing in mind the general run of that class of crittur," said the captain. "But I interrupt."

"My brother considered that our father left the good name to us, to keep clear and true."

"Your brother considered right," said the captain; "and you couldn't take care of a better legacy. But again I interrupt."

"No; for I have nothing more to say. We know that Hugh lived well for the good name, and we feel certain that he died well for the good name. And now it has come into my keeping. And that's all."

"Well spoken!" cried the captain. "Well spoken, young man! Concerning the manner of your brother's death,"--by this time the captain had released the hand he had shaken, and sat with his own broad, brown hands spread out on his knees, and spoke aside,-- "concerning the manner of your brother's death, it may be that I have some information to give you; though it may not be, for I am far from sure. Can we have a little talk alone?"

The young man rose; but not before the captain's quick eye had noticed that, on the pretty sweetheart's turning to the window to greet the young widow with a nod and a wave of the hand, the young widow had held up to her the needlework on which she was engaged, with a patient and pleasant smile. So the captain said, being on his legs, -

"What might she be making now?"

"What is Margaret making, Kitty?" asked the young fisherman,--with one of his arms apparently mislaid somewhere.

As Kitty only blushed in reply, the captain doubled himself up as far as he could, standing, and said, with a slap of his leg, -

"In my country we should call it wedding-clothes. Fact! We should, I do assure you."

But it seemed to strike the captain in another light too; for his laugh was not a long one, and he added, in quite a gentle tone, -

"And it's very pretty, my dear, to see her--poor young thing, with her fatherless child upon her bosom--giving up her thoughts to your home and your happiness. It's very pretty, my dear, and it's very good. May your marriage be more prosperous than hers, and be a comfort to her too. May the blessed sun see you all happy together, in possession of the good name, long after I have done ploughing the great salt field that is never sown!"

Kitty answered very earnestly, "O! Thank you, sir, with all my heart!" And, in her loving little way, kissed her hand to him, and possibly by implication to the young fisherman, too, as the latter held the parlour-door open for the captain to pass out.

CHAPTER II

THE MONEY

"The stairs are very narrow, sir," said Alfred Raybrock to Captain Jorgan.

"Like my cabin-stairs," returned the captain, "on many a voyage."

"And they are rather inconvenient for the head."

"If my head can't take care of itself by this time, after all the knocking about the world it has had," replied the captain, as unconcernedly as if he had no connection with it, "it's not worth looking after."

Thus they came into the young fisherman's bedroom, which was as perfectly neat and clean as the shop and parlour below; though it was but a little place, with a sliding window, and a phrenological ceiling expressive of all the peculiarities of the house-roof. Here the captain sat down on the foot of the bed, and glancing at a dreadful libel on Kitty which ornamented the wall,--the production of some wandering limner, whom the captain secretly admired as having studied portraiture from the figure-heads of ships,--motioned to the young man to take the rush-chair on the other side of the small round table. That done, the captain put his hand in the deep breast-pocket of his long-skirted blue coat, and took out of it a strong square case-bottle,--not a large bottle, but such as may be seen in any ordinary ship's medicine-chest. Setting this bottle on the table without removing his hand from it, Captain Jorgan then spake as follows:-

"In my last voyage homeward-bound," said the captain, "and that's the voyage off of which I now come straight, I encountered such weather off the Horn as is not very often met with, even there. I have rounded that stormy Cape pretty often, and I believe I first beat about there in the identical storms that blew the Devil's horns and tail off, and led to the horns being worked up into tooth-picks for the plantation overseers in my country, who may be seen (if you travel down South, or away West, fur enough) picking their teeth with 'em, while the whips, made of the tail, flog hard. In this last voyage, homeward-bound for Liverpool from South America, I say to you, my young friend, it blew. Whole measures! No half measures, nor making believe to blow; it blew! Now I warn't blown clean out of the water into the sky,--though I expected to be even that,--but I was blown clean out of my course; and when at last it fell calm, it fell dead calm, and a strong current set one way, day and night, night and day, and I drifted--drifted--drifted--out of all the ordinary tracks and courses of ships, and drifted yet, and yet drifted. It behooves a man who takes charge of fellow-critturs' lives, never to rest from making himself master of his calling. I never did rest, and consequently I knew pretty well ('specially looking over the side in the dead calm of that strong current) what dangers to expect, and what precautions to take against 'em. In short, we were driving head on to an island. There was no island in the chart, and, therefore, you may say it was ill-manners in the island to be there; I don't dispute its bad breeding, but there it was. Thanks be to Heaven, I was as ready for the island as the island was ready for me. I made it out myself from the masthead, and I got enough way upon her in good time to keep her off. I ordered a boat to be lowered and manned, and went in that boat myself to explore the island. There was a reef outside it, and, floating in a corner of the smooth water within the reef, was a heap of sea-weed, and entangled in that sea-weed was this bottle."

Here the captain took his hand from the bottle for a moment, that the young fisherman might direct a wondering glance at it; and then replaced his band and went on:-

"If ever you come--or even if ever you don't come--to a desert place, use you your eyes and your spy-glass well; for the smallest thing you see may prove of use to you; and may have some information or some warning in it. That's the principle on which I came to see this bottle. I picked up the bottle and ran the boat alongside the island, and made fast and went ashore armed, with a part of my boat's crew. We found that every scrap of vegetation on the island (I give it you as my opinion, but scant and scrubby at the best of times) had been consumed by fire. As we were making our way, cautiously and toilsomely, over the pulverised embers, one of my people sank into the earth breast-high. He turned pale, and 'Haul me out smart, shipmates,' says he, 'for my feet are among bones.' We soon got him on his legs again, and then we dug up the spot, and we found that the man was right, and that his feet had been among bones. More than that, they were human bones; though whether the remains of one man, or of two or three men, what with calcination and ashes, and what with a poor practical knowledge of anatomy, I can't undertake to say. We examined the whole island and made out nothing else, save and except that, from its opposite side, I sighted a considerable tract of land, which land I was able to identify, and according to the bearings of which (not to trouble you with my log) I took a fresh departure. When I got aboard again I opened the bottle, which was oilskin-covered as you see, and glass- stoppered as you see. Inside of it," pursued the captain, suiting his action to his words, "I found this little crumpled, folded paper, just as you see. Outside of it was written, as you see, these words: 'Whoever finds this, is solemnly entreated by the dead to convey it unread to Alfred Raybrock, Steepways, North Devon, England.' A sacred charge," said the captain, concluding his narrative, "and, Alfred Raybrock, there it is!"

"This is my poor brother's writing!"

"I suppose so," said Captain Jorgan. "I'll take a look out of this little window while you read it."

"Pray no, sir! I should be hurt. My brother couldn't know it would fall into such hands as yours."

The captain sat down again on the foot of the bed, and the young man opened the folded paper with a trembling hand, and spread it on the table. The ragged paper, evidently creased and torn both before and after being written on, was much blotted and stained, and the ink had faded and run, and many words were wanting. What the captain and the young fisherman made out together, after much re-reading and much humouring of the folds of the paper, is given on the next page.

The young fisherman had become more and more agitated, as the writing had become clearer to him. He now left it lying before the captain, over whose shoulder he had been reading it, and dropping into his former seat, leaned forward on the table and laid his face in his hands.

"What, man," urged the captain, "don't give in! Be up and doing like a man!"

"It is selfish, I know,--but doing what, doing what?" cried the young fisherman, in complete despair, and stamping his sea-boot on the ground.

"Doing what?" returned the captain. "Something! I'd go down to the little breakwater below yonder, and take a wrench at one of the salt-rusted iron rings there, and either wrench it up by the roots or wrench my teeth out of my head, sooner than I'd do nothing. Nothing!" ejaculated the captain. "Any fool or fainting heart can do that, and nothing can come of nothing,--which was pretended to be found out, I believe, by one of them Latin critters," said the captain with the deepest disdain; "as if Adam hadn't found it out, afore ever he so much as named the beasts!"

Yet the captain saw, in spite of his bold words, that there was some greater reason than he yet understood for the young man's distress. And he eyed him with a sympathising curiosity.

"Come, come!" continued the captain, "Speak out. What is it, boy!"

"You have seen how beautiful she is, sir," said the young man, looking up for the moment, with a flushed face and rumpled hair.

"Did any man ever say she warn't beautiful?" retorted the captain. "If so, go and lick him."

The young man laughed fretfully in spite of himself, and said -

"It's not that, it's not that."

"Wa'al, then, what is it?" said the captain in a more soothing tone.

The young fisherman mournfully composed himself to tell the captain what it was, and began: "We were to have been married next Monday week--"

"Were to have been!" interrupted Captain Jorgan. "And are to be? Hey?"

Young Raybrock shook his head, and traced out with his fore-finger the words, "poor father's five hundred pounds," in the written paper.

"Go along," said the captain. "Five hundred pounds? Yes?"

"That sum of money," pursued the young fisherman, entering with the greatest earnestness on his demonstration, while the captain eyed him with equal earnestness, "was all my late father possessed. When he died, he owed no man more than he left means to pay, but he had been able to lay by only five hundred pounds."

"Five hundred pounds," repeated the captain. "Yes?"

"In his lifetime, years before, he had expressly laid the money aside to leave to my mother,--like to settle upon her, if I make myself understood."

"Yes?"

"He had risked it once--my father put down in writing at that time, respecting the money--and was resolved never to risk it again."

"Not a spectator," said the captain. "My country wouldn't have suited him. Yes?"

"My mother has never touched the money till now. And now it was to have been laid out, this very next week, in buying me a handsome share in our neighbouring fishery here, to settle me in life with Kitty."

The captain's face fell, and he passed and repassed his sun-browned right hand over his thin hair, in a discomfited manner.

"Kitty's father has no more than enough to live on, even in the sparing way in which we live about here. He is a kind of bailiff or steward of manor rights here, and they are not much, and it is but a poor little office. He was better off once, and Kitty must never marry to mere drudgery and hard living."

The captain still sat stroking his thin hair, and looking at the young fisherman.

"I am as certain that my father had no knowledge that any one was wronged as to this money, or that any restitution ought to be made, as I am certain that the sun now shines. But, after this solemn warning from my brother's grave in the sea, that the money is Stolen Money," said Young Raybrock, forcing himself to the utterance of the words, "can I doubt it? Can I touch it?"

"About not doubting, I ain't so sure," observed the captain; "but about not touching--no--I don't think you can."

"See then," said Young Raybrock, "why I am so grieved. Think of Kitty. Think what I have got to tell her!"

His heart quite failed him again when he had come round to that, and he once more beat his sea-boot softly on the floor. But not for long; he soon began again, in a quietly resolute tone.

"However! Enough of that! You spoke some brave words to me just now, Captain Jorgan, and they shall not be spoken in vain. I have got to do something. What I have got to do, before all other things, is to trace out the meaning of this paper, for the sake of the Good Name that has no one else to put it right. And still for the sake of the Good Name, and my father's memory, not a word of this writing must be breathed to my mother, or to Kitty, or to any human creature. You agree in this?"

"I don't know what they'll think of us below," said the captain, "but for certain I can't oppose it. Now, as to tracing. How will you do?"

They both, as by consent, bent over the paper again, and again carefully puzzled out the whole of the writing.

"I make out that this would stand, if all the writing was here, 'Inquire among the old men living there, for'--some one. Most like, you'll go to this village named here?" said the captain, musing, with his finger on the name.

"Yes! And Mr. Tregarthen is a Cornishman, and--to be sure!--comes from Lanrean."

"Does he?" said the captain quietly. "As I ain't acquainted with him, who may he be?"

"Mr. Tregarthen is Kitty's father."

"Ay, ay!" cried the captain. "Now you speak! Tregarthen knows this village of Lanrean, then?"

"Beyond all doubt he does. I have often heard him mention it, as being his native place. He knows it well."

"Stop half a moment," said the captain. "We want a name here. You could ask Tregarthen (or if you couldn't I could) what names of old men he remembers in his time in those diggings? Hey?"

"I can go straight to his cottage, and ask him now."

"Take me with you," said the captain, rising in a solid way that had a most comfortable reliability in it, "and just a word more first. I have knocked about harder than you, and have got along further than you. I have had, all my sea-going life long, to keep my wits polished bright with acid and friction, like the brass cases of the ship's instruments. I'll keep you company on this expedition. Now you don't live by talking any more than I do. Clench that hand of yours in this hand of mine, and that's a speech on both sides."

Captain Jorgan took command of the expedition with that hearty shake. He at once refolded the paper exactly as before, replaced it in the bottle, put the stopper in, put the oilskin over the stopper, confided the whole to Young Raybrock's keeping, and led the way down-stairs.

But it was harder navigation below-stairs than above. The instant they set foot in the parlour the quick, womanly eye detected that there was something wrong. Kitty exclaimed, frightened, as she ran to her lover's side, "Alfred! What's the matter?" Mrs. Raybrock cried out to the captain, "Gracious! what have you done to my son to change him like this all in a minute?" And the young widow--who was there with her work upon her arm--was at first so agitated that she frightened the little girl she held in her hand, who hid her face in her mother's skirts and screamed. The captain, conscious of being held responsible for this domestic change, contemplated it with quite a guilty expression of countenance, and looked to the young fisherman to come to his rescue.

"Kitty, darling," said Young Raybrock, "Kitty, dearest love, I must go away to Lanrean, and I don't know where else or how much further, this very day. Worse than that--our marriage, Kitty, must be put off, and I don't know for how long."

Kitty stared at him, in doubt and wonder and in anger, and pushed him from her with her hand.

"Put off?" cried Mrs. Raybrock. "The marriage put off? And you going to Lanrean! Why, in the name of the dear Lord?"

"Mother dear, I can't say why; I must not say why. It would be dishonourable and undutiful to say why."

"Dishonourable and undutiful?" returned the dame. "And is there nothing dishonourable or undutiful in the boy's breaking the heart of his own plighted love, and his mother's heart too, for the sake of the dark secrets and counsels of a wicked stranger? Why did you ever come here?" she apostrophised the innocent captain. "Who wanted you? Where did you come from? Why couldn't you rest in your own bad place, wherever it is, instead of disturbing the peace of quiet unoffending folk like us?"

"And what," sobbed the poor little Kitty, "have I ever done to you, you hard and cruel captain, that you should come and serve me so?"

And then they both began to weep most pitifully, while the captain could only look from the one to the other, and lay hold of himself by the coat collar.

"Margaret," said the poor young fisherman, on his knees at Kitty's feet, while Kitty kept both her hands before her tearful face, to shut out the traitor from her view,--but kept her fingers wide asunder and looked at him all the time,--"Margaret, you have suffered so much, so uncomplainingly, and are always so careful and considerate! Do take my part, for poor Hugh's sake!"

The quiet Margaret was not appealed to in vain. "I will, Alfred," she returned, "and I do. I wish this gentleman had never come near us;" whereupon the captain laid hold of himself the tighter; "but I take your part for all that. I am sure you have some strong reason and some sufficient reason for what you do, strange as it is, and even for not saying why you do it, strange as that is. And, Kitty darling, you are bound to think so more than any one, for true love believes everything, and bears everything, and trusts everything. And, mother dear, you are bound to think so too, for you know you have been blest with good sons, whose word was always as good as their oath, and who were brought up in as true a sense of honour as any gentleman in this land. And I am sure you have no more call, mother, to doubt your living son than to doubt your dead son; and for the sake of the dear dead, I stand up for the dear living."

"Wa'al now," the captain struck in, with enthusiasm, "this I say, That whether your opinions flatter me or not, you are a young woman of sense, and spirit, and feeling; and I'd sooner have you by my side in the hour of danger, than a good half of the men I've ever fallen in with--or fallen out with, ayther."

Margaret did not return the captain's compliment, or appear fully to reciprocate his good opinion, but she applied herself to the consolation of Kitty, and of Kitty's mother-in-law that was to have been next Monday week, and soon restored the parlour to a quiet condition.

"Kitty, my darling," said the young fisherman, "I must go to your father to entreat him still to trust me in spite of this wretched change and mystery, and to ask him for some directions concerning Lanrean. Will you come home? Will you come with me, Kitty?"

Kitty answered not a word, but rose sobbing, with the end of her simple head-dress at her eyes. Captain Jorgan followed the lovers out, quite sheepishly, pausing in the shop to give an instruction to Mr. Pettifer.

"Here, Tom!" said the captain, in a low voice. "Here's something in your line. Here's an old lady poorly and low in her spirits. Cheer her up a bit, Tom. Cheer 'em all up."

Mr. Pettifer, with a brisk nod of intelligence, immediately assumed his steward face, and went with his quiet, helpful, steward step into the parlour, where the captain had the great satisfaction of seeing him, through the glass door, take the child in his arms (who offered no objection), and bend over Mrs. Raybrock, administering soft words of consolation.

"Though what he finds to say, unless he's telling her that 't'll soon be over, or that most people is so at first, or that it'll do her good afterward, I cannot imagine!" was the captain's reflection as he followed the lovers.

He had not far to follow them, since it was but a short descent down the stony ways to the cottage of Kitty's father. But short as the distance was, it was long enough to enable the captain to observe that he was fast becoming the village Ogre; for there was not a woman standing working at her door, or a fisherman coming up or going down, who saw Young Raybrock unhappy and little Kitty in tears, but he or she instantly darted a suspicious and indignant glance at the captain, as the foreigner who must somehow be responsible for this unusual spectacle. Consequently, when they came into Tregarthen's little garden,--which formed the platform from which the captain had seen Kitty peeping over the wall,--the captain brought to, and stood off and on at the gate, while Kitty hurried to hide her tears in her own room, and Alfred spoke with her father, who was working in the garden. He was a rather infirm man, but could scarcely be called old yet, with an agreeable face and a promising air of making the best of things. The conversation began on his side with great cheerfulness and good humour, but soon became distrustful, and soon angry. That was the captain's cue for striking both into the conversation and the garden.

"Morning, sir!" said Captain Jorgan. "How do you do?"

"The gentleman I am going away with," said the young fisherman to Tregarthen.

"O!" returned Kitty's father, surveying the unfortunate captain with a look of extreme disfavour. "I confess that I can't say I am glad to see you."

"No," said the captain, "and, to admit the truth, that seems to be the general opinion in these parts. But don't be hasty; you may think better of me by-and-by."

"I hope so," observed Tregarthen.

"Wa'al, I hope so," observed the captain, quite at his ease; "more than that, I believe so,--though you don't. Now, Mr. Tregarthen, you don't want to exchange words of mistrust with me; and if you did, you couldn't, because I wouldn't. You and I are old enough to know better than to judge against experience from surfaces and appearances; and if you haven't lived to find out the evil and injustice of such judgments, you are a lucky man."

The other seemed to shrink under this remark, and replied, "Sir, I have lived to feel it deeply."

"Wa'al," said the captain, mollified, "then I've made a good cast without knowing it. Now, Tregarthen, there stands the lover of your only child, and here stand I who know his secret. I warrant it a righteous secret, and none of his making, though bound to be of his keeping. I want to help him out with it, and tewwards that end we ask you to favour us with the names of two or three old residents in the village of Lanrean. As I am taking out my pocket-book and pencil to put the names down, I may as well observe to you that this, wrote atop of the first page here, is my name and address: 'Silas Jonas Jorgan, Salem, Massachusetts, United States.' If ever you take it in your head to run over any morning, I shall be glad to welcome you. Now, what may be the spelling of these said names?"

"There was an elderly man," said Tregarthen, "named David Polreath. He may be dead."

"Wa'al," said the captain, cheerfully, "if Polreath's dead and buried, and can be made of any service to us, Polreath won't object to our digging of him up. Polreath's down, anyhow."

"There was another named Penrewen. I don't know his Christian name."

"Never mind his Chris'en name," said the captain; "Penrewen, for short."

"There was another named John Tredgear."

"And a pleasant-sounding name, too," said the captain; "John Tredgear's booked."

"I can recall no other except old Parvis."

"One of old Parvis's fam'ly I reckon," said the captain, "kept a dry-goods store in New York city, and realised a handsome competency by burning his house to ashes. Same name, anyhow. David Polreath, Unchris'en Penrewen,

John Tredgear, and old Arson Parvis."

"I cannot recall any others at the moment."

"Thank'ee," said the captain. "And so, Tregarthen, hoping for your good opinion yet, and likewise for the fair Devonshire Flower's, your daughter's, I give you my hand, sir, and wish you good day."

Young Raybrock accompanied him disconsolately; for there was no Kitty at the window when he looked up, no Kitty in the garden when he shut the gate, no Kitty gazing after them along the stony ways when they begin to climb back.

"Now I tell you what," said the captain. "Not being at present calculated to promote harmony in your family, I won't come in. You go and get your dinner at home, and I'll get mine at the little hotel. Let our hour of meeting be two o'clock, and you'll find me smoking a cigar in the sun afore the hotel door. Tell Tom Pettifer, my steward, to consider himself on duty, and to look after your people till we come back; you'll find he'll have made himself useful to 'em already, and will be quite acceptable."

All was done as Captain Jorgan directed. Punctually at two o'clock the young fisherman appeared with his knapsack at his back; and punctually at two o'clock the captain jerked away the last feather- end of his cigar.

"Let me carry your baggage, Captain Jorgan; I can easily take it with mine."

"Thank'ee," said the captain. "I'll carry it myself. It's only a comb."

They climbed out of the village, and paused among the trees and fern on the summit of the hill above, to take breath, and to look down at the beautiful sea. Suddenly the captain gave his leg a resounding slap, and cried, "Never knew such a right thing in all my life!"-- and ran away.

The cause of this abrupt retirement on the part of the captain was little Kitty among the trees. The captain went out of sight and waited, and kept out of sight and waited, until it occurred to him to beguile the time with another cigar. He lighted it, and smoked it out, and still he was out of sight and waiting. He stole within sight at last, and saw the lovers, with their arms entwined and their bent heads touching, moving slowly among the trees. It was the golden time of the afternoon then, and the captain said to himself, "Golden sun, golden sea, golden sails, golden leaves, golden love, golden youth,--a golden state of things altogether!"

Nevertheless the captain found it necessary to hail his young companion before going out of sight again. In a few moments more he came up and they began their journey.

"That still young woman with the fatherless child," said Captain Jorgan, as they fell into step, "didn't throw her words away; but good honest words are never thrown away. And now that I am conveying you off from that tender little thing that loves, and relies, and hopes, I feel just as if I was the snarling crittur in the picters, with the tight legs, the long nose, and the feather in his cap, the tips of whose moustaches get up nearer to his eyes the wickeder he gets."

The young fisherman knew nothing of Mephistopheles; but he smiled when the captain stopped to double himself up and slap his leg, and they went along in right goodfellowship.

CHAPTER V

{1}--THE RESTITUTION

Captain Jorgan, up and out betimes, had put the whole village of Lanrean under an amicable cross-examination, and was returning to the King Arthur's Arms to breakfast, none the wiser for his trouble, when he beheld the young fisherman advancing to meet him, accompanied by a stranger. A glance at this stranger assured the captain that he could be no other than the Seafaring Man; and the captain was about to hail him as a fellow-craftsman, when the two stood still and silent before the captain, and the captain stood still, silent, and wondering before them.

"Why, what's this?" cried the captain, when at last he broke the silence. "You two are alike. You two are much alike. What's this?"

Not a word was answered on the other side, until after the sea- faring brother had got hold of the captain's right hand, and the fisherman brother had got hold of the captain's left hand; and if ever the captain had had his fill of hand-shaking, from his birth to that hour, he had it then. And presently up and spoke the two brothers, one at a time, two at a time, two dozen at a time for the bewilderment into which they plunged the captain, until he gradually had Hugh Raybrock's deliverance made clear to him, and also unravelled the fact that the person referred to in the half- obliterated paper was Tregarthen himself.

"Formerly, dear Captain Jorgan," said Alfred, "of Lanrean, you recollect? Kitty and her father came to live at Steepways after Hugh shipped on his last voyage."

"Ay, ay!" cried the captain, fetching a breath. "Now you have me in tow. Then your brother here don't know his sister-in-law that is to be so much as by name?"

"Never saw her; never heard of her!"

"Ay, ay, ay!" cried the captain. "Why then we every one go back together-- paper, writer, and all--and take Tregarthen into the secret we kept from him?"

"Surely," said Alfred, "we can't help it now. We must go through with our duty."

"Not a doubt," returned the captain. "Give me an arm apiece, and let us set this ship-shape."

So walking up and down in the shrill wind on the wild moor, while the neglected breakfast cooled within, the captain and the brothers settled their course of action.

It was that they should all proceed by the quickest means they could secure to Barnstaple, and there look over the father's books and papers in the lawyer's keeping; as Hugh had proposed to himself to do if ever he reached home. That, enlightened or unenlightened, they should then return to

Steepways and go straight to Mr. Tregarthen, and tell him all they knew, and see what came of it, and act accordingly. Lastly, that when they got there they should enter the village with all precautions against Hugh's being recognised by any chance; and that to the captain should be consigned the task of preparing his wife and mother for his restoration to this life.

"For you see," quoth Captain Jorgan, touching the last head, "it requires caution any way, great joys being as dangerous as great griefs, if not more dangerous, as being more uncommon (and therefore less provided against) in this round world of ours. And besides, I should like to free my name with the ladies, and take you home again at your brightest and luckiest; so don't let's throw away a chance of success."

The captain was highly lauded by the brothers for his kind interest and foresight.

"And now stop!" said the captain, coming to a standstill, and looking from one brother to the other, with quite a new rigging of wrinkles about each eye; "you are of opinion," to the elder, "that you are ra'ather slow?"

"I assure you I am very slow," said the honest Hugh.

"Wa'al," replied the captain, "I assure you that to the best of my belief I am ra'ather smart. Now a slow man ain't good at quick business, is he?"

That was clear to both.

"You," said the captain, turning to the younger brother, "are a little in love; ain't you?"

"Not a little, Captain Jorgan."

"Much or little, you're sort preoccupied; ain't you?"

It was impossible to be denied.

"And a sort preoccupied man ain't good at quick business, is he?" said the captain.

Equally clear on all sides.

"Now," said the captain, "I ain't in love myself, and I've made many a smart run across the ocean, and I should like to carry on and go ahead with this affair of yours, and make a run slick through it. Shall I try? Will you hand it over to me?"

They were both delighted to do so, and thanked him heartily.

"Good," said the captain, taking out his watch. "This is half-past eight a.m., Friday morning. I'll jot that down, and we'll compute how many hours we've been out when we run into your mother's post- office. There! The entry's made, and now we go ahead."

They went ahead so well that before the Barnstaple lawyer's office was open next morning, the captain was sitting whistling on the step of the door, waiting for the clerk to come down the street with his key and open it. But instead of the clerk there came the master, with whom the captain fraternised on the spot to an extent that utterly confounded him.

As he personally knew both Hugh and Alfred, there was no difficulty in obtaining immediate access to such of the father's papers as were in his keeping. These were chiefly old letters and cash accounts; from which the captain, with a shrewdness and despatch that left the lawyer far behind, established with perfect clearness, by noon, the following particulars:-

That one Lawrence Clissold had borrowed of the deceased, at a time when he was a thriving young tradesman in the town of Barnstaple, the sum of five hundred pounds. That he had borrowed it on the written statement that it was to be laid out in furtherance of a speculation which he expected would raise him to independence; he being, at the time of writing that letter, no more than a clerk in the house of Dringworth Brothers, America Square, London. That the money was borrowed for a stipulated period; but that, when the term was out, the aforesaid speculation failed, and Clissold was without means of repayment. That, hereupon, he had written to his creditor, in no very persuasive terms, vaguely requesting further time. That the creditor had refused this concession, declaring that he could not afford delay.

That Clissold then paid the debt, accompanying the remittance of the money with an angry letter describing it as having been advanced by a relative to save him from ruin. That, in acknowlodging the receipt, Raybrock had cautioned Clissold to seek to borrow money of him no more, as he would never so risk money again.

Before the lawyer the captain said never a word in reference to these discoveries. But when the papers had been put back in their box, and he and his two companions were well out of the office, his right leg suffered for it, and he said, -

"So far this run's begun with a fair wind and a prosperous; for don't you see that all this agrees with that dutiful trust in his father maintained by the slow member of the Raybrock family?"

Whether the brothers had seen it before or no, they saw it now. Not that the captain gave them much time to contemplate the state of things at their ease, for he instantly whipped them into a chaise again, and bore them off to Steepways. Although the afternoon was but just beginning to decline when they reached it, and it was broad day-light, still they had no difficulty, by dint of muffing the returned sailor up, and ascending the village rather than descending it, in reaching Tregarthen's cottage unobserved. Kitty was not visible, and they surprised Tregarthen sitting writing in the small bay-window of his little room.

"Sir," said the captain, instantly shaking hands with him, pen and all, "I'm glad to see you, sir. How do you do, sir? I told you you'd think better of me by-and-by, and I congratulate you on going to do it."

Here the captain's eye fell on Tom Pettifer Ho, engaged in preparing some cookery at the fire.

"That critter," said the captain, smiting his leg, "is a born steward, and never ought to have been in any other way of life. Stop where you are, Tom, and make yourself useful. Now, Tregarthen, I'm going to try a chair."

Accordingly the captain drew one close to him, and went on:-

"This loving member of the Raybrock family you know, sir. This slow member of the same family you don't know, sir. Wa'al, these two are brothers,--fact! Hugh's come to life again, and here he stands. Now see here, my friend! You don't want to be told that he was cast away, but you do want to be told (for there's a purpose in it) that he was cast away with another man. That man by name was Lawrence Clissold."

At the mention of this name Tregarthen started and changed colour. "What's the matter?" said the captain.

"He was a fellow-clerk of mine thirty--five-and-thirty--years ago."

"True," said the captain, immediately catching at the clew: "Dringworth Brothers, America Square, London City."

The other started again, nodded, and said, "That was the house."

"Now," pursued the captain, "between those two men cast away there arose a mystery concerning the round sum of five hundred pound."

Again Tregarthen started, changing colour. Again the captain said, "What's the matter?"

As Tregarthen only answered, "Please to go on," the captain recounted, very tersely and plainly, the nature of Clissold's wanderings on the barren island, as he had condensed them in his mind from the seafaring man. Tregarthen became greatly agitated during this recital, and at length exclaimed, -

"Clissold was the man who ruined me! I have suspected it for many a long year, and now I know it."

"And how," said the captain, drawing his chair still closer to Tregarthen, and clapping his hand upon his shoulder,--"how may you know it?"

"When we were fellow-clerks," replied Tregarthen, "in that London house, it was one of my duties to enter daily in a certain book an account of the sums received that day by the firm, and afterward paid into the bankers'. One memorable day,--a Wednesday, the black day of my life,--among the sums I so entered was one of five hundred pounds."

"I begin to make it out," said the captain. "Yes?"

"It was one of Clissold's duties to copy from this entry a memorandum of the sums which the clerk employed to go to the bankers' paid in there. It was my duty to hand the money to Clissold; it was Clissold's to hand it to the clerk, with that memorandum of his writing. On that Wednesday I entered a sum of five hundred pounds received. I handed that sum, as I handed the other sums in the day's entry, to Clissold. I was absolutely certain of it at the time; I have been absolutely certain of it ever since. A sum of five hundred pounds was afterward found by the house to have been that day wanting from the bag, from Clissold's memorandum, and from the entries in my book. Clissold, being questioned, stood upon his perfect clearness in the matter, and emphatically declared that he asked no better than to be tested by 'Tregarthen's book.' My book was examined, and the entry of five hundred pounds was not there."

"How not there," said the captain, "when you made it yourself?"

Tregarthen continued:-

"I was then questioned. Had I made the entry? Certainly I had. The house produced my book, and it was not there. I could not deny my book; I could not deny my writing. I knew there must be forgery by some one; but the writing was wonderfully like mine, and I could impeach no one if the house could not. I was required to pay the money back. I did so; and I left the house, almost broken-hearted, rather than remain there,--even if I could have done so,--with a dark shadow of suspicion always on me. I returned to my native place, Lanrean, and remained there, clerk to a mine, until I was appointed to my little post here."

"I well remember," said the captain, "that I told you that if you had no experience of ill judgments on deceiving appearances, you were a lucky man. You went hurt at that, and I see why. I'm sorry."

"Thus it is," said Tregarthen. "Of my own innocence I have of course been sure; it has been at once my comfort and my trial. Of Clissold I have always had suspicions almost amounting to certainty; but they have never been confirmed until now. For my daughter's sake and for my own I have carried this subject in my own heart, as the only secret of my life, and have long believed that it would die with me."

"Wa'al, my good sir," said the captain cordially, "the present question is, and will be long, I hope, concerning living, and not dying. Now, here are our two honest friends, the loving Raybrock and the slow. Here they stand, agreed on one point, on which I'd back 'em round the world, and right across it from north to south, and then again from east to west, and through it, from your deepest Cornish mine to China. It is, that they will never use this same so-often-mentioned sum of money, and that restitution of it must be made to you. These two, the loving member and the slow, for the sake of the right and of their father's memory, will have it ready for you to-morrow. Take it, and ease their minds and mine, and end a most unfortunate transaction."

Tregarthen took the captain by the hand, and gave his hand to each of the young men, but positively and finally answered No. He said, they trusted to his word, and he was glad of it, and at rest in his mind; but there was no proof, and the money must remain as it was. All were very earnest over this; and earnestness in men, when they are right and true, is so impressive, that Mr. Pettifer deserted his cookery and looked on quite moved.

"And so," said the captain, "so we come--as that lawyer-crittur over yonder where we were this morning might--to mere proof; do we? We must have it; must we? How? From this Clissold's wanderings, and from what you say, it ain't hard to make out that there was a neat forgery of your writing committed by the too smart rowdy that was grease and ashes when I made his acquaintance, and a substitution of a forged leaf in your book for a real and torn leaf torn out. Now was that real and true leaf then and there destroyed? No,--for says he, in his drunken way, he slipped it into a crack in his own desk, because you came into the office before there was time to burn it, and could never get back to it arterwards. Wait a bit. Where is that desk now? Do you consider it likely to be in America Square, London City?"

Tregarthen shook his head.

"The house has not, for years, transacted business in that place. I have heard of it, and read of it, as removed, enlarged, every way altered. Things alter so fast in these times."

"You think so," returned the captain, with compassion; "but you should come over and see me afore you talk about that. Wa'al, now. This desk, this paper,--this paper, this desk," said the captain, ruminating and walking about, and looking, in his uneasy abstraction, into Mr. Pettifer's hat on a table, among other things. "This desk, this paper,--this paper, this desk," the captain continued, musing and roaming about the room, "I'd give--"

However, he gave nothing, but took up his steward's hat instead, and stood looking into it, as if he had just come into church. After that he roamed again, and again said, "This desk, belonging to this house of Dringworth Brothers, America Square, London City--"

Mr. Pettifer, still strangely moved, and now more moved than before, cut the captain off as he backed across the room, and bespake him thus:-

"Captain Jorgan, I have been wishful to engage your attention, but I couldn't do it. I am unwilling to interrupt Captain Jorgan, but I must do it. I knew something about that house."

The captain stood stock-still and looked at him,--with his (Mr. Pettifer's) hat under his arm.

"You're aware," pursued his steward, "that I was once in the broking business, Captain Jorgan?"

"I was aware," said the captain, "that you had failed in that calling, and in half the businesses going, Tom."

"Not quite so, Captain Jorgan; but I failed in the broking business. I was partners with my brother, sir. There was a sale of old office furniture at Dringworth Brothers' when the house was moved from America Square, and me and my brother made what we call in the trade a Deal there, sir. And I'll make bold to say, sir, that the only thing I ever had from my brother, or from any relation,--for my relations have mostly taken property from me instead of giving me any,--was an old desk we bought at that same sale, with a crack in it. My brother wouldn't have given me even that, when we broke partnership, if it had been worth anything."

"Where is that desk now?" said the captain.

"Well, Captain Jorgan," replied the steward, "I couldn't say for certain where it is now; but when I saw it last,--which was last time we were outward bound,--it was at a very nice lady's at Wapping, along with a little chest of mine which was detained for a small matter of a bill owing."

The captain, instead of paying that rapt attention to his steward which was rendered by the other three persons present, went to Church again, in respect of the steward's hat. And a most especially agitated and memorable face the captain produced from it, after a short pause.

"Now, Tom," said the captain, "I spoke to you, when we first came here, respecting your constitutional weakness on the subject of sunstroke."

"You did, sir."

"Will my slow friend," said the captain, "lend me his arm, or I shall sink right back'ards into this blessed steward's cookery? Now, Tom," pursued the captain, when the required assistance was given, "on your oath as a steward, didn't you take that desk to pieces to make a better one of it, and put it together fresh,--or something of the kind?"

"On my oath I did, sir," replied the steward.

"And by the blessing of Heaven, my friends, one and all," cried the captain, radiant with joy,--"of the Heaven that put it into this Tom Pettifer's head to take so much care of his head against the bright sun,--he lined his hat with the original leaf in Tregarthen's writing,--and here it is!"

With that the captain, to the utter destruction of Mr. Pettifer's favourite hat, produced the book-leaf, very much worn, but still legible, and gave both his legs such tremendous slaps that they were heard far off in the bay, and never accounted for.

"A quarter past five p.m.," said the captain, pulling out his watch, "and that's thirty-three hours and a quarter in all, and a pritty run!"

How they were all overpowered with delight and triumph; how the money was restored, then and there, to Tregarthen; how Tregarthen, then and there, gave it all to his daughter; how the captain undertook to go to Dringworth Brothers and re-establish the reputation of their forgotten old clerk; how Kitty came in, and was nearly torn to pieces, and the marriage was reappointed, needs not to be told. Nor how she and the young fisherman went home to the post-office to prepare the way for the captain's coming, by declaring him to be the mightiest of men, who had made all their fortunes,-- and then dutifully withdrew together, in order that he might have the domestic coast entirely to himself. How he availed himself of it is all that remains to tell.

Deeply delighted with his trust, and putting his heart into it, he raised the latch of the post-office parlour where Mrs. Raybrock and the young widow sat, and said, -

"May I come in?"

"Sure you may, Captain Jorgan!" replied the old lady. "And good reason you have to be free of the house, though you have not been too well used in it by some who ought to have known better. I ask your pardon."

"No you don't, ma'am," said the captain, "for I won't let you. Wa'al, to be sure!"

By this time he had taken a chair on the hearth between them.

"Never felt such an evil spirit in the whole course of my life! There! I tell you! I could a'most have cut my own connection. Like the dealer in my country, away West, who when he had let himself be outdone in a bargain, said to himself, 'Now I tell you what! I'll never speak to you again.' And he never did, but joined a settlement of oysters, and translated the multiplication table into their language,--which is a fact that can be proved. If you doubt it, mention it to any oyster you come across, and see if he'll have the face to contradict it."

He took the child from her mother's lap and set it on his knee.

"Not a bit afraid of me now, you see. Knows I am fond of small people. I have a child, and she's a girl, and I sing to her sometimes."

"What do you sing?" asked Margaret.

"Not a long song, my dear.

Silas Jorgan Played the organ.

That's about all. And sometimes I tell her stories,--stories of sailors supposed to be lost, and recovered after all hope was abandoned." Here the captain musingly went back to his song, -

Silas Jorgan Played the organ;

repeating it with his eyes on the fire, as he softly danced the child on his knee. For he felt that Margaret had stopped working.

"Yes," said the captain, still looking at the fire, "I make up stories and tell 'em to that child. Stories of shipwreck on desert islands, and long delay in getting back to civilised lauds. It is to stories the like of that, mostly, that

Silas Jorgan Plays the organ."

There was no light in the room but the light of the fire; for the shades of night were on the village, and the stars had begun to peep out of the sky one by one, as the houses of the village peeped out from among the foliage when the night departed. The captain felt that Margaret's eyes were upon him, and thought it discreetest to keep his own eyes on the fire.

"Yes; I make 'em up," said the captain. "I make up stories of brothers brought together by the good providence of GOD,--of sons brought back to mothers, husbands brought back to wives, fathers raised from the deep, for little children like herself."

Margaret's touch was on his arm, and he could not choose but look round now. Next moment her hand moved imploringly to his breast, and she was on her knees before him,--supporting the mother, who was also kneeling.

"What's the matter?" said the captain. "What's the matter?

Silas Jorgan Played the -

Their looks and tears were too much for him, and he could not finish the song, short as it was.

"Mistress Margaret, you have borne ill fortune well. Could you bear good fortune equally well, if it was to come?"

"I hope so. I thankfully and humbly and earnestly hope so!"

"Wa'al, my dear," said the captain, "p'rhaps it has come. He's-- don't be frightened--shall I say the word--"

"Alive?"

"Yes!"

The thanks they fervently addressed to Heaven were again too much for the captain, who openly took out his handkerchief and dried his eyes.

"He's no further off," resumed the captain, "than my country. Indeed, he's no further off than his own native country. To tell you the truth, he's no further off than Falmouth. Indeed, I doubt if he's quite so fur. Indeed, if you was sure you could bear it nicely, and I was to do no more than whistle for him--"

The captain's trust was discharged. A rush came, and they were all together again.

This was a fine opportunity for Tom Pettifer to appear with a tumbler of cold water, and he presently appeared with it, and administered it to the ladies; at the same time soothing them, and composing their dresses, exactly as if they had been passengers crossing the Channel. The extent to which the captain slapped his legs, when Mr. Pettifer acquitted himself of this act of stewardship, could have been thoroughly appreciated by no one but himself; inasmuch as he must have slapped them black and blue, and they must have smarted tremendously.

He couldn't stay for the wedding, having a few appointments to keep at the irreconcilable distance of about four thousand miles. So next morning all the village cheered him up to the level ground above, and there he shook hands with a complete Census of its population, and invited the whole, without exception, to come and stay several months with him at Salem, Mass., U.S. And there as he stood on the spot where he had seen that little golden picture of love and parting, and from which he could that morning contemplate another golden picture with a vista of golden years in it, little Kitty put her arms around his neck, and kissed him on both his bronzed cheeks, and laid her pretty face upon his storm-beaten breast, in sight of all,-- ashamed to have called such a noble captain names. And there the captain waved his hat over his head three final times; and there he was last seen, going away accompanied by Tom Pettifer Ho, and carrying his hands in his pockets. And there, before that ground was softened with the fallen leaves of three more summers, a rosy little boy took his first unsteady run to a fair young mother's breast, and the name of that infant fisherman was Jorgan Raybrock.

Footnotes:

{1} Dicken's didn't write chapters three and four and they are omitted in this edition. The story continues with Captain Jorgan and Alfred at Lanrean.

Captain Boldheart & the Latin-Grammar Master

by Charles Dickens

A HOLIDAY ROMANCE FROM THE PEN OF LIEUT-COL. ROBIN REDFORTH AGED 9.

FOREWORD

The story contained herein was written by Charles Dickens in 1867. It is the third of four stories entitled "Holiday Romance" and was published originally in a children's magazine in America. It purports to be written by a child aged nine. It was republished in England in "All the Year Round" in 1868. For this and four other Christmas pieces Dickens received ?,000.

"Holiday Romance" was published in book form by Messrs Chapman & Hall in 1874, with "Edwin Drood" and other stories.

For this reprint the text of the story as it appeared in "All the Year Round" has been followed.

CAPTAIN BOLDHEART AND THE LATIN-GRAMMAR MASTER

The subject of our present narrative would appear to have devoted himself to the Pirate profession at a comparatively early age. We find him in command of a splendid schooner of one hundred guns, loaded to the muzzle, 'ere yet he had had a party in honour of his tenth birthday.

It seems that our hero, considering himself spited by a Latin-Grammar-Master, demanded the satisfaction due from one man of honour to another. Not getting it, he privately withdrew his haughty spirit from such low company, bought a second-hand pocket-pistol, folded up some sandwiches in a paper bag, made a bottle of Spanish liquorice-water, and entered on a career of valour.

It were tedious to follow Boldheart (for such was his name) through the commencing stages of his history. Suffice it that we find him bearing the rank of Captain Boldheart, reclining in full uniform on a crimson hearth-rug spread out upon the quarter-deck of his schooner the Beauty, in the China Seas. It was a lovely evening, and as his crew lay grouped about him, he favoured them with the following melody:

O landsmen are folly! O Pirates are jolly! O Diddleum Dolly, Di! (Chorus) Heave yo.

The soothing effect of these animated sounds floating over the waters, as the common sailors united their rough voices to take up the rich tones of

Boldheart, may be more easily conceived than described.

It was under these circumstances that the lookout at the masthead gave the word, "Whales!"

All was now activity.

"Where away?" cried Captain Boldheart, starting up.

"On the larboard bow, sir," replied the fellow at the masthead, touching his hat. For such was the height of discipline on board of the Beauty, that even at that height he was obliged to mind it or be shot through the head.

"This adventure belongs to me," said Boldheart. "Boy, my harpoon. Let no man follow;" and leaping alone into his boat, the captain rowed with admirable dexterity in the direction of the monster.

All was now excitement.

"He nears him!" said an elderly seaman, following the captain through his spy-glass.

"He strikes him!" said another seaman, a mere stripling, but also with a spy-glass.

"He tows him towards us!" said another seaman, a man in the full vigour of life, but also with a spy-glass.

In fact the captain was seen approaching, with the huge bulk following. We will not dwell on the deafening cries of "Boldheart! Boldheart!" with which he was received, when, carelessly leaping on the quarter-deck, he presented his prize to his men. They afterwards made two thousand four hundred and seventeen pound ten and sixpence by it.

Ordering the sails to be braced up, the captain now stood W.N.W. The Beauty flew rather than floated over the dark blue waters. Nothing particular occurred for a fortnight, except taking, with considerable slaughter, four Spanish galleons, and a Snow from South America, all richly laden. Inaction began to tell upon the spirits of the men. Captain Boldheart called all hands aft, and said:

"My lads, I hear there are discontented ones among ye. Let any such stand forth."

After some murmuring, in which the expressions, "Aye, aye, sir!" "Union Jack!" "Avast," "Starboard," "Port," "Bowsprit," and similar indications of a mutinous undercurrent, though subdued, were audible, Bill Boozey, captain of the foretop, came out from the rest. His form was that of a giant, but he quailed under the captain's eye.

"What are your wrongs?" said the captain.

"Why, d'ye see, Captain Boldheart," replied the towering mariner, "I've sailed man and boy for many a year, but I never yet know'd the milk served out for the ship's company's teas to be so sour as 'tis aboard this craft."

At this moment the thrilling cry, "Man overboard!" announced to the astonished crew that Boozey, in stepping back, as the captain (in mere thoughtfulness) laid his hand upon the faithful pocket-pistol which he wore in his belt, had lost his balance, and was struggling with the foaming tide.

All was now stupefaction.

But, with Captain Boldheart, to throw off his uniform coat regardless of the various rich orders with which it was decorated, and to plunge into the sea after the drowning giant, was the work of a moment. Maddening was the excitement when boats were lowered; intense the joy when the captain was seen holding up the drowning man with his teeth; deafening the cheering when both were restored to the main deck of the Beauty. And from the instant of his changing his wet clothes for dry ones, Captain Boldheart had no such devoted though humble friend as William Boozey.

Boldheart now pointed to the horizon, and called the attention of his crew to the taper spars of a ship lying snug in harbour under the guns of a fort.

"She shall be ours at sunrise," said he. "Serve out a double allowance of grog, and prepare for action."

All was now preparation.

When morning dawned after a sleepless night, it was seen that the stranger was crowding on all sail to come out of the harbour and offer battle. As the two ships came nearer to each other, the stranger fired a gun and hoisted Roman colours. Boldheart then perceived her to be the Latin-Grammar-Master's bark. Such indeed she was, and had been tacking about the world in unavailing pursuit, from the time of his first taking to a roving life.

Boldheart now addressed his men, promising to blow them up if he should feel convinced that their reputation required it, and giving orders that the Latin-Grammar-Master should be taken alive. He then dismissed them to their quarters, and the fight began with a broadside from The Beauty. She then veered round, and poured in another. The Scorpion (so was the bark of the Latin-Grammar-Master appropriately called) was not slow to return her fire, and a terrific cannonading ensued, in which the guns of The Beauty did tremendous execution.

The Latin-Grammar-Master was seen upon the poop, in the midst of the smoke and fire, encouraging his men. To do him justice, he was no Craven, though his white hat, his short grey trousers, and his long snuff-coloured surtout reaching to his heels--the self-same coat in which he had spited Boldheart--contrasted most unfavourably with the brilliant uniform of the latter. At this moment Boldheart, seizing a pike and putting himself at the head of his men, gave the word to board.

A desperate conflict ensued in the hammock nettings--or somewhere in about that direction--until the Latin-Grammar-Master, having all his masts gone, his hull and rigging shot through and through, and seeing Boldheart slashing a path towards him, hauled down his flag himself, gave up his sword to Boldheart, and asked for quarter. Scarce had he been put into the captain's boat, 'ere The Scorpion went down with all on board.

On Captain Boldheart's now assembling his men, a circumstance occurred. He found it necessary with one blow of his cutlass to kill the Cook, who, having lost his brother in the late action, was making at the Latin-Grammar-

Master in an infuriated state, intent on his destruction with a carving-knife.

Captain Boldheart then turned to the Latin-Grammar-Master, severely reproaching him with his perfidy, and put it to his crew what they considered that a master who spited a boy deserved?

They answered with one voice, "Death."

"It may be so," said the Captain; "but it shall never be said that Boldheart stained his hour of triumph with the blood of his enemy. Prepare the cutter."

The cutter was immediately prepared.

"Without taking your life," said the Captain, "I must yet for ever deprive you of the power of spiting other boys. I shall turn you adrift in this boat. You will find in her two oars, a compass, a bottle of rum, a small cask of water, a piece of pork, a bag of biscuit, and my Latin grammar. Go! and spite the natives, if you can find any."

Deeply conscious of this bitter sarcasm, the unhappy wretch was put into the cutter, and was soon left far behind. He made no effort to row, but was seen lying on his back with his legs up, when last made out by the ship's telescopes.

A stiff breeze now beginning to blow, Captain Boldheart gave orders to keep her S.S.W., easing her a little during the night by falling off a point or two W. by W., or even by W.S., if she complained much. He then retired for the night, having in truth much need of repose. In addition to the fatigues he had undergone, this brave officer had received sixteen wounds in the engagement, but had not mentioned it.

In the morning a white squall came on, and was succeeded by other squalls of various colours. It thundered and lightened heavily for six weeks. Hurricanes then set in for two months. Waterspouts and tornadoes followed. The oldest sailor on board--and he was a very old one--had never seen such weather. The Beauty lost all idea where she was, and the carpenter reported six feet two of water in the hold. Everybody fell senseless at the pumps every day.

Provisions now ran very low. Our hero put the crew on short allowance, and put himself on shorter allowance than any man in the ship. But his spirit kept him fat. In this extremity, the gratitude of Boozey, the captain of the foretop whom our readers may remember, was truly affecting. The loving though lowly William repeatedly requested to be killed, and preserved for the captain's table.

We now approach a change in affairs.

One day during a gleam of sunshine and when the weather had moderated, the man at the masthead--too weak now to touch his hat, besides its having been blown away--called out,

"Savages!"

All was now expectation.

Presently fifteen hundred canoes, each paddled by twenty savages, were seen advancing in excellent order. They were a light green colour (the Savages were), and sang, with great energy, the following strain:

Choo a choo a choo tooth. Muntch, muntch. Nycey! Choo a choo a choo tooth. Muntch, muntch. Nyce!

As the shades of night were by this time closing in, these expressions were supposed to embody this simple people's views of the Evening Hymn. But it too soon appeared that the song was a translation of "For what we are going to receive," &c.

The chief, imposingly decorated with feathers of lively colours, and having the majestic appearance of a fighting Parrot, no sooner understood (he understood English perfectly) that the ship was The Beauty, Captain Boldheart, than he fell upon his face on the deck, and could not be persuaded to rise until the captain had lifted him up, & told him he wouldn't hurt him. All the rest of the savages also fell on their faces with marks of terror, and had also to be lifted up one by one. Thus the fame of the great Boldheart had gone before him, even among these children of Nature.

Turtles and oysters were now produced in astonishing numbers, and on these and yams the people made a hearty meal. After dinner the Chief told Captain Boldheart that there was better feeding up at the village, and that he would be glad to take him and his officers there. Apprehensive of treachery, Boldheart ordered his boat's crew to attend him completely armed. And well were it for other commanders if their precautions--but let us not anticipate.

When the canoes arrived at the beach, the darkness of the night was illumined by the light of an immense fire. Ordering his boat's crew (with the intrepid though illiterate William at their head) to keep close and be upon their guard, Boldheart bravely went on, arm-in-arm with the Chief.

But how to depict the captain's surprise when he found a ring of Savages singing in chorus that barbarous translation of "For what we are going to receive, &c.," which has been given above, and dancing hand-in-hand round the Latin-Grammar-Master, in a hamper with his head shaved, while two savages floured him, before putting him to the fire to be cooked!

Boldheart now took counsel with his officers on the course to be adopted. In the mean time, the miserable captive never ceased begging pardon and imploring to be delivered. On the generous Boldheart's proposal, it was at length resolved that he should not be cooked, but should be allowed to remain raw, on two conditions. Namely,

1. That he should never under any circumstances presume to teach any boy any thing any more.

2. That, if taken back to England, he should pass his life in travelling to find out boys who wanted their exercises done, and should do their exercises for those boys for nothing, and never say a word about it.

Drawing his sword from its sheath, Boldheart swore him to these conditions on its shining blade. The prisoner wept bitterly, and appeared acutely to feel the errors of his past career.

The captain then ordered his boat's crew to make ready for a volley, and after firing to re-load quickly. "And expect a score or two on ye to go head over heels," murmured William Boozey; "for I'm a looking at ye." With those words the derisive though deadly William took a good aim.

"Fire!"

The ringing voice of Boldheart was lost in the report of the guns and the screeching of the savages. Volley after volley awakened the numerous echoes. Hundreds of savages were killed, hundreds wounded, and thousands ran howling into the woods. The Latin-Grammar-Master had a spare night-cap lent him, and a longtail coat which he wore hind side before. He presented a ludicrous though pitiable appearance, and serve him right.

We now find Captain Boldheart, with this rescued wretch on board, standing off for other islands. At one of these, not a cannibal island, but a pork and vegetable one, he married (only in fun on his part) the King's daughter. Here he rested some time, receiving from the natives great quantities of precious stones, gold dust, elephants' teeth, and sandal wood, and getting very rich. This, too, though he almost every day made presents of enormous value to his men.

The ship being at length as full as she could hold of all sorts of valuable things, Boldheart gave orders to weigh the anchor, and turn the Beauty's head towards England. These orders were obeyed with three cheers, and ere the sun went down full many a hornpipe had been danced on deck by the uncouth though agile William.

We next find Captain Boldheart about three leagues off Madeira, surveying through his spy-glass a stranger of suspicious appearance making sail towards him. On his firing a gun ahead of her to bring her to, she ran up a flag, which he instantly recognized as the flag from the mast in the back-garden at home.

Inferring from this, that his father had put to sea to seek his long-lost son, the captain sent his own boat on board the stranger, to inquire if this was so, and if so, whether his father's intentions were strictly honourable. The boat came back with a present of greens and fresh meat, and reported that the stranger was The Family of twelve hundred tons, and had not only the captain's father on board, but also his mother, with the majority of his aunts and uncles, and all his cousins. It was further reported to Boldheart that the whole of these relations had expressed themselves in a becoming manner, and were anxious to embrace him and thank him for the glorious credit he had done them. Boldheart at once invited them to breakfast next morning on board the Beauty, and gave orders for a brilliant ball that should last all day.

It was in the course of the night that the captain discovered the hopelessness of reclaiming the Latin-Grammar-Master. That thankless traitor was found out, as the two ships lay near each other, communicating with The Family by signals, and offering to give up Boldheart. He was hanged at the yard-arm the first thing in the morning, after having it impressively pointed out to him by Boldheart that this was what spiters came to.

The meeting between the captain and his parents was attended with tears. His uncles and aunts would have attended their meeting with tears too, but he wasn't going to stand that. His cousins were very much astonished by the size of his ship and the discipline of his men, and were greatly overcome by the splendour of his uniform. He kindly conducted them round the vessel, and pointed out every thing worthy of notice. He also fired his hundred guns, and found it amusing to witness their alarm.

The entertainment surpassed everything ever seen on board ship, and lasted from ten in the morning until seven the next morning. Only one disagreeable incident occurred. Captain Boldheart found himself obliged to put his cousin Tom in irons, for being disrespectful. On the boy's promising amendment, however, he was humanely released after a few hours' close confinement.

Boldheart now took his mother down into the great cabin, and asked after the young lady with whom, it was well known to the world, he was in love. His mother replied that the object of his affections was then at school at Margate, for the benefit of sea-bathing (it was the month of September), but that she feared the young lady's friends were still opposed to the union. Boldheart at once resolved, if necessary, to bombard the town.

Taking the command of his ship with this intention, and putting all but fighting men on board The Family, with orders to that vessel to keep in company, Boldheart soon anchored in Margate Roads. Here he went ashore well-armed, and attended by his boat's crew (at their head the faithful though ferocious William), and demanded to see the Mayor, who came out of his office.

"Dost know the name of yon ship, Mayor?" asked Boldheart fiercely.

[Illustration: "DOST KNOW THE NAME OF YON SHIP, MAYOR?"]

[Illustration: STANDING SENTRY OVER HIM]

"No," said the Mayor, rubbing his eyes, which he could scarce believe when he saw the goodly vessel riding at anchor.

"She is named the Beauty," said the captain.

"Hah!" exclaimed the Mayor, with a start. "And you, then, are Captain Boldheart?"

"The same."

A pause ensued. The Mayor trembled.

"Now, Mayor," said the captain, "choose. Help me to my Bride, or be bombarded."

The Mayor begged for two hours' grace, in which to make inquiries respecting the young lady. Boldheart accorded him but one; and during that one placed William Boozey sentry over him, with a drawn sword and instructions to accompany him wherever he went, and to run him through the body if he showed a sign of playing false.

At the end of the hour, the Mayor re-appeared more dead than alive, closely waited on by Boozey more alive than dead.

"Captain," said the Mayor, "I have ascertained that the young lady is going to bathe. Even now she waits her turn for a machine. The tide is low, though rising. I, in one of our town-boats, shall not be suspected. When she comes forth in her bathing-dress into the shallow water from behind the hood of the machine, my boat shall intercept her and prevent her return. Do you the rest."

"Mayor," returned Capt. Boldheart, "thou hast saved thy town."

The captain then signalled his boat to take him off, and steering her himself ordered her crew to row towards the bathing-ground, and there to rest upon their oars. All happened as had been arranged. His lovely bride came forth, the Mayor glided in behind her, she became confused and had floated out of her depth, when, with one skilful touch of the rudder and one quivering stroke from the boat's crew, her adoring Boldheart held her in his strong arms. There her shrieks of terror were changed to cries of joy.

Before the Beauty could get under weigh, the hoisting of all the flags in the town and harbour, and the ringing of all the bells, announced to the brave Boldheart that he had nothing to fear. He therefore determined to be married on the spot, and signalled for a clergyman and clerk, who came off promptly in a sailing-boat named the Skylark. Another great entertainment was then given on board the Beauty, in the midst of which the Mayor was called out by a messenger. He returned with the news that Government had sent down to know whether Captain Boldheart, in acknowledgment of the great services he had done his country by being a Pirate, would consent to be made a Lieutenant-Colonel. For himself he would have spurned the worthless boon, but his Bride wished it and he consented.

Only one thing further happened before the good ship Family was dismissed, with rich presents to all on board. It is painful to record (but such is human nature in some cousins) that Captain Boldheart's unmannerly cousin Tom was actually tied up to receive three dozen with a rope's end "for cheekyness and making games," when Captain Boldheart's lady begged for him and he was spared. The Beauty then refitted, and the Captain and his Bride departed for the Indian Ocean to enjoy themselves for evermore.

THE END.

George Silverman's Explanation

by Charles Dickens

FIRST CHAPTER

IT happened in this wise -

But, sitting with my pen in my hand looking at those words again, without descrying any hint in them of the words that should follow, it comes into my mind that they have an abrupt appearance. They may serve, however, if I let them remain, to suggest how very difficult I find it to begin to explain my explanation. An uncouth phrase: and yet I do not see my way to a better.

SECOND CHAPTER

IT happened in THIS wise -

But, looking at those words, and comparing them with my former opening, I find they are the self-same words repeated. This is the more surprising to me, because I employ them in quite a new connection. For indeed I declare that my intention was to discard the commencement I first had in my thoughts, and to give the preference to another of an entirely different nature, dating my explanation from an anterior period of my life. I will make a third trial, without erasing this second failure, protesting that it is not my design to conceal any of my infirmities, whether they be of head or heart.

THIRD CHAPTER

NOT as yet directly aiming at how it came to pass, I will come upon it by degrees. The natural manner, after all, for God knows that is how it came upon me.

My parents were in a miserable condition of life, and my infant home was a cellar in Preston. I recollect the sound of father's Lancashire clogs on the street pavement above, as being different in my young hearing from the sound of all other clogs; and I recollect, that, when mother came down the cellar-steps, I used tremblingly to speculate on her feet having a good or an ill- tempered look, - on her knees, - on her waist, - until finally her face came into view, and settled the question. From this it will be seen that I was timid, and that the cellar-steps were steep, and that the doorway was very low.

Mother had the gripe and clutch of poverty upon her face, upon her figure, and not least of all upon her voice. Her sharp and high- pitched words were squeezed out of her, as by the compression of bony fingers on a leathern bag; and she had a way of rolling her eyes about and about the cellar, as she scolded, that was gaunt and hungry. Father, with his shoulders rounded, would sit quiet on a three-legged stool, looking at the empty grate, until she would pluck the stool from under him, and bid him go bring some money home. Then he would dismally ascend the steps; and I, holding my ragged shirt and trousers together with a hand (my only braces), would feint and dodge from mother's pursuing grasp at my hair.

A worldly little devil was mother's usual name for me. Whether I cried for that I was in the dark, or for that it was cold, or for that I was hungry, or whether I squeezed myself into a warm corner when there was a fire, or ate voraciously when there was food, she would still say, 'O, you worldly little devil!' And the sting of it was, that I quite well knew myself to be a worldly little devil. Worldly as to wanting to be housed and warmed, worldly as to wanting to be fed, worldly as to the greed with which I inwardly compared how much I got of those good things with how much father and mother got, when, rarely, those good things were going.

Sometimes they both went away seeking work; and then I would be locked up in the cellar for a day or two at a time. I was at my worldliest then. Left alone, I yielded myself up to a worldly yearning for enough of anything (except misery), and for the death of mother's father, who was a machine-maker at Birmingham, and on whose decease, I had heard mother say, she would come into a whole courtful of houses 'if she had her rights.' Worldly little devil, I would stand about, musingly fitting my cold bare feet into cracked bricks and crevices of the damp cellar-floor, - walking over my grandfather's body, so to speak, into the courtful of houses, and selling them for meat and drink, and clothes to wear.

At last a change came down into our cellar. The universal change came down even as low as that, - so will it mount to any height on which a human creature can perch, - and brought other changes with it.

We had a heap of I don't know what foul litter in the darkest corner, which we called 'the bed.' For three days mother lay upon it without getting up, and then began at times to laugh. If I had ever heard her laugh before, it had been so seldom that the strange sound frightened me. It frightened father too; and we took it by turns to give her water. Then she began to move her head from side to side, and sing. After that, she getting no better, father fell a-laughing and a-singing; and then there was only I to give them both water, and they both died.

FOURTH CHAPTER

WHEN I was lifted out of the cellar by two men, of whom one came peeping down alone first, and ran away and brought the other, I could hardly bear the light of the street. I was sitting in the road-way, blinking at it, and at a ring of people collected around me, but not close to me, when, true to my character of worldly little devil, I broke silence by saying, 'I am hungry and thirsty!'

'Does he know they are dead?' asked one of another.

'Do you know your father and mother are both dead of fever?' asked a third of me severely.

'I don't know what it is to be dead. I supposed it meant that, when the cup rattled against their teeth, and the water spilt over them. I am hungry and thirsty.' That was all I had to say about it.

The ring of people widened outward from the inner side as I looked around me; and I smelt vinegar, and what I know to be camphor, thrown in towards where I sat. Presently some one put a great vessel of smoking vinegar on the ground near me; and then they all looked at me in silent horror as I ate and drank of what was brought for me. I knew at the time they had a horror of me, but I couldn't help it.

I was still eating and drinking, and a murmur of discussion had begun to arise respecting what was to be done with me next, when I heard a cracked voice somewhere in the ring say, 'My name is Hawkyard, Mr. Verity Hawkyard, of West Bromwich.' Then the ring split in one place; and a yellow-faced, peak-nosed gentleman, clad all in iron-gray to his gaiters, pressed forward with a policeman and another official of some sort. He came forward close to the vessel of smoking vinegar; from which he sprinkled himself carefully, and me copiously.

'He had a grandfather at Birmingham, this young boy, who is just dead too,' said Mr. Hawkyard.

I turned my eyes upon the speaker, and said in a ravening manner, 'Where's his houses?'

'Hah! Horrible worldliness on the edge of the grave,' said Mr. Hawkyard, casting more of the vinegar over me, as if to get my devil out of me. 'I have undertaken a slight - a very slight - trust in behalf of this boy; quite a voluntary trust: a matter of mere honour, if not of mere sentiment: still I have taken it upon myself, and it shall be (O, yes, it shall be!) discharged.'

The bystanders seemed to form an opinion of this gentleman much more favourable than their opinion of me.

'He shall be taught,' said Mr. Hawkyard, '(O, yes, he shall be taught!) but what is to be done with him for the present? He may be infected. He may disseminate infection.' The ring widened considerably. 'What is to be done with him?'

He held some talk with the two officials. I could distinguish no word save 'Farm-house.' There was another sound several times repeated, which was wholly meaningless in my ears then, but which I knew afterwards to be 'Hoghton Towers.'

'Yes,' said Mr. Hawkyard. 'I think that sounds promising; I think that sounds hopeful. And he can be put by himself in a ward, for a night or two, you say?'

It seemed to be the police-officer who had said so; for it was he who replied, Yes! It was he, too, who finally took me by the arm, and walked me before him through the streets, into a whitewashed room in a bare building, where I had a chair to sit in, a table to sit at, an iron bedstead and good mattress to lie upon, and a rug and blanket to cover me. Where I had enough to eat too, and was shown how to clean the tin porringer in which it was conveyed to me, until it was as good as a looking-glass. Here, likewise, I was put in a bath, and had new clothes brought to me; and my old rags were burnt, and I was camphored and vinegared and disinfected in a variety of ways.

When all this was done, - I don't know in how many days or how few, but it matters not, - Mr. Hawkyard stepped in at the door, remaining close to it, and said, 'Go and stand against the opposite wall, George Silverman. As far off as you can. That'll do. How do you feel?'

I told him that I didn't feel cold, and didn't feel hungry, and didn't feel thirsty. That was the whole round of human feelings, as far as I knew, except the pain of being beaten.

'Well,' said he, 'you are going, George, to a healthy farm-house to be purified. Keep in the air there as much as you can. Live an out-of-door life there, until you are fetched away. You had better not say much - in fact, you had better be very careful not to say anything - about what your parents died of, or they might not like to take you in. Behave well, and I'll put you to school; O, yes! I'll put you to school, though I'm not obliged to do it. I am a servant of the Lord, George; and I have been a good servant to him, I have, these five-and-thirty years. The Lord has had a good servant in me, and he knows it.'

What I then supposed him to mean by this, I cannot imagine. As little do I know when I began to comprehend that he was a prominent member of some obscure denomination or congregation, every member of which held forth to the rest when so inclined, and among whom he was called Brother Hawkyard. It was enough for me to know, on that day in the ward, that the farmer's cart was waiting for me at the street corner. I was not slow to get into it; for it was the first ride I ever had in my life.

It made me sleepy, and I slept. First, I stared at Preston streets as long as they lasted; and, meanwhile, I may have had some small dumb wondering within me whereabouts our cellar was; but I doubt it. Such a worldly little devil was I, that I took no thought who would bury father and mother, or where they would be buried, or when. The question whether the eating and drinking by day, and the covering by night, would be as good at the farm-house as at the ward superseded those questions.

The jolting of the cart on a loose stony road awoke me; and I found that we were mounting a steep hill, where the road was a rutty by- road through a field. And so, by fragments of an ancient terrace, and by some rugged outbuildings that had once been fortified, and passing under a ruined gateway we came to the old farm-house in the thick stone wall outside the old quadrangle of Hoghton Towers: which I looked at like a stupid savage, seeing no specially in, seeing no antiquity in; assuming all farm-houses to resemble it; assigning the decay I noticed to the one potent cause of all ruin that I knew, - poverty; eyeing the pigeons in their flights, the cattle in their stalls, the ducks in the pond, and the fowls pecking about the yard, with a hungry hope that plenty of them might be killed for dinner while I stayed there; wondering whether the scrubbed dairy vessels, drying in the sunlight, could be goodly porringers out of which the master ate his belly-filling food, and which he polished when he had done, according to my ward experience; shrinkingly doubtful whether the shadows, passing over that airy height on the bright spring day, were not something in the nature of frowns, - sordid, afraid, unadmiring, - a small brute to shudder at.

To that time I had never had the faintest impression of duty. I had had no knowledge whatever that there was anything lovely in this life. When I had occasionally slunk up the cellar-steps into the street, and glared in at shop-windows, I had done so with no higher feelings than we may suppose to animate a mangy young dog or wolf-cub. It is equally the fact that I had never been alone, in the sense of holding unselfish converse with myself. I had been solitary often enough, but nothing better.

Such was my condition when I sat down to my dinner that day, in the kitchen of the old farm-house. Such was my condition when I lay on my bed in the old farm-house that night, stretched out opposite the narrow mullioned window, in the cold light of the moon, like a young vampire.

FIFTH CHAPTER

WHAT do I know of Hoghton Towers? Very little; for I have been gratefully unwilling to disturb my first impressions. A house, centuries old, on high ground a mile or so removed from the road between Preston and Blackburn, where the first James of England, in his hurry to make money by making baronets, perhaps made some of those remunerative dignitaries. A house, centuries old, deserted and falling to pieces, its woods and gardens long since grass-land or ploughed up, the Rivers Ribble and Darwen glancing below it, and a vague haze of smoke, against which not even the supernatural prescience of the first Stuart could foresee a counter-blast, hinting at steam-power, powerful in two distances.

What did I know then of Hoghton Towers? When I first peeped in at the gate of the lifeless quadrangle, and started from the mouldering statue becoming visible to me like its guardian ghost; when I stole round by the back of the farm-house, and got in among the ancient rooms, many of them with their floors and ceilings falling, the beams and rafters hanging dangerously down, the plaster dropping as I trod, the oaken panels stripped away, the windows half walled up, half broken; when I discovered a gallery commanding the old kitchen, and looked down between balustrades upon a massive old table and benches, fearing to see I know not what dead-alive creatures come in and seat themselves, and look up with I know not what dreadful eyes, or lack of eyes, at me; when all over the house I was awed by gaps and chinks where the sky stared sorrowfully at me, where the birds passed, and the ivy rustled, and the stains of winter weather blotched the rotten floors; when down at the bottom of dark pits of staircase, into which the stairs had sunk, green leaves trembled, butterflies fluttered, and bees hummed in and out through the broken door-ways; when encircling the whole ruin were sweet scents, and sights of fresh green growth, and ever-renewing life, that I had never dreamed of, - I say, when I passed into such clouded perception of these things as my dark soul could compass, what did I know then of Hoghton Towers?

I have written that the sky stared sorrowfully at me. Therein have I anticipated the answer. I knew that all these things looked sorrowfully at me; that they seemed to sigh or whisper, not without pity for me, 'Alas! poor worldly little devil!'

There were two or three rats at the bottom of one of the smaller pits of broken staircase when I craned over and looked in. They were scuffling for some prey that was there; and, when they started and hid themselves close together in the dark, I thought of the old life (it had grown old already) in the cellar.

How not to be this worldly little devil? how not to have a repugnance towards myself as I had towards the rats? I hid in a corner of one of the smaller chambers, frightened at myself, and crying (it was the first time I had ever cried for any cause not purely physical), and I tried to think about it. One of the farm- ploughs came into my range of view just then; and it seemed to help me as it went on with its two horses up and down the field so peacefully and quietly.

There was a girl of about my own age in the farm-house family, and she sat opposite to me at the narrow table at meal-times. It had come into my mind, at our first dinner, that she might take the fever from me. The thought had not disquieted me then. I had only speculated how she would look under the altered circumstances, and whether she would die. But it came into my mind now, that I might try to prevent her taking the fever by keeping away from her. I knew I should have but scrambling board if I did; so much the less worldly and less devilish the deed would be, I thought.

From that hour, I withdrew myself at early morning into secret corners of the ruined house, and remained hidden there until she went to bed. At first, when meals were ready, I used to hear them calling me; and then my resolution weakened. But I strengthened it again by going farther off into the ruin, and getting out of hearing. I often watched for her at the dim windows; and, when I saw that she was fresh and rosy, felt much happier.

Out of this holding her in my thoughts, to the humanising of myself, I suppose some childish love arose within me. I felt, in some sort, dignified by the pride of protecting her, - by the pride of making the sacrifice for her. As my heart swelled with that new feeling, it insensibly softened about mother and father. It seemed to have been frozen before, and now to be thawed. The old ruin and all the lovely things that haunted it were not sorrowful for me only, but sorrowful for mother and father as well. Therefore did I cry again, and often too.

The farm-house family conceived me to be of a morose temper, and were very short with me; though they never stinted me in such broken fare as was to be got out of regular hours. One night when I lifted the kitchen latch at my usual time, Sylvia (that was her pretty name) had but just gone out of the room. Seeing her ascending the opposite stairs, I stood still at the door. She had heard the clink of the latch, and looked round.

'George,' she called to me in a pleased voice, 'to-morrow is my birthday; and we are to have a fiddler, and there's a party of boys and girls coming in a cart, and we shall dance. I invite you. Be sociable for once, George.'

'I am very sorry, miss,' I answered; 'but I - but, no; I can't come.'

'You are a disagreeable, ill-humoured lad,' she returned disdainfully; 'and I ought not to have asked you. I shall never speak to you again.'

As I stood with my eyes fixed on the fire, after she was gone, I felt that the farmer bent his brows upon me.

'Eh, lad!' said he; 'Sylvy's right. You're as moody and broody a lad as never I set eyes on yet.'

I tried to assure him that I meant no harm; but he only said coldly, 'Maybe not, maybe not! There, get thy supper, get thy supper; and then thou canst sulk to thy heart's content again.'

Ah! if they could have seen me next day, in the ruin, watching for the arrival of the cart full of merry young guests; if they could have seen me at night, gliding out from behind the ghostly statue, listening to the music and the fall of dancing feet, and watching the lighted farm-house windows from the quadrangle when all the ruin was dark; if they could have read my heart, as I crept up to bed by the back way, comforting myself with the reflection, 'They will take no hurt from me,' - they would not have thought mine a morose or an unsocial nature.

It was in these ways that I began to form a shy disposition; to be of a timidly silent character under misconstruction; to have an inexpressible, perhaps a morbid, dread of ever being sordid or worldly. It was in these ways that my nature came to shape itself to such a mould, even before it was affected by the influences of the studious and retired life of a poor scholar.

SIXTH CHAPTER

BROTHER HAWKYARD (as he insisted on my calling him) put me to school, and told me to work my way. 'You are all right, George,' he said. 'I have been the best servant the Lord has had in his service for this five-and-thirty year (O, I have!); and he knows the value of such a servant as I have been to him (O, yes, he does!); and he'll prosper your schooling as a part of my reward. That's what HE'll do, George. He'll do it for me.'

From the first I could not like this familiar knowledge of the ways of the sublime, inscrutable Almighty, on Brother Hawkyard's part. As I grew a little wiser, and still a little wiser, I liked it less and less. His manner, too, of confirming himself in a parenthesis, - as if, knowing himself, he doubted his own word, - I found distasteful. I cannot tell how much these dislikes cost me; for I had a dread that they were worldly.

As time went on, I became a Foundation-boy on a good foundation, and I cost Brother Hawkyard nothing. When I had worked my way so far, I worked yet harder, in the hope of ultimately getting a presentation to college and a fellowship. My health has never been strong (some vapour from the Preston cellar cleaves to me, I think); and what with much work and some weakness, I came again to be regarded - that is, by my fellow-students - as unsocial.

All through my time as a foundation-boy, I was within a few miles of Brother Hawkyard's congregation; and whenever I was what we called a leave-boy on a Sunday, I went over there at his desire. Before the knowledge became forced upon me that outside their place of meeting these brothers and sisters were no better than the rest of the human family, but on the whole were, to put the case mildly, as bad as most, in respect of giving short weight in their shops, and not speaking the truth, - I say, before this knowledge became forced upon me, their prolix addresses, their inordinate conceit, their daring ignorance, their investment of the Supreme Ruler of heaven and earth with their own miserable meannesses and littlenesses, greatly shocked me. Still, as their term for the frame of mind that could not perceive them to be in an exalted state of grace was the 'worldly' state, I did for a time suffer tortures under my inquiries of myself whether that young worldly- devilish spirit of mine could secretly be lingering at the bottom of my non-appreciation.

Brother Hawkyard was the popular expounder in this assembly, and generally occupied the platform (there was a little platform with a table on it, in lieu of a pulpit) first, on a Sunday afternoon. He was by trade a drysalter. Brother Gimblet, an elderly man with a crabbed face, a large dog's-eared shirt-collar, and a spotted blue neckerchief reaching up behind to the crown of his head, was also a drysalter and an expounder. Brother Gimblet professed the greatest admiration for Brother Hawkyard, but (I had thought more than once) bore him a jealous grudge.

Let whosoever may peruse these lines kindly take the pains here to read twice my solemn pledge, that what I write of the language and customs of the congregation in question I write scrupulously, literally, exactly, from the life and the truth.

On the first Sunday after I had won what I had so long tried for, and when it was certain that I was going up to college, Brother Hawkyard concluded a long exhortation thus:

'Well, my friends and fellow-sinners, now I told you when I began, that I didn't know a word of what I was going to say to you (and no, I did not!), but that it was all one to me, because I knew the Lord would put into my mouth the words I wanted.'

('That's it!' from Brother Gimblet.)

'And he did put into my mouth the words I wanted.'

('So he did!' from Brother Gimblet.)

'And why?'

('Ah, let's have that!' from Brother Gimblet.)

'Because I have been his faithful servant for five-and-thirty years, and because he knows it. For five-and-thirty years! And he knows it, mind you! I got those words that I wanted on account of my wages. I got 'em from the Lord, my fellow-sinners. Down! I said, "Here's a heap of wages due; let us have something down, on account." And I got it down, and I paid it over to you; and you won't wrap it up in a napkin, nor yet in a towel, nor yet pocketankercher, but you'll put it out at good interest. Very well. Now, my brothers and sisters and fellow-sinners, I am going to conclude with a question, and I'll make it so plain (with the help of the Lord, after five-and-thirty years, I should rather hope!) as that the Devil shall not be able to confuse it in your heads, - which he would be overjoyed to do.'

('Just his way. Crafty old blackguard!' from Brother Gimblet.)

'And the question is this, Are the angels learned?'

('Not they. Not a bit on it!' from Brother Gimblet, with the greatest confidence.)

'Not they. And where's the proof? sent ready-made by the hand of the Lord. Why, there's one among us here now, that has got all the learning that can be crammed into him. I got him all the learning that could be crammed into him. His grandfather' (this I had never heard before) 'was a brother of ours. He was Brother Parksop. That's what he was. Parksop; Brother Parksop. His worldly name was Parksop, and he was a brother of this brotherhood. Then wasn't he Brother Parksop?'

('Must be. Couldn't help hisself!' from Brother Gimblet.)

'Well, he left that one now here present among us to the care of a brother-sinner of his (and that brother-sinner, mind you, was a sinner of a bigger size in his time than any of you; praise the Lord!), Brother Hawkyard. Me. I got him without fee or reward, - without a morsel of myrrh, or frankincense, nor yet amber, letting alone the honeycomb, - all the learning that could be crammed into him. Has it brought him into our temple, in the spirit? No. Have we had any ignorant brothers and sisters that didn't know round O from crooked S, come in among us meanwhile? Many. Then the angels are NOT learned; then they don't so much as know their alphabet. And now, my friends and fellow-sinners, having brought it to that, perhaps some brother present - perhaps you, Brother Gimblet - will pray a bit for us?'

Brother Gimblet undertook the sacred function, after having drawn his sleeve across his mouth, and muttered, 'Well! I don't know as I see my way to hitting any of you quite in the right place neither.' He said this with a dark smile, and then began to bellow. What we were specially to be preserved from, according to his solicitations, was, despoilment of the orphan, suppression of testamentary intentions on the part of a father or (say) grandfather, appropriation of the orphan's house-property, feigning to give in charity to the wronged one from whom we withheld his due; and that class of sins. He ended with the petition, 'Give us peace!' which, speaking for myself, was very much needed after twenty minutes of his bellowing.

Even though I had not seen him when he rose from his knees, steaming with perspiration, glance at Brother Hawkyard, and even though I had not heard Brother Hawkyard's tone of congratulating him on the vigour with which he had roared, I should have detected a malicious application in this prayer. Unformed suspicions to a similar effect had sometimes passed through my mind in my earlier school-days, and had always caused me great distress; for they were worldly in their nature, and wide, very wide, of the spirit that had drawn me from Sylvia. They were sordid suspicions, without a shadow of proof. They were worthy to have originated in the unwholesome cellar. They were not only without proof, but against proof; for was I not myself a living proof of what Brother Hawkyard had done? and without him, how should I ever have seen the sky look sorrowfully down upon that wretched boy at Hoghton Towers?

Although the dread of a relapse into a stage of savage selfishness was less strong upon me as I approached manhood, and could act in an increased degree for myself, yet I was always on my guard against any tendency to such relapse. After getting these suspicions under my feet, I had been troubled by not being able to like Brother Hawkyard's manner, or his professed religion. So it came about, that, as I walked back that Sunday evening, I thought it would be an act of reparation for any such injury my struggling thoughts had unwillingly done him, if I wrote, and placed in his hands, before going to college, a full acknowledgment of his goodness to me, and an ample tribute of thanks. It might serve as an implied vindication of him against any dark scandal from a rival brother and expounder, or from any other quarter.

Accordingly, I wrote the document with much care. I may add with much feeling too; for it affected me as I went on. Having no set studies to pursue, in the brief interval between leaving the Foundation and going to Cambridge, I determined to walk out to his place of business, and give it into his own hands.

It was a winter afternoon, when I tapped at the door of his little counting-house, which was at the farther end of his long, low shop. As I did so (having entered by the back yard, where casks and boxes were taken in, and where there was the inscription, 'Private way to the counting-house'), a shopman called to me from the counter that he was engaged.

'Brother Gimblet' (said the shopman, who was one of the brotherhood) 'is with him.'

I thought this all the better for my purpose, and made bold to tap again. They were talking in a low tone, and money was passing; for I heard it being counted out.

'Who is it?' asked Brother Hawkyard, sharply.

'George Silverman,' I answered, holding the door open. 'May I come in?'

Both brothers seemed so astounded to see me that I felt shyer than usual. But they looked quite cadaverous in the early gaslight, and perhaps that accidental circumstance exaggerated the expression of their faces.

'What is the matter?' asked Brother Hawkyard.

'Ay! what is the matter?' asked Brother Gimblet.

'Nothing at all,' I said, diffidently producing my document: 'I am only the bearer of a letter from myself.'

'From yourself, George?' cried Brother Hawkyard.

'And to you,' said I.

'And to me, George?'

He turned paler, and opened it hurriedly; but looking over it, and seeing generally what it was, became less hurried, recovered his colour, and said, 'Praise the Lord!'

'That's it!' cried Brother Gimblet. 'Well put! Amen.'

Brother Hawkyard then said, in a livelier strain, 'You must know, George, that Brother Gimblet and I are going to make our two businesses one. We are going into partnership. We are settling it now. Brother Gimblet is to take one clear half of the profits (O, yes! he shall have it; he shall have it to the last farthing).'

'D.V.!' said Brother Gimblet, with his right fist firmly clinched on his right leg.

'There is no objection,' pursued Brother Hawkyard, 'to my reading this aloud, George?'

As it was what I expressly desired should be done, after yesterday's prayer, I more than readily begged him to read it aloud. He did so; and Brother Gimblet listened with a crabbed smile.

'It was in a good hour that I came here,' he said, wrinkling up his eyes. 'It was in a good hour, likewise, that I was moved yesterday to depict for the terror of evil-doers a character the direct opposite of Brother Hawkyard's. But it was the Lord that done it: I felt him at it while I was perspiring.'

After that it was proposed by both of them that I should attend the congregation once more before my final departure. What my shy reserve would undergo, from being expressly preached at and prayed at, I knew beforehand. But I reflected that it would be for the last time, and that it might add to the weight of my letter. It was well known to the brothers and sisters that there was no place taken for me in THEIR paradise; and if I showed this last token of deference to Brother Hawkyard, notoriously in despite of my own sinful inclinations, it might go some little way in aid of my statement that he had been good to me, and that I was grateful to him. Merely stipulating, therefore, that no express endeavour should be made for my conversion, - which would involve the rolling of several brothers and sisters on the floor, declaring that they felt all their sins in a heap on their left side, weighing so many pounds avoirdupois, as I knew from what I had seen of those repulsive mysteries, - I promised.

Since the reading of my letter, Brother Gimblet had been at intervals wiping one eye with an end of his spotted blue neckerchief, and grinning to himself.

It was, however, a habit that brother had, to grin in an ugly manner even when expounding. I call to mind a delighted snarl with which he used to detail from the platform the torments reserved for the wicked (meaning all human creation except the brotherhood), as being remarkably hideous.

I left the two to settle their articles of partnership, and count money; and I never saw them again but on the following Sunday. Brother Hawkyard died within two or three years, leaving all he possessed to Brother Gimblet, in virtue of a will dated (as I have been told) that very day.

Now I was so far at rest with myself, when Sunday came, knowing that I had conquered my own mistrust, and righted Brother Hawkyard in the jaundiced vision of a rival, that I went, even to that coarse chapel, in a less sensitive state than usual. How could I foresee that the delicate, perhaps the diseased, corner of my mind, where I winced and shrunk when it was touched, or was even approached, would be handled as the theme of the whole proceedings?

On this occasion it was assigned to Brother Hawkyard to pray, and to Brother Gimblet to preach. The prayer was to open the ceremonies; the discourse was to come next. Brothers Hawkyard and Gimblet were both on the platform; Brother Hawkyard on his knees at the table, unmusically ready to pray; Brother Gimblet sitting against the wall, grinningly ready to preach.

'Let us offer up the sacrifice of prayer, my brothers and sisters and fellow-sinners.' Yes; but it was I who was the sacrifice. It was our poor, sinful, worldly-minded brother here present who was wrestled for. The now-opening career of this our unawakened brother might lead to his becoming a minister of what was called 'the church.' That was what HE looked to. The church. Not the chapel, Lord. The church. No rectors, no vicars, no archdeacons, no bishops, no archbishops, in the chapel, but, O Lord! many such in the church. Protect our sinful brother from his love of lucre. Cleanse from our unawakened brother's breast his sin of worldly- mindedness. The prayer said infinitely more in words, but nothing more to any intelligible effect.

Then Brother Gimblet came forward, and took (as I knew he would) the text, 'My kingdom is not of this world.' Ah! but whose was, my fellow-sinners? Whose? Why, our brother's here present was. The only kingdom he had an idea of was of this world. ('That's it!' from several of the congregation.) What did the woman do when she lost the piece of money? Went and looked for it. What should our brother do when he lost his way? ('Go and look for it,' from a sister.) Go and look for it, true. But must he look for it in the right direction, or in the wrong? ('In the right,' from a brother.) There spake the prophets! He must look for it in the right direction, or he couldn't find it. But he had turned his back upon the right direction, and he wouldn't find it. Now, my fellow-sinners, to show you the difference betwixt worldly- mindedness and unworldly-mindedness, betwixt kingdoms not of this world and kingdoms OF this world, here was a letter wrote by even our worldly-minded brother unto Brother Hawkyard. Judge, from hearing of it read, whether Brother Hawkyard was the faithful steward that the Lord had in his mind only t'other day, when, in this very place, he drew you the picter of the unfaithful one; for it was him that done it, not me. Don't doubt that!

Brother Gimblet then groaned and bellowed his way through my composition, and subsequently through an hour. The service closed with a hymn, in which the brothers unanimously roared, and the sisters unanimously shrieked at me, That I by wiles of worldly gain was mocked, and they on waters of sweet love were rocked; that I with mammon struggled in the dark, while they were floating in a second ark.

I went out from all this with an aching heart and a weary spirit: not because I was quite so weak as to consider these narrow creatures interpreters of the Divine Majesty and Wisdom, but because I was weak enough to feel as though it were my hard fortune to be misrepresented and misunderstood, when I most tried to subdue any risings of mere worldliness within me, and when I most hoped that, by dint of trying earnestly, I had succeeded.

SEVENTH CHAPTER

MY timidity and my obscurity occasioned me to live a secluded life at college, and to be little known. No relative ever came to visit me, for I had no relative. No intimate friends broke in upon my studies, for I made no intimate friends. I supported myself on my scholarship, and read much. My college time was otherwise not so very different from my time at Hoghton Towers.

Knowing myself to be unfit for the noisier stir of social existence, but believing myself qualified to do my duty in a moderate, though earnest way, if I could obtain some small preferment in the Church, I applied my mind to the clerical profession. In due sequence I took orders, was ordained, and began to look about me for employment. I must observe that I had taken a good degree, that I had succeeded in winning a good fellowship, and that my means were ample for my retired way of life. By this time I had read with several young men; and the occupation increased my income, while it was highly interesting to me. I once accidentally overheard our greatest don say, to my boundless joy, 'That he heard it reported of Silverman that his gift of quiet explanation, his patience, his amiable temper, and his conscientiousness made him the best of coaches.' May my 'gift of quiet explanation' come more seasonably and powerfully to my aid in this present explanation than I think it will!

It may be in a certain degree owing to the situation of my college- rooms (in a corner where the daylight was sobered), but it is in a much larger degree referable to the state of my own mind, that I seem to myself, on looking back to this time of my life, to have been always in the peaceful shade. I can see others in the sunlight; I can see our boats' crews and our athletic young men on the glistening water, or speckled with the moving lights of sunlit leaves; but I myself am always in the shadow looking on. Not unsympathetically, - God forbid! - but looking on alone, much as I looked at Sylvia from the shadows of the ruined house, or looked at the red gleam shining through the farmer's windows, and listened to the fall of dancing feet, when all the ruin was dark that night in the quadrangle.

I now come to the reason of my quoting that laudation of myself above given. Without such reason, to repeat it would have been mere boastfulness.

Among those who had read with me was Mr. Fareway, second son of Lady Fareway, widow of Sir Gaston Fareway, baronet. This young gentleman's abilities were much above the average; but he came of a rich family, and was idle and luxurious. He presented himself to me too late, and afterwards came to me too irregularly, to admit of my being of much service to him. In the end, I considered it my duty to dissuade him from going up for an examination which he could never pass; and he left college without a degree. After his departure, Lady Fareway wrote to me, representing the justice of my returning half my fee, as I had been of so little use to her son. Within my knowledge a similar demand had not been made in any other case; and I most freely admit that the justice of it had not occurred to me until it was pointed out. But I at once perceived it, yielded to it, and returned the money -

Mr. Fareway had been gone two years or more, and I had forgotten him, when he one day walked into my rooms as I was sitting at my books.

Said he, after the usual salutations had passed, 'Mr. Silverman, my mother is in town here, at the hotel, and wishes me to present you to her.'

I was not comfortable with strangers, and I dare say I betrayed that I was a little nervous or unwilling. 'For,' said he, without my having spoken, 'I think the interview may tend to the advancement of your prospects.'

It put me to the blush to think that I should be tempted by a worldly reason, and I rose immediately.

Said Mr. Fareway, as we went along, 'Are you a good hand at business?'

'I think not,' said I.

Said Mr. Fareway then, 'My mother is.'

'Truly?' said I.

'Yes: my mother is what is usually called a managing woman. Doesn't make a bad thing, for instance, even out of the spendthrift habits of my eldest brother abroad. In short, a managing woman. This is in confidence.'

He had never spoken to me in confidence, and I was surprised by his doing so. I said I should respect his confidence, of course, and said no more on the delicate subject. We had but a little way to walk, and I was soon in his mother's company. He presented me, shook hands with me, and left us two (as he said) to business.

I saw in my Lady Fareway a handsome, well-preserved lady of somewhat large stature, with a steady glare in her great round dark eyes that embarrassed me.

Said my lady, 'I have heard from my son, Mr. Silverman, that you would be glad of some preferment in the church.' I gave my lady to understand that was so.

'I don't know whether you are aware,' my lady proceeded, 'that we have a presentation to a living? I say WE have; but, in point of fact, I have.'

I gave my lady to understand that I had not been aware of this.

Said my lady, 'So it is: indeed I have two presentations, - one to two hundred a year, one to six. Both livings are in our county, - North Devonshire, - as you probably know. The first is vacant. Would you like it?'

What with my lady's eyes, and what with the suddenness of this proposed gift, I was much confused.

'I am sorry it is not the larger presentation,' said my lady, rather coldly; 'though I will not, Mr. Silverman, pay you the bad compliment of supposing that YOU are, because that would be mercenary, - and mercenary I am persuaded you are not.'

Said I, with my utmost earnestness, 'Thank you, Lady Fareway, thank you, thank you! I should be deeply hurt if I thought I bore the character.'

'Naturally,' said my lady. 'Always detestable, but particularly in a clergyman. You have not said whether you will like the living?'

With apologies for my remissness or indistinctness, I assured my lady that I accepted it most readily and gratefully. I added that I hoped she would not estimate my appreciation of the generosity of her choice by my flow of words; for I was not a ready man in that respect when taken by surprise or touched at heart.

'The affair is concluded,' said my lady; 'concluded. You will find the duties very light, Mr. Silverman. Charming house; charming little garden, orchard, and all that. You will be able to take pupils. By the bye! No: I will return to the word afterwards. What was I going to mention, when it put me out?'

My lady stared at me, as if I knew. And I didn't know. And that perplexed me afresh.

Said my lady, after some consideration, 'O, of course, how very dull of me! The last incumbent, - least mercenary man I ever saw, - in consideration of the duties being so light and the house so delicious, couldn't rest, he said, unless I permitted him to help me with my correspondence, accounts, and various little things of that kind; nothing in themselves, but which it worries a lady to cope with. Would Mr. Silverman also like to -? Or shall I -?'

I hastened to say that my poor help would be always at her ladyship's service.

'I am absolutely blessed,' said my lady, casting up her eyes (and so taking them off me for one moment), 'in having to do with gentlemen who cannot endure an approach to the idea of being mercenary!' She shivered at the word. 'And now as to the pupil.'

'The -?' I was quite at a loss.

'Mr. Silverman, you have no idea what she is. She is,' said my lady, laying her touch upon my coat-sleeve, 'I do verily believe, the most extraordinary girl in this world. Already knows more Greek and Latin than Lady Jane Grey. And taught herself! Has not yet, remember, derived a moment's advantage from Mr. Silverman's classical acquirements. To say nothing of mathematics, which she is bent upon becoming versed in, and in which (as I hear from my son and others) Mr. Silverman's reputation is so deservedly high!'

Under my lady's eyes I must have lost the clue, I felt persuaded; and yet I did not know where I could have dropped it.

'Adelina,' said my lady, 'is my only daughter. If I did not feel quite convinced that I am not blinded by a mother's partiality; unless I was absolutely sure that when you know her, Mr. Silverman, you will esteem it a high and unusual privilege to direct her studies, - I should introduce a mercenary element into this conversation, and ask you on what terms - '

I entreated my lady to go no further. My lady saw that I was troubled, and did me the honour to comply with my request.

EIGHTH CHAPTER

EVERYTHING in mental acquisition that her brother might have been, if he would, and everything in all gracious charms and admirable qualities that no one but herself could be, - this was Adelina.

I will not expatiate upon her beauty; I will not expatiate upon her intelligence, her quickness of perception, her powers of memory, her sweet consideration, from the first moment, for the slow-paced tutor who ministered to her wonderful gifts. I was thirty then; I am over sixty now: she is ever present to me in these hours as she was in those, bright and beautiful and young, wise and fanciful and good.

When I discovered that I loved her, how can I say? In the first day? in the first week? in the first month? Impossible to trace. If I be (as I am) unable to represent to myself any previous period of my life as quite separable from her attracting power, how can I answer for this one detail?

Whensoever I made the discovery, it laid a heavy burden on me. And yet, comparing it with the far heavier burden that I afterwards took up, it does not seem to me now to have been very hard to bear. In the knowledge that I did love her, and that I should love her while my life lasted, and that I was ever to hide my secret deep in my own breast, and she was never to find it, there was a kind of sustaining joy or pride, or comfort, mingled with my pain.

But later on, - say, a year later on, - when I made another discovery, then indeed my suffering and my struggle were strong. That other discovery was -

These words will never see the light, if ever, until my heart is dust; until her bright spirit has returned to the regions of which, when imprisoned here, it surely retained some unusual glimpse of remembrance; until all the pulses that ever beat around us shall have long been quiet; until all the fruits of all the tiny victories and defeats achieved in our little breasts shall have withered away. That discovery was that she loved me.

She may have enhanced my knowledge, and loved me for that; she may have over-valued my discharge of duty to her, and loved me for that; she may have refined upon a playful compassion which she would sometimes show for what she called my want of wisdom, according to the light of the world's dark lanterns, and loved me for that; she may - she must - have confused the borrowed light of what I had only learned, with its brightness in its pure, original rays; but she loved me at that time, and she made me know it.

Pride of family and pride of wealth put me as far off from her in my lady's eyes as if I had been some domesticated creature of another kind. But they could not put me farther from her than I put myself when I set my merits against hers. More than that. They could not put me, by millions of fathoms, half so low beneath her as I put myself when in imagination I took advantage of her noble trustfulness, took the fortune that I knew she must possess in her own right, and left her to find herself, in the zenith of her beauty and genius, bound to poor rusty, plodding me.

No! Worldliness should not enter here at any cost. If I had tried to keep it out of other ground, how much harder was I bound to try to keep it out from this sacred place!

But there was something daring in her broad, generous character, that demanded at so delicate a crisis to be delicately and patiently addressed. And many and many a bitter night (O, I found I could cry for reasons not purely physical, at this pass of my life!) I took my course.

My lady had, in our first interview, unconsciously overstated the accommodation of my pretty house. There was room in it for only one pupil. He was a young gentleman near coming of age, very well connected, but what is called a poor relation. His parents were dead. The charges of his living and reading with me were defrayed by an uncle; and he and I were to do our utmost together for three years towards qualifying him to make his way. At this time he had entered into his second year with me. He was well-looking, clever, energetic, enthusiastic; bold; in the best sense of the term, a thorough young Anglo-Saxon.

I resolved to bring these two together.

NINTH CHAPTER

SAID I, one night, when I had conquered myself, 'Mr. Granville,' - Mr. Granville Wharton his name was, - 'I doubt if you have ever yet so much as seen Miss Fareway.'

'Well, sir,' returned he, laughing, 'you see her so much yourself, that you hardly leave another fellow a chance of seeing her.'

'I am her tutor, you know,' said I.

And there the subject dropped for that time. But I so contrived as that they should come together shortly afterwards. I had previously so contrived as to keep them asunder; for while I loved her, - I mean before I had determined on my sacrifice, - a lurking jealousy of Mr. Granville lay within my unworthy breast.

It was quite an ordinary interview in the Fareway Park but they talked easily together for some time: like takes to like, and they had many points of resemblance. Said Mr. Granville to me, when he and I sat at our supper that night, 'Miss Fareway is remarkably beautiful, sir, remarkably engaging. Don't you think so?' 'I think so,' said I. And I stole a glance at him, and saw that he had reddened and was thoughtful. I remember it most vividly, because the mixed feeling of grave pleasure and acute pain that the slight circumstance caused me was the first of a long, long series of such mixed impressions under which my hair turned slowly gray.

I had not much need to feign to be subdued; but I counterfeited to be older than I was in all respects (Heaven knows! my heart being all too young the while), and feigned to be more of a recluse and bookworm than I had really become, and gradually set up more and more of a fatherly manner towards Adelina. Likewise I made my tuition less imaginative than before; separated myself from my poets and philosophers; was careful to present them in their own light, and me, their lowly servant, in my own shade. Moreover, in the matter of apparel I was equally mindful; not that I had ever been dapper that way; but that I was slovenly now.

As I depressed myself with one hand, so did I labour to raise Mr. Granville with the other; directing his attention to such subjects as I too well knew interested her, and fashioning him (do not deride or misconstrue the expression, unknown reader of this writing; for I have suffered!) into a greater resemblance to myself in my solitary one strong aspect. And gradually, gradually, as I saw him take more and more to these thrown-out lures of mine, then did I come to know better and better that love was drawing him on, and was drawing her from me.

So passed more than another year; every day a year in its number of my mixed impressions of grave pleasure and acute pain; and then these two, being of age and free to act legally for themselves, came before me hand in hand (my hair being now quite white), and entreated me that I would unite them together. 'And indeed, dear tutor,' said Adelina, 'it is but consistent in you that you should do this thing for us, seeing that we should never have spoken together that first time but for you, and that but for you we could never have met so often afterwards.' The whole of which was literally true; for I had availed myself of my many business attendances on, and conferences with, my lady, to take Mr. Granville to the house, and leave him in the outer room with Adelina.

I knew that my lady would object to such a marriage for her daughter, or to any marriage that was other than an exchange of her for stipulated lands, goods, and moneys. But looking on the two, and seeing with full eyes that they were both young and beautiful; and knowing that they were alike in the tastes and acquirements that will outlive youth and beauty; and considering that Adelina had a fortune now, in her own keeping; and considering further that Mr. Granville, though for the present poor, was of a good family that had never lived in a cellar in Preston; and believing that their love would endure, neither having any great discrepancy to find out in the other, - I told them of my readiness to do this thing which Adelina asked of her dear tutor, and to send them forth, husband and wife, into the shining world with golden gates that awaited them.

It was on a summer morning that I rose before the sun to compose myself for the crowning of my work with this end; and my dwelling being near to the sea, I walked down to the rocks on the shore, in order that I might behold the sun in his majesty.

The tranquillity upon the deep, and on the firmament, the orderly withdrawal of the stars, the calm promise of coming day, the rosy suffusion of the sky and waters, the ineffable splendour that then burst forth, attuned my mind afresh after the discords of the night. Methought that all I looked on said to me, and that all I heard in the sea and in the air said to me, 'Be comforted, mortal, that thy life is so short. Our preparation for what is to follow has endured, and shall endure, for unimaginable ages.'

I married them. I knew that my hand was cold when I placed it on their hands clasped together; but the words with which I had to accompany the action I could say without faltering, and I was at peace.

They being well away from my house and from the place after our simple breakfast, the time was come when I must do what I had pledged myself to them that I would do, - break the intelligence to my lady.

I went up to the house, and found my lady in her ordinary business- room. She happened to have an unusual amount of commissions to intrust to me that day; and she had filled my hands with papers before I could originate a word.

'My lady,' I then began, as I stood beside her table.

'Why, what's the matter?' she said quickly, looking up.

'Not much, I would fain hope, after you shall have prepared yourself, and considered a little.'

'Prepared myself; and considered a little! You appear to have prepared YOURSELF but indifferently, anyhow, Mr. Silverman.' This mighty scornfully, as I experienced my usual embarrassment under her stare.

Said I, in self-extenuation once for all, 'Lady Fareway, I have but to say for myself that I have tried to do my duty.'

'For yourself?' repeated my lady. 'Then there are others concerned, I see. Who are they?'

I was about to answer, when she made towards the bell with a dart that stopped me, and said, 'Why, where is Adelina?'

'Forbear! be calm, my lady. I married her this morning to Mr. Granville Wharton.'

She set her lips, looked more intently at me than ever, raised her right hand, and smote me hard upon the cheek.

'Give me back those papers! give me back those papers!' She tore them out of my hands, and tossed them on her table. Then seating herself defiantly in her great chair, and folding her arms, she stabbed me to the heart with the unlooked-for reproach, 'You worldly wretch!'

'Worldly?' I cried. 'Worldly?'

'This, if you please,' - she went on with supreme scorn, pointing me out as if there were some one there to see, - 'this, if you please, is the disinterested scholar, with not a design beyond his books! This, if you please, is the simple creature whom any one could overreach in a bargain! This, if you please, is Mr. Silverman! Not of this world; not he! He has too much simplicity for this world's cunning. He has too much singleness of purpose to be a match for this world's double-dealing. What did he give you for it?'

'For what? And who?'

'How much,' she asked, bending forward in her great chair, and insultingly tapping the fingers of her right hand on the palm of her left, - 'how much does Mr. Granville Wharton pay you for getting him Adelina's money? What is the amount of your percentage upon Adelina's fortune? What were the terms of the agreement that you proposed to this boy when you, the Rev. George Silverman, licensed to marry, engaged to put him in possession of this girl? You made good terms for yourself, whatever they were. He would stand a poor chance against your keenness.'

Bewildered, horrified, stunned by this cruel perversion, I could not speak. But I trust that I looked innocent, being so.

'Listen to me, shrewd hypocrite,' said my lady, whose anger increased as she gave it utterance; 'attend to my words, you cunning schemer, who have carried this plot through with such a practised double face that I have never suspected you. I had my projects for my daughter; projects for family connection; projects for fortune. You have thwarted them, and overreached me; but I am not one to be thwarted and overreached without retaliation. Do you mean to hold this living another month?'

'Do you deem it possible, Lady Fareway, that I can hold it another hour, under your injurious words?'

'Is it resigned, then?'

'It was mentally resigned, my lady, some minutes ago.'

Don't equivocate, sir. IS it resigned?'

'Unconditionally and entirely; and I would that I had never, never come near it!'

'A cordial response from me to THAT wish, Mr. Silverman! But take this with you, sir. If you had not resigned it, I would have had you deprived of it. And though you have resigned it, you will not get quit of me as easily as you think for. I will pursue you with this story. I will make this nefarious conspiracy of yours, for money, known. You have made money by it, but you have at the same time made an enemy by it. YOU will take good care that the money sticks to you; I will take good care that the enemy sticks to you.'

Then said I finally, 'Lady Fareway, I think my heart is broken. Until I came into this room just now, the possibility of such mean wickedness as you have imputed to me never dawned upon my thoughts. Your suspicions - '

'Suspicions! Pah!' said she indignantly. 'Certainties.'

'Your certainties, my lady, as you call them, your suspicions as I call them, are cruel, unjust, wholly devoid of foundation in fact. I can declare no more; except that I have not acted for my own profit or my own pleasure. I have not in this proceeding considered myself. Once again, I think my heart is broken. If I have unwittingly done any wrong with a righteous motive, that is some penalty to pay.'

She received this with another and more indignant 'Pah!' and I made my way out of her room (I think I felt my way out with my hands, although my eyes were open), almost suspecting that my voice had a repulsive sound, and that I was a repulsive object.

There was a great stir made, the bishop was appealed to, I received a severe reprimand, and narrowly escaped suspension. For years a cloud hung over me, and my name was tarnished.

But my heart did not break, if a broken heart involves death; for I lived through it.

They stood by me, Adelina and her husband, through it all. Those who had known me at college, and even most of those who had only known me there by reputation, stood by me too. Little by little, the belief widened that I was not capable of what was laid to my charge. At length I was presented to a college-living in a sequestered place, and there I now pen my explanation. I pen it at my open window in the summer-time, before me, lying in the churchyard, equal resting-place for sound hearts, wounded hearts, and broken hearts. I pen it for the relief of my own mind, not foreseeing whether or no it will ever have a reader.

Going into Society

by Charles Dickens

At one period of its reverses, the House fell into the occupation of a Showman. He was found registered as its occupier, on the parish books of the time when he rented the House, and there was therefore no need of any clue to his name. But, he himself was less easy to be found; for, he had led a wandering life, and settled people had lost sight of him, and people who plumed themselves on being respectable were shy of admitting that they had ever known anything of him. At last, among the marsh lands near the river's level, that lie about Deptford and the neighbouring market-gardens, a

Grizzled Personage in velveteen, with a face so cut up by varieties of weather that he looked as if he had been tattooed, was found smoking a pipe at the door of a wooden house on wheels. The wooden house was laid up in ordinary for the winter, near the mouth of a muddy creek; and everything near it, the foggy river, the misty marshes, and the steaming market-gardens, smoked in company with the grizzled man. In the midst of this smoking party, the funnel-chimney of the wooden house on wheels was not remiss, but took its pipe with the rest in a companionable manner.

On being asked if it were he who had once rented the House to Let, Grizzled Velveteen looked surprised, and said yes. Then his name was Magsman? That was it, Toby Magsman--which lawfully christened Robert; but called in the line, from a infant, Toby. There was nothing agin Toby Magsman, he believed? If there was suspicion of such--mention it!

There was no suspicion of such, he might rest assured. But, some inquiries were making about that House, and would he object to say why he left it?

Not at all; why should he? He left it, along of a Dwarf.

Along of a Dwarf?

Mr. Magsman repeated, deliberately and emphatically, Along of a Dwarf.

Might it be compatible with Mr. Magsman's inclination and convenience to enter, as a favour, into a few particulars?

Mr. Magsman entered into the following particulars.

It was a long time ago, to begin with;--afore lotteries and a deal more was done away with. Mr. Magsman was looking about for a good pitch, and he see that house, and he says to himself, "I'll have you, if you're to be had. If money'll get you, I'll have you."

The neighbours cut up rough, and made complaints; but Mr. Magsman don't know what they WOULD have had. It was a lovely thing. First of all, there was the canvass, representin the picter of the Giant, in Spanish trunks and a ruff, who was himself half the heighth of the house, and was run up with a line and pulley to a pole on the roof, so that his Ed was coeval with the parapet. Then, there was the canvass, representin the picter of the Albina lady, showing her white air to the Army and Navy in correct uniform. Then, there was the canvass, representin the picter of the Wild Indian a scalpin a member of some foreign nation. Then, there was the canvass, representin the picter of a child of a British Planter, seized by two Boa Constrictors--not that WE never had no child, nor no Constrictors neither. Similarly, there was the canvass, representin the picter of the Wild Ass of the Prairies--not that WE never had no wild asses, nor wouldn't have had 'em at a gift. Last, there was the canvass, representin the picter of the Dwarf, and like him too (considerin), with George the Fourth in such a state of astonishment at him as His Majesty couldn't with his utmost politeness and stoutness express. The front of the House was so covered with canvasses, that there wasn't a spark of daylight ever visible on that side. "MAGSMAN'S AMUSEMENTS," fifteen foot long by two foot high, ran over the front door and parlour winders. The passage was a Arbour of green baize and gardenstuff. A barrel-organ performed there unceasing. And as to respectability,--if threepence ain't respectable, what is?

But, the Dwarf is the principal article at present, and he was worth the money. He was wrote up as MAJOR TPSCHOFFKI, OF THE IMPERIAL BULGRADERIAN BRIGADE. Nobody couldn't pronounce the name, and it never was intended anybody should. The public always turned it, as a regular rule, into Chopski. In the line he was called Chops; partly on that account, and partly because his real name, if he ever had any real name (which was very dubious), was Stakes.

He was a un-common small man, he really was. Certainly not so small as he was made out to be, but where IS your Dwarf as is? He was a most uncommon small man, with a most uncommon large Ed; and what he had inside that Ed, nobody ever knowed but himself: even supposin himself to have ever took stock of it, which it would have been a stiff job for even him to do.

The kindest little man as never growed! Spirited, but not proud. When he travelled with the Spotted Baby--though he knowed himself to be a nat'ral Dwarf, and knowed the Baby's spots to be put upon him artificial, he nursed that Baby like a mother. You never heerd him give a ill-name to a Giant. He DID allow himself to break out into strong language respectin the Fat Lady from Norfolk; but that was an affair of the 'art; and when a man's 'art has been trifled with by a lady, and the preference giv to a Indian, he ain't master of his actions.

He was always in love, of course; every human nat'ral phenomenon is. And he was always in love with a large woman; I never knowed the Dwarf as could be got to love a small one. Which helps to keep 'em the Curiosities they are.

One sing'ler idea he had in that Ed of his, which must have meant something, or it wouldn't have been there. It was always his opinion that he was entitled to property. He never would put his name to anything. He had been taught to write, by the young man without arms, who got his living with his toes (quite a writing master HE was, and taught scores in the line), but Chops would have starved to death, afore he'd have gained a bit of bread by putting his hand to a paper. This is the more curious to bear in mind, because HE had no property, nor hope of property, except his house and a sarser. When I say his house, I mean the box, painted and got up outside like a reg'lar six-roomer, that he used to creep into, with a diamond ring (or quite as good to look at) on his forefinger, and ring a little bell out of what the Public believed to be the Drawing-room winder. And when I say a sarser, I mean a Chaney sarser in which he made a collection for himself at the end of every Entertainment. His cue for that, he took from me: "Ladies and gentlemen, the little man will now walk three times round the Cairawan, and retire behind the curtain." When he said anything important, in private life, he mostly wound it up with this form of words, and they was generally the last thing he said to me at night afore he went to bed.

He had what I consider a fine mind--a poetic mind. His ideas respectin his property never come upon him so strong as when he sat upon a barrel-organ and had the handle turned. Arter the wibration had run through him a little time, he would screech out, "Toby, I feel my property coming--grind away! I'm counting my guineas by thousands, Toby--grind away! Toby, I shall be a man of fortun! I feel the Mint a jingling in me, Toby, and I'm swelling out into the Bank of England!" Such is the influence of music on a poetic mind. Not that he was partial to any other music but a barrel-organ; on the contrary, hated it.

He had a kind of a everlasting grudge agin the Public: which is a thing you may notice in many phenomenons that get their living out of it. What riled him most in the nater of his occupation was, that it kep him out of Society. He was continiwally saying, "Toby, my ambition is, to go into Society. The curse of my position towards the Public is, that it keeps me hout of Society. This don't signify to a low beast of a Indian; he an't formed for Society. This don't signify to a Spotted Baby; HE an't formed for Society.--I am."

Nobody never could make out what Chops done with his money. He had a good salary, down on the drum every Saturday as the day came round, besides having the run of his teeth--and he was a Woodpecker to eat--but all Dwarfs are. The sarser was a little income, bringing him in so many halfpence that he'd carry 'em for a week together, tied up in a pocket-handkercher. And yet he never had money. And it couldn't be the Fat Lady from Norfolk, as was once supposed; because it stands to reason that when you have a animosity towards a Indian, which makes you grind your teeth at him to his face, and which can hardly hold you from Goosing him audible when he's going through his War-Dance--it stands to reason you wouldn't under them circumstances deprive yourself, to support that Indian in the lap of luxury.

Most unexpected, the mystery come out one day at Egham Races. The Public was shy of bein pulled in, and Chops was ringin his little bell out of his drawing-room winder, and was snarlin to me over his shoulder as he kneeled down with his legs out at the back-door--for he couldn't be shoved into his house without kneeling down, and the premises wouldn't accommodate his legs--was snarlin, "Here's a precious Public for you; why the Devil don't they tumble up?" when a man in the crowd holds up a carrier-pigeon, and cries out, "If there's any person here as has got a ticket, the Lottery's just drawed, and the number as has come up for the great prize is three, seven, forty-two! Three, seven, forty-two!" I was givin the man to the Furies myself, for calling off the Public's attention--for the Public will turn away, at any time, to look at anything in preference to the thing showed 'em; and if you doubt it, get 'em together for any indiwidual purpose on the face of the earth, and send only two people in late, and see if the whole company an't far more interested in takin particular notice of them two than of you-- I say, I wasn't best pleased with the man for callin out, and wasn't blessin him in my own mind, when I see Chops's little bell fly out of winder at a old lady, and he gets up and kicks his box over, exposin the whole secret, and he catches hold of the calves of my legs and he says to me, "Carry me into the wan, Toby, and throw a pail of water over me or I'm a dead man, for I've come into my property!"

Twelve thousand odd hundred pound, was Chops's winnins. He had bought a half-ticket for the twenty-five thousand prize, and it had come up. The first use he made of his property, was, to offer to fight the Wild Indian for five hundred pound a side, him with a poisoned darnin-needle and the Indian with a club; but the Indian being in want of backers to that amount, it went no further.

Arter he had been mad for a week--in a state of mind, in short, in which, if I had let him sit on the organ for only two minutes, I believe he would have bust--but we kep the organ from him--Mr. Chops come round, and behaved liberal and beautiful to all. He then sent for a young man he knowed, as had a wery genteel appearance and was a Bonnet at a gaming-booth (most respectable brought up, father havin been imminent in the livery stable line but unfort'nate in a commercial crisis, through paintin a old gray, ginger-bay, and sellin him with a Pedigree), and Mr. Chops said to this Bonnet, who said his name was Normandy, which it wasn't:

"Normandy, I'm a goin into Society. Will you go with me?"

Says Normandy: "Do I understand you, Mr. Chops, to hintimate that the 'ole of the expenses of that move will be borne by yourself?"

"Correct," says Mr. Chops. "And you shall have a Princely allowance too."

The Bonnet lifted Mr. Chops upon a chair, to shake hands with him, and replied in poetry, with his eyes seemingly full of tears:

"My boat is on the shore, And my bark is on the sea, And I do not ask for more, But I'll Go:- along with thee."

They went into Society, in a chay and four grays with silk jackets. They took lodgings in Pall Mall, London, and they blazed away.

In consequence of a note that was brought to Bartlemy Fair in the autumn of next year by a servant, most wonderful got up in milk- white cords and tops, I cleaned myself and went to Pall Mall, one evening appinted. The gentlemen was at their wine arter dinner, and Mr. Chops's eyes was more fixed in that Ed of his than I thought good for him. There was three of 'em (in company, I mean), and I knowed the third well. When last met, he had on a white Roman shirt, and a bishop's mitre covered with leopard-skin, and played the clarionet all wrong, in a band at a Wild Beast Show.

This gent took on not to know me, and Mr. Chops said: "Gentlemen, this is a old friend of former days:" and Normandy looked at me through a eye-glass, and said, "Magsman, glad to see you!"--which I'll take my oath he wasn't. Mr. Chops, to git him convenient to the table, had his chair on a throne (much of the form of George the Fourth's in the canvass), but he hardly appeared to me to be King there in any other pint of view, for his two gentlemen ordered about like Emperors. They was all dressed like May-Day--gorgeous!--And as to Wine, they swam in all sorts.

I made the round of the bottles, first separate (to say I had done it), and then mixed 'em all together (to say I had done it), and then tried two of 'em as half-and-half, and then t'other two. Altogether, I passed a pleasin evenin, but with a tendency to feel muddled, until I considered it good manners to get up and say, "Mr. Chops, the best of friends must part, I thank you for the wariety of foreign drains you have stood so 'ansome, I looks towards you in red wine, and I takes my leave." Mr. Chops replied, "If you'll just hitch me out of this over your right arm, Magsman, and carry me down-stairs, I'll see you out." I said I couldn't think of such a thing, but he would have it, so I lifted him off his throne. He smelt strong of Maideary, and I couldn't help thinking as I carried him down that it was like carrying a large bottle full of wine, with a rayther ugly stopper, a good deal out of proportion.

When I set him on the door-mat in the hall, he kep me close to him by holding on to my coat-collar, and he whispers:

"I ain't 'appy, Magsman."

"What's on your mind, Mr. Chops?"

"They don't use me well. They an't grateful to me. They puts me on the mantel-piece when I won't have in more Champagne-wine, and they locks me in the sideboard when I won't give up my property."

"Get rid of 'em, Mr. Chops."

"I can't. We're in Society together, and what would Society say?"

"Come out of Society!" says I.

"I can't. You don't know what you're talking about. When you have once gone into Society, you mustn't come out of it."

"Then if you'll excuse the freedom, Mr. Chops," were my remark, shaking my head grave, "I think it's a pity you ever went in."

Mr. Chops shook that deep Ed of his, to a surprisin extent, and slapped it half a dozen times with his hand, and with more Wice than I thought were in him. Then, he says, "You're a good fellow, but you don't understand. Good-night, go along. Magsman, the little man will now walk three times round the Cairawan, and retire behind the curtain." The last I see of him on that occasion was his tryin, on the extremest werge of insensibility, to climb up the stairs, one by one, with his hands and knees. They'd have been much too steep for him, if he had been sober; but he wouldn't be helped.

It warn't long after that, that I read in the newspaper of Mr. Chops's being presented at court. It was printed, "It will be recollected"--and I've noticed in my life, that it is sure to be printed that it WILL be recollected, whenever it won't--"that Mr. Chops is the individual of small stature, whose brilliant success in the last State Lottery attracted so much attention." Well, I says to myself, Such is Life! He has been and done it in earnest at last. He has astonished George the Fourth!

(On account of which, I had that canvass new-painted, him with a bag of money in his hand, a presentin it to George the Fourth, and a lady in Ostrich Feathers fallin in love with him in a bag-wig, sword, and buckles correct.)

I took the House as is the subject of present inquiries--though not the honour of bein acquainted--and I run Magsman's Amusements in it thirteen months--sometimes one thing, sometimes another, sometimes nothin particular, but always all the canvasses outside. One night, when we had played the last company out, which was a shy company, through its raining Heavens hard, I was takin a pipe in the one pair back along with the young man with the toes, which I had taken on for a month (though he never drawed--except on paper), and I heard a kickin at the street door. "Halloa!" I says to the young man, "what's up!" He rubs his eyebrows with his toes, and he says, "I can't imagine, Mr. Magsman"--which he never could imagine nothin, and was monotonous company.

The noise not leavin off, I laid down my pipe, and I took up a candle, and I went down and opened the door. I looked out into the street; but nothin could I see, and nothin was I aware of, until I turned round quick, because some creetur run between my legs into the passage. There was Mr. Chops!

"Magsman," he says, "take me, on the old terms, and you've got me; if it's done, say done!"

I was all of a maze, but I said, "Done, sir."

"Done to your done, and double done!" says he. "Have you got a bit of supper in the house?"

Bearin in mind them sparklin warieties of foreign drains as we'd guzzled away at in Pall Mall, I was ashamed to offer him cold sassages and gin-and-water; but he took 'em both and took 'em free; havin a chair for his table, and sittin down at it on a stool, like hold times. I, all of a maze all the while.

It was arter he had made a clean sweep of the sassages (beef, and to the best of my calculations two pound and a quarter), that the wisdom as was in that little man began to come out of him like prespiration.

"Magsman," he says, "look upon me! You see afore you, One as has both gone into Society and come out."

"O! You ARE out of it, Mr. Chops? How did you get out, sir?"

"SOLD OUT!" says he. You never saw the like of the wisdom as his Ed expressed, when he made use of them two words.

"My friend Magsman, I'll impart to you a discovery I've made. It's wallable; it's cost twelve thousand five hundred pound; it may do you good in life--The secret of this matter is, that it ain't so much that a person goes into Society, as that Society goes into a person."

Not exactly keepin up with his meanin, I shook my head, put on a deep look, and said, "You're right there, Mr. Chops."

"Magsman," he says, twitchin me by the leg, "Society has gone into me, to the tune of every penny of my property."

I felt that I went pale, and though nat'rally a bold speaker, I couldn't hardly say, "Where's Normandy?"

"Bolted. With the plate," said Mr. Chops.

"And t'other one?" meaning him as formerly wore the bishop's mitre.

"Bolted. With the jewels," said Mr. Chops.

I sat down and looked at him, and he stood up and looked at me.

"Magsman," he says, and he seemed to myself to get wiser as he got hoarser; "Society, taken in the lump, is all dwarfs. At the court of St. James's, they was all a doing my old business--all a goin three times round the Cairawan, in the hold court-suits and properties. Elsewheres, they was most of 'em ringin their little bells out of make-believes. Everywheres, the sarser was a goin round. Magsman, the sarser is the uniwersal Institution!"

I perceived, you understand, that he was soured by his misfortunes, and I felt for Mr. Chops.

"As to Fat Ladies," he says, giving his head a tremendious one agin the wall, "there's lots of THEM in Society, and worse than the original. HERS was a outrage upon Taste--simply a outrage upon Taste--awakenin contempt-- carryin its own punishment in the form of a Indian." Here he giv himself another tremendious one. "But THEIRS, Magsman, THEIRS is mercenary outrages. Lay in Cashmeer shawls, buy bracelets, strew 'em and a lot of 'andsome fans and things about your rooms, let it be known that you give away like water to all as come to admire, and the Fat Ladies that don't exhibit for so much down upon the drum, will come from all the pints of the compass to flock about you, whatever you are. They'll drill holes in your 'art, Magsman, like a Cullender. And when you've no more left to give, they'll laugh at you to your face, and leave you to have your bones picked dry by Wulturs, like the dead Wild Ass of the Prairies that you deserve to be!" Here he giv himself the most tremendious one of all, and dropped.

I thought he was gone. His Ed was so heavy, and he knocked it so hard, and he fell so stoney, and the sassagerial disturbance in him must have been so immense, that I thought he was gone. But, he soon come round with care, and he sat up on the floor, and he said to me, with wisdom comin out of his eyes, if ever it come:

"Magsman! The most material difference between the two states of existence through which your unhappy friend has passed;" he reached out his poor little hand, and his tears dropped down on the moustachio which it was a credit to him to have done his best to grow, but it is not in mortals to command success,--"the difference this. When I was out of Society, I was paid light for being seen. When I went into Society, I paid heavy for being seen. I prefer the former, even if I wasn't forced upon it. Give me out through the trumpet, in the hold way, to-morrow."

Arter that, he slid into the line again as easy as if he had been iled all over. But the organ was kep from him, and no allusions was ever made, when a company was in, to his property. He got wiser every day; his views of Society and the Public was luminous, bewilderin, awful; and his Ed got bigger and bigger as his Wisdom expanded it.

He took well, and pulled 'em in most excellent for nine weeks. At the expiration of that period, when his Ed was a sight, he expressed one evenin, the last Company havin been turned out, and the door shut, a wish to have a little music.

"Mr. Chops," I said (I never dropped the "Mr." with him; the world might do it, but not me); "Mr. Chops, are you sure as you are in a state of mind and body to sit upon the organ?"

His answer was this: "Toby, when next met with on the tramp, I forgive her and the Indian. And I am."

It was with fear and trembling that I began to turn the handle; but he sat like a lamb. I will be my belief to my dying day, that I see his Ed expand as he sat; you may therefore judge how great his thoughts was. He sat out all the changes, and then he come off.

"Toby," he says, with a quiet smile, "the little man will now walk three times round the Cairawan, and retire behind the curtain."

When we called him in the morning, we found him gone into a much better Society than mine or Pall Mall's. I giv Mr. Chops as comfortable a funeral as lay in my power, followed myself as Chief, and had the George the Fourth canvass carried first, in the form of a banner. But, the House was so dismal arterwards, that I giv it up, and took to the Wan again.

"I don't triumph," said Jarber, folding up the second manuscript, and looking hard at Trottle. "I don't triumph over this worthy creature. I merely ask him if he is satisfied now?"

"How can he be anything else?" I said, answering for Trottle, who sat obstinately silent. "This time, Jarber, you have not only read us a delightfully amusing story, but you have also answered the question about the House. Of course it stands empty now. Who would think of taking it after it had been turned into a caravan?" I looked at Trottle, as I said those last words, and Jarber waved his hand indulgently in the same direction.

"Let this excellent person speak," said Jarber. "You were about to say, my good man?" -

"I only wished to ask, sir," said Trottle doggedly, "if you could kindly oblige me with a date or two in connection with that last story?"

"A date!" repeated Jarber. "What does the man want with dates!"

"I should be glad to know, with great respect," persisted Trottle, "if the person named Magsman was the last tenant who lived in the House. It's my opinion--if I may be excused for giving it--that he most decidedly was not."

With those words, Trottle made a low bow, and quietly left the room.

There is no denying that Jarber, when we were left together, looked sadly discomposed. He had evidently forgotten to inquire about dates; and, in spite of his magnificent talk about his series of discoveries, it was quite as plain that the two stories he had just read, had really and truly exhausted his present stock. I thought myself bound, in common gratitude, to help him out of his embarrassment by a timely suggestion. So I proposed that he should come to tea again, on the next Monday evening, the thirteenth, and should make such inquiries in the meantime, as might enable him to dispose triumphantly of Trottle's objection.

He gallantly kissed my hand, made a neat little speech of acknowledgment, and took his leave. For the rest of the week I would not encourage Trottle by allowing him to refer to the House at all. I suspected he was making his own inquiries about dates, but I put no questions to him.

On Monday evening, the thirteenth, that dear unfortunate Jarber came, punctual to the appointed time. He looked so terribly harassed, that he was really quite a spectacle of feebleness and fatigue. I saw, at a glance, that the question of dates had gone against him, that Mr. Magsman had not been the last tenant of the House, and that the reason of its emptiness was still to seek.

"What I have gone through," said Jarber, "words are not eloquent enough to tell. O Sophonisba, I have begun another series of discoveries! Accept the last two as stories laid on your shrine; and wait to blame me for leaving your curiosity unappeased, until you have heard Number Three."

Number Three looked like a very short manuscript, and I said as much. Jarber explained to me that we were to have some poetry this time. In the course of his investigations he had stepped into the Circulating Library, to seek for information on the one important subject. All the Library-people knew about the House was, that a female relative of the last tenant, as they believed, had, just after that tenant left, sent a little manuscript poem to them which she described as referring to events that had actually passed in the House; and which she wanted the proprietor of the Library to publish. She had written no address on her letter; and the proprietor had kept the manuscript ready to be given back to her (the publishing of poems not being in his line) when she might call for it. She had never called for it; and the poem had been lent to Jarber, at his express request, to read to me.

Before he began, I rang the bell for Trottle; being determined to have him present at the new reading, as a wholesome check on his obstinacy. To my surprise Peggy answered the bell, and told me, that Trottle had stepped out without saying where. I instantly felt the strongest possible conviction that he was at his old tricks: and that his stepping out in the evening, without leave, meant-- Philandering.

Controlling myself on my visitor's account, I dismissed Peggy, stifled my indignation, and prepared, as politely as might be, to listen to Jarber.

Hunted Down

by Charles Dickens

I.

Most of us see some romances in life. In my capacity as Chief Manager of a Life Assurance Office, I think I have within the last thirty years seen more romances than the generality of men, however unpromising the opportunity may, at first sight, seem.

As I have retired, and live at my ease, I possess the means that I used to want, of considering what I have seen, at leisure. My experiences have a more remarkable aspect, so reviewed, than they had when they were in progress. I have come home from the Play now, and can recall the scenes of the Drama upon which the curtain has fallen, free from the glare, bewilderment, and bustle of the Theatre.

Let me recall one of these Romances of the real world.

There is nothing truer than physiognomy, taken in connection with manner. The art of reading that book of which Eternal Wisdom obliges every human creature to present his or her own page with the individual character written on it, is a difficult one, perhaps, and is little studied. It may require some natural aptitude, and it must require (for everything does) some patience and some pains. That these are not usually given to it, - that numbers of people accept a few stock commonplace expressions of the face as the whole list of characteristics, and neither seek nor know the refinements that are truest, - that You, for instance, give a great deal of time and attention to the reading of music, Greek, Latin, French, Italian, Hebrew, if you please, and do not qualify yourself to read the face of the master or mistress looking over your shoulder teaching it to you, - I assume to be five hundred times more probable than improbable. Perhaps a little self-sufficiency may be at the bottom of this; facial expression requires no study from you, you think; it comes by nature to you to know enough about it, and you are not to be taken in.

I confess, for my part, that I HAVE been taken in, over and over again. I have been taken in by acquaintances, and I have been taken in (of course) by friends; far oftener by friends than by any other class of persons. How came I to be so deceived? Had I quite misread their faces?

No. Believe me, my first impression of those people, founded on face and manner alone, was invariably true. My mistake was in suffering them to come nearer to me and explain themselves away.

II.

The partition which separated my own office from our general outer office in the City was of thick plate-glass. I could see through it what passed in the outer office, without hearing a word. I had it put up in place of a wall that had been there for years, - ever since the house was built. It is no matter whether I did or did not make the change in order that I might derive my first impression of strangers, who came to us on business, from their faces alone, without being influenced by anything they said. Enough to mention that I turned my glass partition to that account, and that a Life Assurance Office is at all times exposed to be practised upon by the most crafty and cruel of the human race.

It was through my glass partition that I first saw the gentleman whose story I am going to tell.

He had come in without my observing it, and had put his hat and umbrella on the broad counter, and was bending over it to take some papers from one of the clerks. He was about forty or so, dark, exceedingly well dressed in black, - being in mourning, - and the hand he extended with a polite air, had a particularly well-fitting black-kid glove upon it. His hair, which was elaborately brushed and oiled, was parted straight up the middle; and he presented this parting to the clerk, exactly (to my thinking) as if he had said, in so many words: 'You must take me, if you please, my friend, just as I show myself. Come straight up here, follow the gravel path, keep off the grass, I allow no trespassing.'

I conceived a very great aversion to that man the moment I thus saw him.

He had asked for some of our printed forms, and the clerk was giving them to him and explaining them. An obliged and agreeable smile was on his face, and his eyes met those of the clerk with a sprightly look. (I have known a vast quantity of nonsense talked about bad men not looking you in the face. Don't trust that conventional idea. Dishonesty will stare honesty out of countenance, any day in the week, if there is anything to be got by it.)

I saw, in the corner of his eyelash, that he became aware of my looking at him. Immediately he turned the parting in his hair toward the glass partition, as if he said to me with a sweet smile, 'Straight up here, if you please. Off the grass!'

In a few moments he had put on his hat and taken up his umbrella, and was gone.

I beckoned the clerk into my room, and asked, 'Who was that?'

He had the gentleman's card in his hand. 'Mr. Julius Slinkton, Middle Temple.'

'A barrister, Mr. Adams?'

'I think not, sir.'

'I should have thought him a clergyman, but for his having no Reverend here,' said I.

'Probably, from his appearance,' Mr. Adams replied, 'he is reading for orders.'

I should mention that he wore a dainty white cravat, and dainty linen altogether.

'What did he want, Mr. Adams?'

'Merely a form of proposal, sir, and form of reference.'

'Recommended here? Did he say?'

'Yes, he said he was recommended here by a friend of yours. He noticed you, but said that as he had not the pleasure of your personal acquaintance he would not trouble you.'

'Did he know my name?'

'O yes, sir! He said, "There IS Mr. Sampson, I see!"'

'A well-spoken gentleman, apparently?'

'Remarkably so, sir.'

'Insinuating manners, apparently?'

'Very much so, indeed, sir.'

'Hah!' said I. 'I want nothing at present, Mr. Adams.'

Within a fortnight of that day I went to dine with a friend of mine, a merchant, a man of taste, who buys pictures and books, and the first man I saw among the company was Mr. Julius Slinkton. There he was, standing before the fire, with good large eyes and an open expression of face; but still

(I thought) requiring everybody to come at him by the prepared way he offered, and by no other.

I noticed him ask my friend to introduce him to Mr. Sampson, and my friend did so. Mr. Slinkton was very happy to see me. Not too happy; there was no over-doing of the matter; happy in a thoroughly well-bred, perfectly unmeaning way.

'I thought you had met,' our host observed.

'No,' said Mr. Slinkton. 'I did look in at Mr. Sampson's office, on your recommendation; but I really did not feel justified in troubling Mr. Sampson himself, on a point in the everyday, routine of an ordinary clerk.'

I said I should have been glad to show him any attention on our friend's introduction.

'I am sure of that,' said he, 'and am much obliged. At another time, perhaps, I may be less delicate. Only, however, if I have real business; for I know, Mr. Sampson, how precious business time is, and what a vast number of impertinent people there are in the world.'

I acknowledged his consideration with a slight bow. 'You were thinking,' said I, 'of effecting a policy on your life.'

'O dear no! I am afraid I am not so prudent as you pay me the compliment of supposing me to be, Mr. Sampson. I merely inquired for a friend. But you know what friends are in such matters. Nothing may ever come of it. I have the greatest reluctance to trouble men of business with inquiries for friends, knowing the probabilities to be a thousand to one that the friends will never follow them up. People are so fickle, so selfish, so inconsiderate. Don't you, in your business, find them so every day, Mr. Sampson?'

I was going to give a qualified answer; but he turned his smooth, white parting on me with its 'Straight up here, if you please!' and I answered 'Yes.'

'I hear, Mr. Sampson,' he resumed presently, for our friend had a new cook, and dinner was not so punctual as usual, 'that your profession has recently suffered a great loss.'

'In money?' said I.

He laughed at my ready association of loss with money, and replied, 'No, in talent and vigour.'

Not at once following out his allusion, I considered for a moment. 'HAS it sustained a loss of that kind?' said I. 'I was not aware of it.'

'Understand me, Mr. Sampson. I don't imagine that you have retired. It is not so bad as that. But Mr. Meltham - '

'O, to be sure!' said I. 'Yes! Mr. Meltham, the young actuary of the "Inestimable."'

'Just so,' he returned in a consoling way.

'He is a great loss. He was at once the most profound, the most original, and the most energetic man I have ever known connected with Life Assurance.'

I spoke strongly; for I had a high esteem and admiration for Meltham; and my gentleman had indefinitely conveyed to me some suspicion that he wanted to sneer at him. He recalled me to my guard by presenting that trim pathway up his head, with its internal 'Not on the grass, if you please - the gravel.'

'You knew him, Mr. Slinkton.'

'Only by reputation. To have known him as an acquaintance or as a friend, is an honour I should have sought if he had remained in society, though I might never have had the good fortune to attain it, being a man of far inferior mark. He was scarcely above thirty, I suppose?'

'About thirty.'

'Ah!' he sighed in his former consoling way. 'What creatures we are! To break up, Mr. Sampson, and become incapable of business at that time of life!

- Any reason assigned for the melancholy fact?'

('Humph!' thought I, as I looked at him. 'But I WON'T go up the track, and I WILL go on the grass.')

'What reason have you heard assigned, Mr. Slinkton?' I asked, point-blank.

'Most likely a false one. You know what Rumour is, Mr. Sampson. I never repeat what I hear; it is the only way of paring the nails and shaving the head of Rumour. But when YOU ask me what reason I have heard assigned for Mr. Meltham's passing away from among men, it is another thing. I am not gratifying idle gossip then. I was told, Mr. Sampson, that Mr. Meltham had relinquished all his avocations and all his prospects, because he was, in fact, broken-hearted. A disappointed attachment I heard, - though it hardly seems probable, in the case of a man so distinguished and so attractive.'

'Attractions and distinctions are no armour against death,' said I.

'O, she died? Pray pardon me. I did not hear that. That, indeed, makes it very, very sad. Poor Mr. Meltham! She died? Ah, dear me! Lamentable, lamentable!'

I still thought his pity was not quite genuine, and I still suspected an unaccountable sneer under all this, until he said, as we were parted, like the other knots of talkers, by the announcement of dinner:

'Mr. Sampson, you are surprised to see me so moved on behalf of a man whom I have never known. I am not so disinterested as you may suppose. I have suffered, and recently too, from death myself. I have lost one of two charming nieces, who were my constant companions. She died young - barely three-and-twenty; and even her remaining sister is far from strong. The world is a grave!'

He said this with deep feeling, and I felt reproached for the coldness of my manner. Coldness and distrust had been engendered in me, I knew, by my bad experiences; they were not natural to me; and I often thought how much I had lost in life, losing trustfulness, and how little I had gained, gaining hard caution. This state of mind being habitual to me, I troubled myself more about this conversation than I might have troubled myself about a greater matter. I listened to his talk at dinner, and observed how readily other men responded to it, and with what a graceful instinct he adapted his subjects to the knowledge and habits of those he talked with. As, in talking with me, he had easily started the subject I might be supposed to understand best, and to be the most interested in, so, in talking with others, he guided himself by the same rule. The company was of a varied character; but he was not at fault, that I could discover, with any member of it. He knew just as much of each man's pursuit as made him agreeable to that man in reference to it, and just as little as made it natural in him to seek modestly for information when the theme was broached.

As he talked and talked - but really not too much, for the rest of us seemed to force it upon him - I became quite angry with myself. I took his face to pieces in my mind, like a watch, and examined it in detail. I could not say much against any of his features separately; I could say even less against them when they were put together. 'Then is it not monstrous,' I asked myself, 'that because a man happens to part his hair straight up the middle of his head, I should permit myself to suspect, and even to detest him?'

(I may stop to remark that this was no proof of my sense. An observer of men who finds himself steadily repelled by some apparently trifling thing in a stranger is right to give it great weight. It may be the clue to the whole mystery. A hair or two will show where a lion is hidden. A very little key will open a very heavy door.)

I took my part in the conversation with him after a time, and we got on remarkably well. In the drawing-room I asked the host how long he had known Mr. Slinkton. He answered, not many months; he had met him at the house of a celebrated painter then present, who had known him well when he was travelling with his nieces in Italy for their health. His plans in life being broken by the death of one of them, he was reading with the intention of going back to college as a matter of form, taking his degree, and going into orders. I could not but argue with myself that here was the true explanation of his interest in poor Meltham, and that I had been almost brutal in my distrust on that simple head.

III.

On the very next day but one I was sitting behind my glass partition, as before, when he came into the outer office, as before. The moment I saw him again without hearing him, I hated him worse than ever.

It was only for a moment that I had this opportunity; for he waved his tight-fitting black glove the instant I looked at him, and came straight in.

'Mr. Sampson, good-day! I presume, you see, upon your kind permission to intrude upon you. I don't keep my word in being justified by business, for my business here - if I may so abuse the word - is of the slightest nature.'

I asked, was it anything I could assist him in?

'I thank you, no. I merely called to inquire outside whether my dilatory friend had been so false to himself as to be practical and sensible. But, of course, he has done nothing. I gave him your papers with my own hand, and he was hot upon the intention, but of course he has done nothing. Apart from the general human disinclination to do anything that ought to be done, I dare say there is a specially about assuring one's life. You find it like will-making. People are so superstitious, and take it for granted they will die soon afterwards.'

'Up here, if you please; straight up here, Mr. Sampson. Neither to the right nor to the left.' I almost fancied I could hear him breathe the words as he sat smiling at me, with that intolerable parting exactly opposite the bridge of my nose.

'There is such a feeling sometimes, no doubt,' I replied; 'but I don't think it obtains to any great extent.'

'Well,' said he, with a shrug and a smile, 'I wish some good angel would influence my friend in the right direction. I rashly promised his mother and sister in Norfolk to see it done, and he promised them that he would do it. But I suppose he never will.'

He spoke for a minute or two on indifferent topics, and went away.

I had scarcely unlocked the drawers of my writing-table next morning, when he reappeared. I noticed that he came straight to the door in the glass partition, and did not pause a single moment outside.

'Can you spare me two minutes, my dear Mr. Sampson?'

'By all means.'

'Much obliged,' laying his hat and umbrella on the table; 'I came early, not to interrupt you. The fact is, I am taken by surprise in reference to this proposal my friend has made.'

'Has he made one?' said I.

'Ye-es,' he answered, deliberately looking at me; and then a bright idea seemed to strike him - 'or he only tells me he has. Perhaps that may be a new way of evading the matter. By Jupiter, I never thought of that!'

Mr. Adams was opening the morning's letters in the outer office. 'What is the name, Mr. Slinkton?' I asked.

'Beckwith.'

I looked out at the door and requested Mr. Adams, if there were a proposal in that name, to bring it in. He had already laid it out of his hand on the counter. It was easily selected from the rest, and he gave it me. Alfred Beckwith. Proposal to effect a policy with us for two thousand pounds. Dated yesterday.

'From the Middle Temple, I see, Mr. Slinkton.'

'Yes. He lives on the same staircase with me; his door is opposite. I never thought he would make me his reference though.'

'It seems natural enough that he should.'

'Quite so, Mr. Sampson; but I never thought of it. Let me see.' He took the printed paper from his pocket. 'How am I to answer all these questions?'

'According to the truth, of course,' said I.

'O, of course!' he answered, looking up from the paper with a smile; 'I meant they were so many. But you do right to be particular. It stands to reason that you must be particular. Will you allow me to use your pen and ink?'

'Certainly.'

'And your desk?'

'Certainly.'

He had been hovering about between his hat and his umbrella for a place to write on. He now sat down in my chair, at my blotting- paper and inkstand, with the long walk up his head in accurate perspective before me, as I stood with my back to the fire.

Before answering each question he ran over it aloud, and discussed it. How long had he known Mr. Alfred Beckwith? That he had to calculate by years upon his fingers. What were his habits? No difficulty about them; temperate in the last degree, and took a little too much exercise, if anything. All the answers were satisfactory. When he had written them all, he looked them over, and finally signed them in a very pretty hand. He supposed he had now done with the business. I told him he was not likely to be troubled any farther. Should he leave the papers there? If he pleased. Much obliged. Good-morning.

I had had one other visitor before him; not at the office, but at my own house. That visitor had come to my bedside when it was not yet daylight, and had been seen by no one else but by my faithful confidential servant.

A second reference paper (for we required always two) was sent down into Norfolk, and was duly received back by post. This, likewise, was satisfactorily answered in every respect. Our forms were all complied with; we accepted the proposal, and the premium for one year was paid.

IV.

For six or seven months I saw no more of Mr. Slinkton. He called once at my house, but I was not at home; and he once asked me to dine with him in the Temple, but I was engaged. His friend's assurance was effected in March. Late in September or early in October I was down at Scarborough for a breath of sea-air, where I met him on the beach. It was a hot evening; he came toward me with his hat in his hand; and there was the walk I had felt so strongly disinclined to take in perfect order again, exactly in front of the bridge of my nose.

He was not alone, but had a young lady on his arm.

She was dressed in mourning, and I looked at her with great interest. She had the appearance of being extremely delicate, and her face was remarkably pale and melancholy; but she was very pretty. He introduced her as his niece, Miss Niner.

'Are you strolling, Mr. Sampson? Is it possible you can be idle?'

It WAS possible, and I WAS strolling.

'Shall we stroll together?'

'With pleasure.'

The young lady walked between us, and we walked on the cool sea sand, in the direction of Filey.

'There have been wheels here,' said Mr. Slinkton. 'And now I look again, the wheels of a hand-carriage! Margaret, my love, your shadow without doubt!'

'Miss Niner's shadow?' I repeated, looking down at it on the sand.

'Not that one,' Mr. Slinkton returned, laughing. 'Margaret, my dear, tell Mr. Sampson.'

'Indeed,' said the young lady, turning to me, 'there is nothing to tell - except that I constantly see the same invalid old gentleman at all times, wherever I go. I have mentioned it to my uncle, and he calls the gentleman my shadow.'

'Does he live in Scarborough?' I asked.

'He is staying here.'

'Do you live in Scarborough?'

'No, I am staying here. My uncle has placed me with a family here, for my health.'

'And your shadow?' said I, smiling.

'My shadow,' she answered, smiling too, 'is - like myself - not very robust, I fear; for I lose my shadow sometimes, as my shadow loses me at other times. We both seem liable to confinement to the house. I have not seen my shadow for days and days; but it does oddly happen, occasionally, that wherever I go, for many days together, this gentleman goes. We have come together in the most unfrequented nooks on this shore.'

'Is this he?' said I, pointing before us.

The wheels had swept down to the water's edge, and described a great loop on the sand in turning. Bringing the loop back towards us, and spinning it out as it came, was a hand-carriage, drawn by a man.

'Yes,' said Miss Niner, 'this really is my shadow, uncle.'

As the carriage approached us and we approached the carriage, I saw within it an old man, whose head was sunk on his breast, and who was enveloped in a variety of wrappers. He was drawn by a very quiet but very keen-looking man, with iron-gray hair, who was slightly lame. They had passed us, when the carriage stopped, and the old gentleman within, putting out his arm, called to me by my name. I went back, and was absent from Mr. Slinkton and his niece for about five minutes.

When I rejoined them, Mr. Slinkton was the first to speak. Indeed, he said to me in a raised voice before I came up with him:

'It is well you have not been longer, or my niece might have died of curiosity to know who her shadow is, Mr. Sampson.'

'An old East India Director,' said I. 'An intimate friend of our friend's, at whose house I first had the pleasure of meeting you. A certain Major Banks. You have heard of him?'

'Never.'

'Very rich, Miss Niner; but very old, and very crippled. An amiable man, sensible - much interested in you. He has just been expatiating on the affection that he has observed to exist between you and your uncle.'

Mr. Slinkton was holding his hat again, and he passed his hand up the straight walk, as if he himself went up it serenely, after me.

'Mr. Sampson,' he said, tenderly pressing his niece's arm in his, 'our affection was always a strong one, for we have had but few near ties. We have still fewer now. We have associations to bring us together, that are not of this world, Margaret.'

'Dear uncle!' murmured the young lady, and turned her face aside to hide her tears.

'My niece and I have such remembrances and regrets in common, Mr. Sampson,' he feelingly pursued, 'that it would be strange indeed if the relations between us were cold or indifferent. If I remember a conversation we once had together, you will understand the reference I make. Cheer up, dear Margaret. Don't droop, don't droop. My Margaret! I cannot bear to see you droop!'

The poor young lady was very much affected, but controlled herself. His feelings, too, were very acute. In a word, he found himself under such great need of a restorative, that he presently went away, to take a bath of sea-water, leaving the young lady and me sitting by a point of rock, and probably presuming - but that you will say was a pardonable indulgence in a luxury - that she would praise him with all her heart.

She did, poor thing! With all her confiding heart, she praised him to me, for his care of her dead sister, and for his untiring devotion in her last illness. The sister had wasted away very slowly, and wild and terrible fantasies had come over her toward the end, but he had never been impatient with her, or at a loss; had always been gentle, watchful, and self-possessed. The sister had known him, as she had known him, to be the best of men, the kindest of men, and yet a man of such admirable strength of character, as to be a very tower for the support of their weak natures while their poor lives endured.

'I shall leave him, Mr. Sampson, very soon,' said the young lady; 'I know my life is drawing to an end; and when I am gone, I hope he will marry and be happy. I am sure he has lived single so long, only for my sake, and for my poor, poor sister's.'

The little hand-carriage had made another great loop on the damp sand, and was coming back again, gradually spinning out a slim figure of eight, half a mile long.

'Young lady,' said I, looking around, laying my hand upon her arm, and speaking in a low voice, 'time presses. You hear the gentle murmur of that sea?'

She looked at me with the utmost wonder and alarm, saying, 'Yes!'

'And you know what a voice is in it when the storm comes?'

'Yes!'

'You see how quiet and peaceful it lies before us, and you know what an awful sight of power without pity it might be, this very night!'

'Yes!'

'But if you had never heard or seen it, or heard of it in its cruelty, could you believe that it beats every inanimate thing in its way to pieces, without mercy, and destroys life without remorse?'

'You terrify me, sir, by these questions!'

'To save you, young lady, to save you! For God's sake, collect your strength and collect your firmness! If you were here alone, and hemmed in by the rising tide on the flow to fifty feet above your head, you could not be in greater danger than the danger you are now to be saved from.'

The figure on the sand was spun out, and straggled off into a crooked little jerk that ended at the cliff very near us.

'As I am, before Heaven and the Judge of all mankind, your friend, and your dead sister's friend, I solemnly entreat you, Miss Niner, without one moment's loss of time, to come to this gentleman with me!'

If the little carriage had been less near to us, I doubt if I could have got her away; but it was so near that we were there before she had recovered the hurry of being urged from the rock. I did not remain there with her two minutes. Certainly within five, I had the inexpressible satisfaction of seeing her - from the point we had sat on, and to which I had returned - half supported and half carried up some rude steps notched in the cliff, by the figure of an active man. With that figure beside her, I knew she was safe anywhere.

I sat alone on the rock, awaiting Mr. Slinkton's return. The twilight was deepening and the shadows were heavy, when he came round the point, with his hat hanging at his button-hole, smoothing his wet hair with one of his hands, and picking out the old path with the other and a pocket-comb.

'My niece not here, Mr. Sampson?' he said, looking about.

'Miss Niner seemed to feel a chill in the air after the sun was down, and has gone home.'

He looked surprised, as though she were not accustomed to do anything without him; even to originate so slight a proceeding.

'I persuaded Miss Niner,' I explained.

'Ah!' said he. 'She is easily persuaded - for her good. Thank you, Mr. Sampson; she is better within doors. The bathing-place was farther than I thought, to say the truth.'

'Miss Niner is very delicate,' I observed.

He shook his head and drew a deep sigh. 'Very, very, very. You may recollect my saying so. The time that has since intervened has not strengthened her. The gloomy shadow that fell upon her sister so early in life seems, in my anxious eyes, to gather over her, ever darker, ever darker. Dear Margaret, dear Margaret! But we must hope.'

The hand-carriage was spinning away before us at a most indecorous pace for an invalid vehicle, and was making most irregular curves upon the sand. Mr. Slinkton, noticing it after he had put his handkerchief to his eyes, said;

'If I may judge from appearances, your friend will be upset, Mr. Sampson.'

'It looks probable, certainly,' said I.

'The servant must be drunk.'

'The servants of old gentlemen will get drunk sometimes,' said I.

'The major draws very light, Mr. Sampson.'

'The major does draw light,' said I.

By this time the carriage, much to my relief, was lost in the darkness. We walked on for a little, side by side over the sand, in silence. After a short while he said, in a voice still affected by the emotion that his niece's state of health had awakened in him,

'Do you stay here long, Mr. Sampson?'

'Why, no. I am going away to-night.'

'So soon? But business always holds you in request. Men like Mr. Sampson are too important to others, to be spared to their own need of relaxation and enjoyment.'

'I don't know about that,' said I. 'However, I am going back.'

'To London?'

'To London.'

'I shall be there too, soon after you.'

I knew that as well as he did. But I did not tell him so. Any more than I told him what defensive weapon my right hand rested on in my pocket, as I walked by his side. Any more than I told him why I did not walk on the sea side of him with the night closing in.

We left the beach, and our ways diverged. We exchanged goodnight, and had parted indeed, when he said, returning,

'Mr. Sampson, MAY I ask? Poor Meltham, whom we spoke of, - dead yet?'

'Not when I last heard of him; but too broken a man to live long, and hopelessly lost to his old calling.'

'Dear, dear, dear!' said he, with great feeling. 'Sad, sad, sad! The world is a grave!' And so went his way.

It was not his fault if the world were not a grave; but I did not call that observation after him, any more than I had mentioned those other things just now enumerated. He went his way, and I went mine with all expedition. This happened, as I have said, either at the end of September or beginning of October. The next time I saw him, and the last time, was late in November.

V.

I had a very particular engagement to breakfast in the Temple. It was a bitter north-easterly morning, and the sleet and slush lay inches deep in the streets. I could get no conveyance, and was soon wet to the knees; but I should have been true to that appointment, though I had to wade to it up to my neck in the same impediments.

The appointment took me to some chambers in the Temple. They were at the top of a lonely corner house overlooking the river. The name, MR. ALFRED BECKWITH, was painted on the outer door. On the door opposite, on the same landing, the name MR. JULIUS SLINKTON. The doors of both sets of chambers stood open, so that anything said aloud in one set could be heard in the other.

I had never been in those chambers before. They were dismal, close, unwholesome, and oppressive; the furniture, originally good, and not yet old, was faded and dirty, - the rooms were in great disorder; there was a strong prevailing smell of opium, brandy, and tobacco; the grate and fire-irons were splashed all over with unsightly blotches of rust; and on a sofa by the fire, in the room where breakfast had been prepared, lay the host, Mr. Beckwith, a man with all the appearances of the worst kind of drunkard, very far advanced upon his shameful way to death.

'Slinkton is not come yet,' said this creature, staggering up when I went in; 'I'll call him. - Halloa! Julius Caesar! Come and drink!' As he hoarsely roared this out, he beat the poker and tongs together in a mad way, as if that were his usual manner of summoning his associate.

The voice of Mr. Slinkton was heard through the clatter from the opposite side of the staircase, and he came in. He had not expected the pleasure of meeting me. I have seen several artful men brought to a stand, but I never saw a man so aghast as he was when his eyes rested on mine.

'Julius Caesar,' cried Beckwith, staggering between us, 'Mist' Sampson! Mist' Sampson, Julius Caesar! Julius, Mist' Sampson, is the friend of my soul. Julius keeps me plied with liquor, morning, noon, and night. Julius is a real benefactor. Julius threw the tea and coffee out of window when I used to have any. Julius empties all the water-jugs of their contents, and fills 'em with spirits. Julius winds me up and keeps me going. - Boil the brandy, Julius!'

There was a rusty and furred saucepan in the ashes, - the ashes looked like the accumulation of weeks, - and Beckwith, rolling and staggering between us as if he were going to plunge headlong into the fire, got the saucepan out, and tried to force it into Slinkton's hand.

'Boil the brandy, Julius Caesar! Come! Do your usual office. Boil the brandy!'

He became so fierce in his gesticulations with the saucepan, that I expected to see him lay open Slinkton's head with it. I therefore put out my hand to check him. He reeled back to the sofa, and sat there panting, shaking, and red-eyed, in his rags of dressing-gown, looking at us both. I noticed then that there was nothing to drink on the table but brandy, and nothing to eat but salted herrings, and a hot, sickly, highly-peppered stew.

'At all events, Mr. Sampson,' said Slinkton, offering me the smooth gravel path for the last time, 'I thank you for interfering between me and this unfortunate man's violence. However you came here, Mr. Sampson, or with whatever motive you came here, at least I thank you for that.'

'Boil the brandy,' muttered Beckwith.

Without gratifying his desire to know how I came there, I said, quietly, 'How is your niece, Mr. Slinkton?'

He looked hard at me, and I looked hard at him.

'I am sorry to say, Mr. Sampson, that my niece has proved treacherous and ungrateful to her best friend. She left me without a word of notice or explanation. She was misled, no doubt, by some designing rascal. Perhaps you may have heard of it.'

'I did hear that she was misled by a designing rascal. In fact, I have proof of it.'

'Are you sure of that?' said he.

'Quite.'

'Boil the brandy,' muttered Beckwith. 'Company to breakfast, Julius Caesar. Do your usual office, - provide the usual breakfast, dinner, tea, and supper. Boil the brandy!'

The eyes of Slinkton looked from him to me, and he said, after a moment's consideration,

'Mr. Sampson, you are a man of the world, and so am I. I will be plain with you.'

'O no, you won't,' said I, shaking my head.

'I tell you, sir, I will be plain with you.'

'And I tell you you will not,' said I. 'I know all about you. YOU plain with any one? Nonsense, nonsense!'

'I plainly tell you, Mr. Sampson,' he went on, with a manner almost composed, 'that I understand your object. You want to save your funds, and escape from your liabilities; these are old tricks of trade with you Office-gentlemen. But you will not do it, sir; you will not succeed. You have not an easy adversary to play against, when you play against me. We shall have to inquire, in due time, when and how Mr. Beckwith fell into his present habits. With that remark, sir, I put this poor creature, and his incoherent wanderings of speech, aside, and wish you a good morning and a better case next time.'

While he was saying this, Beckwith had filled a half-pint glass with brandy. At this moment, he threw the brandy at his face, and threw the glass after it. Slinkton put his hands up, half blinded with the spirit, and cut with the glass across the forehead. At the sound of the breakage, a fourth person came into the room, closed the door, and stood at it; he was a very quiet but very keen-looking man, with iron-gray hair, and slightly lame.

Slinkton pulled out his handkerchief, assuaged the pain in his smarting eyes, and dabbled the blood on his forehead. He was a long time about it, and I saw that in the doing of it, a tremendous change came over him, occasioned by the change in Beckwith, - who ceased to pant and tremble, sat upright, and never took his eyes off him. I never in my life saw a face in which abhorrence and determination were so forcibly painted as in Beckwith's then.

'Look at me, you villain,' said Beckwith, 'and see me as I really am. I took these rooms, to make them a trap for you. I came into them as a drunkard, to bait the trap for you. You fell into the trap, and you will never leave it alive. On the morning when you last went to Mr. Sampson's office, I had seen him first. Your plot has been known to both of us, all along, and you have been counter- plotted all along. What? Having been cajoled into putting that prize of two thousand pounds in your power, I was to be done to death with brandy, and, brandy not proving quick enough, with something quicker? Have I never seen you, when you thought my senses gone, pouring from your little bottle into my glass? Why, you Murderer and Forger, alone here with you in the dead of night, as I have so often been, I have had my hand upon the trigger of a pistol, twenty times, to blow your brains out!'

This sudden starting up of the thing that he had supposed to be his imbecile victim into a determined man, with a settled resolution to hunt him down and be the death of him, mercilessly expressed from head to foot, was, in the first shock, too much for him. Without any figure of speech, he staggered under it. But there is no greater mistake than to suppose that a man who is a calculating criminal, is, in any phase of his guilt, otherwise than true to himself, and perfectly consistent with his whole character. Such a man commits murder, and murder is the natural culmination of his course; such a man has to outface murder, and will do it with hardihood and effrontery. It is a sort of fashion to express surprise that any notorious criminal, having such crime upon his conscience, can so brave it out. Do you think that if he had it on his conscience at all, or had a conscience to have it upon, he would ever have committed the crime?

Perfectly consistent with himself, as I believe all such monsters to be, this Slinkton recovered himself, and showed a defiance that was sufficiently cold and quiet. He was white, he was haggard, he was changed; but only as a sharper who had played for a great stake and had been outwitted and had lost the game.

'Listen to me, you villain,' said Beckwith, 'and let every word you hear me say be a stab in your wicked heart. When I took these rooms, to throw myself in your way and lead you on to the scheme that I knew my appearance and supposed character and habits would suggest to such a devil, how did I know that? Because you were no stranger to me. I knew you well. And I knew you to be the cruel wretch who, for so much money, had killed one innocent girl while she trusted him implicitly, and who was by inches killing another.'

Slinkton took out a snuff-box, took a pinch of snuff, and laughed.

'But see here,' said Beckwith, never looking away, never raising his voice, never relaxing his face, never unclenching his hand. 'See what a dull wolf you have been, after all! The infatuated drunkard who never drank a fiftieth part of the liquor you plied him with, but poured it away, here, there, everywhere - almost before your eyes; who bought over the fellow you set to watch him and to ply him, by outbidding you in his bribe, before he had been at his work three days - with whom you have observed no caution, yet who was so bent on ridding the earth of you as a wild beast, that he would have defeated you if you had been ever so prudent - that drunkard whom you have, many a time, left on the floor of this room, and who has even let you go out of it, alive and undeceived, when you have turned him over with your foot - has, almost as often, on the same night, within an hour, within a few minutes, watched you awake, had his hand at your pillow when you were asleep, turned over your papers, taken samples from your bottles and packets of powder, changed their contents, rifled every secret of your life!'

He had had another pinch of snuff in his hand, but had gradually let it drop from between his fingers to the floor; where he now smoothed it out with his foot, looking down at it the while.

'That drunkard,' said Beckwith, 'who had free access to your rooms at all times, that he might drink the strong drinks that you left in his way and be the sooner ended, holding no more terms with you than he would hold with a tiger, has had his master-key for all your locks, his test for all your poisons, his clue to your cipher- writing. He can tell you, as well as you can tell him, how long it took to complete that deed, what doses there were, what intervals, what signs of gradual decay upon mind and body; what distempered fancies were produced, what observable changes, what physical pain. He can tell you, as well as you can tell him, that all this was recorded day by day, as a lesson of experience for future service. He can tell you, better than you can tell him, where that journal is at this moment.'

Slinkton stopped the action of his foot, and looked at Beckwith.

'No,' said the latter, as if answering a question from him. 'Not in the drawer of the writing-desk that opens with a spring; it is not there, and it never will be there again.'

'Then you are a thief!' said Slinkton.

Without any change whatever in the inflexible purpose, which it was quite terrific even to me to contemplate, and from the power of which I had always felt convinced it was impossible for this wretch to escape, Beckwith returned,

'And I am your niece's shadow, too.'

With an imprecation Slinkton put his hand to his head, tore out some hair, and flung it to the ground. It was the end of the smooth walk; he destroyed it in the action, and it will soon be seen that his use for it was past.

Beckwith went on: 'Whenever you left here, I left here. Although I understood that you found it necessary to pause in the completion of that purpose, to avert suspicion, still I watched you close, with the poor confiding girl. When I had the diary, and could read it word by word, - it was only about the night before your last visit to Scarborough, - you remember the night? you slept with a small flat vial tied to your wrist, - I sent to Mr. Sampson, who was kept out of view. This is Mr. Sampson's trusty servant standing by the door. We three saved your niece among us.'

Slinkton looked at us all, took an uncertain step or two from the place where he had stood, returned to it, and glanced about him in a very curious way, - as one of the meaner reptiles might, looking for a hole to hide in. I noticed at the same time, that a singular change took place in the figure of the man, - as if it collapsed within his clothes, and they consequently became ill-shapen and ill-fitting.

'You shall know,' said Beckwith, 'for I hope the knowledge will be bitter and terrible to you, why you have been pursued by one man, and why, when the whole interest that Mr. Sampson represents would have expended any money in hunting you down, you have been tracked to death at a single individual's charge. I hear you have had the name of Meltham on your lips sometimes?'

I saw, in addition to those other changes, a sudden stoppage come upon his breathing.

'When you sent the sweet girl whom you murdered (you know with what artfully made-out surroundings and probabilities you sent her) to Meltham's office, before taking her abroad to originate the transaction that doomed her to the grave, it fell to Meltham's lot to see her and to speak with her. It did not fall to his lot to save her, though I know he would freely give his own life to have done it. He admired her; - I would say he loved her deeply, if I thought it possible that you could understand the word. When she was sacrificed, he was thoroughly assured of your guilt. Having lost her, he had but one object left in life, and that was to avenge her and destroy you.'

I saw the villain's nostrils rise and fall convulsively; but I saw no moving at his mouth.

'That man Meltham,' Beckwith steadily pursued, 'was as absolutely certain that you could never elude him in this world, if he devoted himself to your destruction with his utmost fidelity and earnestness, and if he divided the sacred duty with no other duty in life, as he was certain that in achieving it he would be a poor instrument in the hands of Providence, and would do well before Heaven in striking you out from among living men. I am that man, and I thank God that I have done my work!'

If Slinkton had been running for his life from swift-footed savages, a dozen miles, he could not have shown more emphatic signs of being oppressed at heart and labouring for breath, than he showed now, when he looked at the pursuer who had so relentlessly hunted him down.

'You never saw me under my right name before; you see me under my right name now. You shall see me once again in the body, when you are tried for your life. You shall see me once again in the spirit, when the cord is round your neck, and the crowd are crying against you!'

When Meltham had spoken these last words, the miscreant suddenly turned away his face, and seemed to strike his mouth with his open hand. At the same instant, the room was filled with a new and powerful odour, and, almost at the same instant, he broke into a crooked run, leap, start, - I have no name for the spasm, - and fell, with a dull weight that shook the heavy old doors and windows in their frames.

That was the fitting end of him.

When we saw that he was dead, we drew away from the room, and Meltham, giving me his hand, said, with a weary air,

'I have no more work on earth, my friend. But I shall see her again elsewhere.'

It was in vain that I tried to rally him. He might have saved her, he said; he had not saved her, and he reproached himself; he had lost her, and he was broken-hearted.

'The purpose that sustained me is over, Sampson, and there is nothing now to hold me to life. I am not fit for life; I am weak and spiritless; I have no hope and no object; my day is done.'

In truth, I could hardly have believed that the broken man who then spoke to me was the man who had so strongly and so differently impressed me when his purpose was before him. I used such entreaties with him, as I could; but he still said, and always said, in a patient, undemonstrative way, - nothing could avail him, - he was broken-hearted.

He died early in the next spring. He was buried by the side of the poor young lady for whom he had cherished those tender and unhappy regrets; and he left all he had to her sister. She lived to be a happy wife and mother; she married my sister's son, who succeeded poor Meltham; she is living now, and her children ride about the garden on my walking-stick when I go to see her.

Sunday Under Three Heads

by Charles Dickens

DEDICATION

To The Right Reverend THE BISHOP OF LONDON

MY LORD,

You were among the first, some years ago, to expatiate on the vicious addiction of the lower classes of society to Sunday excursions; and were thus instrumental in calling forth occasional demonstrations of those extreme opinions on the subject, which are very generally received with derision, if not with contempt.

Your elevated station, my Lord, affords you countless opportunities of increasing the comforts and pleasures of the humbler classes of society--not by the expenditure of the smallest portion of your princely income, but by merely sanctioning with the influence of your example, their harmless pastimes, and innocent recreations.

That your Lordship would ever have contemplated Sunday recreations with so much horror, if you had been at all acquainted with the wants and necessities of the people who indulged in them, I cannot imagine possible. That a Prelate of your elevated rank has the faintest conception of the extent of those wants, and the nature of those necessities, I do not believe.

For these reasons, I venture to address this little Pamphlet to your Lordship's consideration. I am quite conscious that the outlines I have drawn, afford but a very imperfect description of the feelings they are intended to illustrate; but I claim for them one merit--their truth and freedom from exaggeration. I may have fallen short of the mark, but I have never overshot it: and while I have pointed out what appears to me, to be injustice on the part of others, I hope I have carefully abstained from committing it myself.

I am, My Lord, Your Lordship's most obedient, Humble Servant, TIMOTHY SPARKS. June, 1836.

CHAPTER I

There are few things from which I derive greater pleasure, than walking through some of the principal streets of London on a fine Sunday, in summer, and watching the cheerful faces of the lively groups with which they are thronged. There is something, to my eyes at least, exceedingly pleasing in the general desire evinced by the humbler classes of society, to appear neat and clean on this their only holiday. There are many grave old persons, I know, who shake their heads with an air of profound wisdom, and tell you that poor people dress too well now-a-days; that when they were children, folks knew their stations in life better; that you may depend upon it, no good will come of this sort of thing in the end,--and so forth: but I fancy I can discern in the fine bonnet of the working-man's wife, or the feather-bedizened hat of his child, no inconsiderable evidence of good feeling on the part of the man himself, and an affectionate desire to expend the few shillings he can spare from his week's wages, in improving the appearance and adding to the happiness of those who are nearest and dearest to him. This may be a very heinous and unbecoming degree of vanity, perhaps, and the money might possibly be applied to better uses; it must not be forgotten, however, that it might very easily be devoted to worse: and if two or three faces can be rendered happy and contented, by a trifling improvement of outward appearance, I cannot help thinking that the object is very cheaply purchased, even at the expense of a smart gown, or a gaudy riband. There is a great deal of very unnecessary cant about the over- dressing of the common people. There is not a manufacturer or tradesman in existence, who would not employ a man who takes a reasonable degree of pride in the appearance of himself and those about him, in preference to a sullen, slovenly fellow, who works doggedly on, regardless of his own clothing and that of his wife and children, and seeming to take pleasure or pride in nothing.

The pampered aristocrat, whose life is one continued round of licentious pleasures and sensual gratifications; or the gloomy enthusiast, who detests the cheerful amusements he can never enjoy, and envies the healthy feelings he can never know, and who would put down the one and suppress the other, until he made the minds of his fellow-beings as besotted and distorted as his own;--neither of these men can by possibility form an adequate notion of what Sunday really is to those whose lives are spent in sedentary or laborious occupations, and who are accustomed to look forward to it through their whole existence, as their only day of rest from toil, and innocent enjoyment.

The sun that rises over the quiet streets of London on a bright Sunday morning, shines till his setting, on gay and happy faces. Here and there, so early as six o'clock, a young man and woman in their best attire, may be seen hurrying along on their way to the house of some acquaintance, who is included in their scheme of pleasure for the day; from whence, after stopping to take "a bit of breakfast," they sally forth, accompanied by several old people, and a whole crowd of young ones, bearing large hand-baskets full of provisions, and Belcher handkerchiefs done up in bundles, with the neck of a bottle sticking out at the top, and closely-packed apples bulging out at the sides,--and away they hurry along the streets leading to the steam-packet wharfs, which are already plentifully sprinkled with parties bound for the same destination. Their good humour and delight know no bounds--for it is a delightful morning, all blue over head, and nothing like a cloud in the whole sky; and even the air of the river at London Bridge is something to them, shut up as they have been, all the week, in close streets and heated rooms. There are dozens of steamers to all sorts of places- -Gravesend, Greenwich, and Richmond; and such numbers of people, that when you have once sat down on the deck, it is all but a moral impossibility to get up again--to say nothing of walking about, which is entirely out of the question. Away they go, joking and laughing, and eating and drinking, and admiring everything they see, and pleased with everything they hear, to climb Windmill Hill, and catch a glimpse of the rich corn-fields and beautiful orchards of Kent; or to stroll among the fine old trees of Greenwich Park, and survey the wonders of Shooter's Hill and Lady James's Folly; or to glide past the beautiful meadows of Twickenham and Richmond, and to gaze with a delight which only people like them can know, on every lovely object in the fair prospect around. Boat follows boat, and coach succeeds coach, for the next three hours; but all are filled, and all with the same kind of people--neat and clean, cheerful and contented.

They reach their places of destination, and the taverns are crowded; but there is no drunkenness or brawling, for the class of men who commit the enormity of making Sunday excursions, take their families with them: and this in itself would be a check upon them, even if they were inclined to dissipation, which they really are not. Boisterous their mirth may be, for they have all the excitement of feeling that fresh air and green fields can impart to the dwellers in crowded cities, but it is innocent and harmless. The glass is circulated, and the joke goes round; but the one is free from excess, and the other from offence; and nothing but good humour and hilarity prevail.

In streets like Holborn and Tottenham Court Road, which form the central market of a large neighbourhood, inhabited by a vast number of mechanics and poor people, a few shops are open at an early hour of the morning; and a very poor man, with a thin and sickly woman by his side, may be seen with their little basket in hand, purchasing the scanty quantity of necessaries they can afford, which the time at which the man receives his wages, or his having a good deal of work to do, or the woman's having been out charing till a late hour, prevented their procuring over-night. The coffee-shops too, at which clerks and young men employed in counting-houses can procure their breakfasts, are also open. This class comprises, in a place like London, an enormous number of people, whose limited means prevent their engaging for their lodgings any other apartment than a bedroom, and who have consequently no alternative but to take their breakfasts at a coffee-shop, or go without it altogether. All these places, however, are quickly closed; and by the time the church bells begin to ring, all appearance of traffic has ceased. And then, what are the signs of immorality that meet the eye? Churches are well filled, and Dissenters' chapels are crowded to suffocation. There is no preaching to empty benches, while the drunken and dissolute populace run riot in the streets.

Here is a fashionable church, where the service commences at a late hour, for the accommodation of such members of the congregation-- and they are not a few--as may happen to have lingered at the Opera far into the morning of the Sabbath; an excellent contrivance for poising the balance between God and Mammon, and illustrating the ease with which a man's duties to both, may be accommodated and adjusted. How the carriages rattle up, and deposit their richly- dressed burdens beneath the lofty portico! The powdered footmen glide along the aisle, place the richly-bound prayer-books on the pew desks, slam the doors, and hurry away, leaving the fashionable members of the congregation to inspect each other through their glasses, and to dazzle and glitter in the eyes of the few shabby people in the free seats. The organ peals forth, the hired singers commence a short hymn, and the congregation condescendingly rise, stare about them, and converse in whispers. The clergyman enters the reading-desk,--a young man of noble family and elegant demeanour, notorious at Cambridge for his knowledge of horse-flesh and dancers, and celebrated at Eton for his hopeless stupidity. The service commences. Mark the soft voice in which he reads, and the impressive manner in which he applies his white hand, studded with brilliants, to his perfumed hair. Observe the graceful emphasis with which he offers up the prayers for the King, the Royal Family, and all the Nobility; and the nonchalance with which he hurries over the more uncomfortable portions of the service, the seventh commandment for instance, with a studied regard for the taste and feeling of his auditors, only to be equalled by that displayed by the sleek divine who succeeds him, who murmurs, in a voice kept down by rich feeding, most comfortable doctrines for exactly twelve minutes, and then arrives at the anxiously expected 'Now to God,' which is the signal for the dismissal of the congregation. The organ is again heard; those who have been asleep wake up, and those who have kept awake, smile and seem greatly relieved; bows and congratulations are exchanged, the livery servants are all bustle and commotion, bang go the steps, up jump the footmen, and off rattle the carriages: the inmates discoursing on the dresses of the congregation, and congratulating themselves on having set so excellent an example to the community in general, and Sunday-pleasurers in particular.

Enter a less orthodox place of religious worship, and observe the contrast. A small close chapel with a white-washed wall, and plain deal pews and pulpit, contains a closely-packed congregation, as different in dress, as they are opposed in manner, to that we have just quitted. The hymn is sung--not by paid singers, but by the whole assembly at the loudest pitch of their voices, unaccompanied by any musical instrument, the words being given out, two lines at a time, by the clerk. There is something in the sonorous quavering of the harsh voices, in the lank and hollow faces of the men, and the sour solemnity of the women, which bespeaks this a strong-hold of intolerant zeal and ignorant enthusiasm. The preacher enters the pulpit. He is a coarse, hard-faced man of forbidding aspect, clad in rusty black, and bearing in his hand a small plain Bible from which he selects some passage for his text, while the hymn is concluding. The congregation fall upon their knees, and are hushed into profound stillness as he delivers an extempore prayer, in which he calls upon the Sacred Founder of the Christian faith to bless his ministry, in terms of disgusting and impious familiarity not to be described. He begins his oration in a drawling tone, and his hearers listen with silent attention. He grows warmer as he proceeds with his subject, and his gesticulation becomes proportionately violent. He clenches his fists, beats the book upon the desk before him, and swings his arms wildly about his head. The congregation murmur their acquiescence in his doctrines: and a short groan, occasionally bears testimony to the moving nature of his eloquence. Encouraged by these symptoms of approval, and working himself up to a pitch of enthusiasm amounting almost to frenzy, he denounces sabbath-breakers with the direst vengeance of offended Heaven. He stretches his body half out of the pulpit, thrusts forth his arms with frantic gestures, and blasphemously calls upon The Deity to visit with eternal torments, those who turn aside from the word, as interpreted and preached by--himself. A low moaning is heard, the women rock their bodies to and fro, and wring their hands; the preacher's fervour increases, the perspiration starts upon his brow, his face is flushed, and he clenches his hands convulsively, as he draws a hideous and appalling picture of the horrors preparing for the wicked in a future state. A great excitement is visible among his hearers, a scream is heard, and some young girl falls senseless on the floor. There is a momentary rustle, but it is only for a moment--all eyes are turned towards the preacher. He pauses, passes his handkerchief across his face, and looks complacently round. His voice resumes its natural tone, as with mock humility he offers up a thanksgiving for having been successful in his efforts, and having been permitted to rescue one sinner from the path of evil. He sinks back into his seat, exhausted with the violence of his ravings; the girl is removed, a hymn is sung, a petition for some measure for securing the better observance of the Sabbath, which has been prepared by the good man, is read; and his worshipping admirers struggle who shall be the first to sign it.

But the morning service has concluded, and the streets are again crowded with people. Long rows of cleanly-dressed charity children, preceded by a portly beadle and a withered schoolmaster, are returning to their welcome dinner; and it is evident, from the number of men with beer-trays who are running from house to house, that no inconsiderable portion of the population are about to take theirs at this early hour. The bakers' shops in the humbler suburbs especially, are filled with men, women, and children, each anxiously waiting for the Sunday dinner. Look at the group of children who surround that working man who has just emerged from the baker's shop at the corner of the street, with the reeking dish, in which a diminutive joint of mutton simmers above a vast heap of half-browned potatoes. How the young rogues clap their hands, and dance round their father, for very joy at the prospect of the feast: and how anxiously the youngest and chubbiest of the lot, lingers on tiptoe by his side, trying to get a peep into the interior of the dish. They turn up the street, and the chubby-faced boy trots on as fast as his little legs will carry him, to herald the approach of the dinner to 'Mother' who is standing with a baby in her arms on the doorstep, and who seems almost as pleased with the whole scene as the children themselves; whereupon 'baby' not precisely understanding the importance of the business in hand, but clearly perceiving that it is something unusually lively, kicks and crows most lustily, to the unspeakable delight of all the children and both the parents: and the dinner is borne into the house amidst a shouting of small voices, and jumping of fat legs, which would fill Sir Andrew Agnew with astonishment; as well it might, seeing that Baronets, generally speaking, eat pretty comfortable dinners all the week through, and cannot be expected to understand what people feel, who only have a meat dinner on one day out of every seven.

The bakings being all duly consigned to their respective owners, and the beer-man having gone his rounds, the church bells ring for afternoon service, the shops are again closed, and the streets are more than ever thronged with people; some who have not been to church in the morning, going to it now; others who have been to church, going out for a walk; and others--let us admit the full measure of their guilt--going for a walk, who have not been to church at all. I am afraid the smart servant of all work, who has been loitering at the corner of the square for the last ten minutes, is one of the latter class. She is evidently waiting for somebody, and though she may have made up her mind to go to church with him one of these mornings, I don't think they have any such intention on this particular afternoon. Here he is, at last. The white trousers, blue coat, and yellow waistcoat--and more especially that cock of the hat--indicate, as surely as inanimate objects can, that Chalk Farm and not the parish church, is their destination. The girl colours up, and puts out her hand with a very awkward affectation of indifference. He gives it a gallant squeeze, and away they walk, arm in arm, the girl just looking back towards her 'place' with an air of conscious self-importance, and nodding to her fellow-servant who has gone up to the two-pair-of-stairs window, to take a full view of 'Mary's young man,' which being communicated to William, he takes off his hat to the fellow-servant: a proceeding which affords unmitigated satisfaction to all parties, and impels the fellow-servant to inform Miss Emily confidentially, in the course of the evening, 'that the young man as Mary keeps company with, is one of the most genteelest young men as ever she see.'

The two young people who have just crossed the road, and are following this happy couple down the street, are a fair specimen of another class of Sunday--pleasurers. There is a dapper smartness, struggling through very limited means, about the young man, which induces one to set him down at once as a junior clerk to a tradesman or attorney. The girl no one could possibly mistake. You may tell a young woman in the employment of a large dress- maker, at any time, by a certain neatness of cheap finery and humble following of fashion, which pervade her whole attire; but unfortunately there are other tokens not to be misunderstood--the pale face with its hectic bloom, the slight distortion of form which no artifice of dress can wholly conceal, the unhealthy stoop, and the short cough--the effects of hard work and close application to a sedentary employment, upon a tender frame. They turn towards the fields. The girl's countenance brightens, and an unwonted glow rises in her face. They are going to Hampstead or Highgate, to spend their holiday afternoon in some place where they can see the sky, the fields, and trees, and breathe for an hour or two the pure air, which so seldom plays upon that poor girl's form, or exhilarates her spirits.

I would to God, that the iron-hearted man who would deprive such people as these of their only pleasures, could feel the sinking of heart and soul, the wasting exhaustion of mind and body, the utter prostration of present strength and future hope, attendant upon that incessant toil which lasts from day to day, and from month to month; that toil which is too often protracted until the silence of midnight, and resumed with the first stir of morning. How marvellously would his ardent zeal for other men's souls, diminish after a short probation, and how enlightened and comprehensive would his views of the real object and meaning of the institution of the Sabbath become!

The afternoon is far advanced--the parks and public drives are crowded. Carriages, gigs, phaetons, stanhopes, and vehicles of every description, glide smoothly on. The promenades are filled with loungers on foot, and the road is thronged with loungers on horseback. Persons of every class are crowded together, here, in one dense mass. The plebeian, who takes his pleasure on no day but Sunday, jostles the patrician, who takes his, from year's end to year's end. You look in vain for any outward signs of profligacy or debauchery.

You see nothing before you but a vast number of people, the denizens of a large and crowded city, in the needful and rational enjoyment of air and exercise.

It grows dusk. The roads leading from the different places of suburban resort, are crowded with people on their return home, and the sound of merry voices rings through the gradually darkening fields. The evening is hot and sultry. The rich man throws open the sashes of his spacious dining-room, and quaffs his iced wine in splendid luxury. The poor man, who has no room to take his meals in, but the close apartment to which he and his family have been confined throughout the week, sits in the tea-garden of some famous tavern, and drinks his beer in content and comfort. The fields and roads are gradually deserted, the crowd once more pour into the streets, and disperse to their several homes; and by midnight all is silent and quiet, save where a few stragglers linger beneath the window of some great man's house, to listen to the strains of music from within: or stop to gaze upon the splendid carriages which are waiting to convey the guests from the dinner-party of an Earl.

There is a darker side to this picture, on which, so far from its being any part of my purpose to conceal it, I wish to lay particular stress. In some parts of London, and in many of the manufacturing towns of England, drunkenness and profligacy in their most disgusting forms, exhibit in the open streets on Sunday, a sad and a degrading spectacle. We need go no farther than St. Giles's, or Drury Lane, for sights and scenes of a most repulsive nature. Women with scarcely the articles of apparel which common decency requires, with forms bloated by disease, and faces rendered hideous by habitual drunkenness--men reeling and staggering along--children in rags and filth-- whole streets of squalid and miserable appearance, whose inhabitants are lounging in the public road, fighting, screaming, and swearing--these are the common objects which present themselves in, these are the well-known characteristics of, that portion of London to which I have just referred.

And why is it, that all well-disposed persons are shocked, and public decency scandalised, by such exhibitions?

These people are poor--that is notorious. It may be said that they spend in liquor, money with which they might purchase necessaries, and there is no denying the fact; but let it be remembered that even if they applied every farthing of their earnings in the best possible way, they would still be very-- very poor. Their dwellings are necessarily uncomfortable, and to a certain degree unhealthy. Cleanliness might do much, but they are too crowded together, the streets are too narrow, and the rooms too small, to admit of their ever being rendered desirable habitations. They work very hard all the week. We know that the effect of prolonged and arduous labour, is to produce, when a period of rest does arrive, a sensation of lassitude which it requires the application of some stimulus to overcome. What stimulus have they? Sunday comes, and with it a cessation of labour. How are they to employ the day, or what inducement have they to employ it, in recruiting their stock of health? They see little parties, on pleasure excursions, passing through the streets; but they cannot imitate their example, for they have not the means. They may walk, to be sure, but it is exactly the inducement to walk that they require. If every one of these men knew, that by taking the trouble to walk two or three miles he would be enabled to share in a good game of cricket, or some athletic sport, I very much question whether any of them would remain at home.

But you hold out no inducement, you offer no relief from listlessness, you provide nothing to amuse his mind, you afford him no means of exercising his body. Unwashed and unshaven, he saunters moodily about, weary and dejected. In lieu of the wholesome stimulus he might derive from nature, you drive him to the pernicious excitement to be gained from art. He flies to the gin-shop as his only resource; and when, reduced to a worse level than the lowest brute in the scale of creation, he lies wallowing in the kennel, your saintly lawgivers lift up their hands to heaven, and exclaim for a law which shall convert the day intended for rest and cheerfulness, into one of universal gloom, bigotry, and persecution.

CHAPTER II

AS SABBATH BILLS WOULD MAKE IT

The provisions of the bill introduced into the House of Commons by Sir Andrew Agnew, and thrown out by that House on the motion for the second reading, on the 18th of May in the present year, by a majority of 32, may very fairly be taken as a test of the length to which the fanatics, of which the honourable Baronet is the distinguished leader, are prepared to go. No test can be fairer; because while on the one hand this measure may be supposed to exhibit all that improvement which mature reflection and long deliberation may have suggested, so on the other it may very reasonably be inferred, that if it be quite as severe in its provisions, and to the full as partial in its operation, as those which have preceded it and experienced a similar fate, the disease under which the honourable Baronet and his friends labour, is perfectly hopeless, and beyond the reach of cure.

The proposed enactments of the bill are briefly these:- All work is prohibited on the Lord's day, under heavy penalties, increasing with every repetition of the offence. There are penalties for keeping shops open--penalties for drunkenness--penalties for keeping open houses of entertainment--penalties for being present at any public meeting or assembly--penalties for letting carriages, and penalties for hiring them--penalties for travelling in steam-boats, and penalties for taking passengers--penalties on vessels commencing their voyage on Sunday--penalties on the owners of cattle who suffer them to be driven on the Lord's day--penalties on constables who refuse to act, and penalties for resisting them when they do. In addition to these trifles, the constables are invested with arbitrary, vexatious, and most extensive powers; and all this in a bill which sets out with a hypocritical and canting declaration that 'nothing is more acceptable to God than the TRUE AND SINCERE worship of Him according to His holy will, and that it is the bounden duty of Parliament to promote the observance of the Lord's day, by protecting every class of society against being required to sacrifice their comfort, health, religious privileges, and conscience, for the convenience, enjoyment, or supposed advantage of any other class on the Lord's day'! The idea of making a man truly moral through the ministry of constables, and sincerely religious under the influence of penalties, is worthy of the mind which could form such a mass of monstrous absurdity as this bill is composed of.

The House of Commons threw the measure out certainly, and by so doing retrieved the disgrace--so far as it could be retrieved--of placing among the printed papers of Parliament, such an egregious specimen of legislative folly; but there was a degree of delicacy and forbearance about the debate that took place, which I cannot help thinking as unnecessary and uncalled for, as it is unusual in Parliamentary discussions. If it had been the first time of Sir Andrew Agnew's attempting to palm such a measure upon the country, we might well understand, and duly appreciate, the delicate and compassionate feeling due to the supposed weakness and imbecility of the man, which prevented his proposition being exposed in its true colours, and induced this Hon. Member to bear testimony to his excellent motives, and that Noble Lord to regret that he could not- -although he had tried to do so--adopt any portion of the bill. But when these attempts have been repeated, again and again; when Sir Andrew Agnew has renewed them session after session, and when it has become palpably evident to the whole House that

His impudence of proof in every trial, Kens no polite, and heeds no plain denial -

it really becomes high time to speak of him and his legislation, as they appear to deserve, without that gloss of politeness, which is all very well in an ordinary case, but rather out of place when the liberties and comforts of a whole people are at stake.

In the first place, it is by no means the worst characteristic of this bill, that it is a bill of blunders: it is, from beginning to end, a piece of deliberate cruelty, and crafty injustice. If the rich composed the whole population of this country, not a single comfort of one single man would be affected by it. It is directed exclusively, and without the exception of a solitary instance, against the amusements and recreations of the poor. This was the bait held out by the Hon. Baronet to a body of men, who cannot be supposed to have any very strong sympathies in common with the poor, because they cannot understand their sufferings or their struggles. This is the bait, which will in time prevail, unless public attention is awakened, and public feeling exerted, to prevent it.

Take the very first clause, the provision that no man shall be allowed to work on Sunday--'That no person, upon the Lord's day, shall do, or hire, or employ any person to do any manner of labour, or any work of his or her ordinary calling.' What class of persons does this affect? The rich man? No. Menial servants, both male and female, are specially exempted from the operation of the bill. 'Menial servants' are among the poor people. The bill has no regard for them. The Baronet's dinner must be cooked on Sunday, the Bishop's horses must be groomed, and the Peer's carriage must be driven. So the menial servants are put utterly beyond the pale of grace;--unless indeed, they are to go to heaven through the sanctity of their masters, and possibly they might think even that, rather an uncertain passport.

There is a penalty for keeping open, houses of entertainment. Now, suppose the bill had passed, and that half-a-dozen adventurous licensed victuallers, relying upon the excitement of public feeling on the subject, and the consequent difficulty of conviction (this is by no means an improbable supposition), had determined to keep their houses and gardens open, through the whole Sunday afternoon, in defiance of the law. Every act of hiring or working, every act of buying or selling, or delivering, or causing anything to be bought or sold, is specifically made a separate offence--mark the effect. A party, a man and his wife and children, enter a tea- garden, and the informer stations himself in the next box, from whence he can see and hear everything that passes. 'Waiter!' says the father. 'Yes. Sir.' 'Pint of the best ale!' 'Yes, Sir.' Away runs the waiter to the bar, and gets the ale from the landlord. Out comes the informer's note-book--penalty on the father for hiring, on the waiter for delivering, and on the landlord for selling, on the Lord's day. But it does not stop here. The waiter delivers the ale, and darts off, little suspecting the penalties in store for him. 'Hollo,' cries the father, 'waiter!' 'Yes, Sir.' 'Just get this little boy a biscuit, will you?' 'Yes, Sir.' Off runs the waiter again, and down goes another case of hiring, another case of delivering, and another case of selling; and so it would go on ad infinitum, the sum and substance of the matter being, that every time a man or woman cried 'Waiter!' on Sunday, he or she would be fined not less than forty shillings, nor more than a hundred; and every time a waiter replied, 'Yes, Sir,' he and his master would be fined in the same amount: with the addition of a new sort of window duty on the landlord, to wit, a tax of twenty shillings an hour for every hour beyond the first one, during which he should have his shutters down on the Sabbath.

With one exception, there are perhaps no clauses in the whole bill, so strongly illustrative of its partial operation, and the intention of its framer, as those which relate to travelling on Sunday. Penalties of ten, twenty, and thirty pounds, are mercilessly imposed upon coach proprietors who shall run their coaches on the Sabbath; one, two, and ten pounds upon those who hire, or let to hire, horses and carriages upon the Lord's day, but not one syllable about those who have no necessity to hire, because they have carriages and horses of their own; not one word of a penalty on liveried coachmen and footmen. The whole of the saintly venom is directed against the hired cabriolet, the humble fly, or the rumbling hackney-coach, which enables a man of the poorer class to escape for a few hours from the smoke and dirt, in the midst of which he has been confined throughout the week: while the escutcheoned carriage and the dashing cab, may whirl their wealthy owners to Sunday feasts and private oratorios, setting constables, informers, and penalties, at defiance. Again, in the description of the places of public resort which it is rendered criminal to attend on Sunday, there are no words comprising a very fashionable promenade. Public discussions, public debates, public lectures and speeches, are cautiously guarded against; for it is by their means that the people become enlightened enough to deride the last efforts of bigotry and superstition. There is a stringent provision for punishing the poor man who spends an hour in a news- room, but there is nothing to prevent the rich one from lounging away the day in the Zoological Gardens.

There is, in four words, a mock proviso, which affects to forbid travelling 'with any animal' on the Lord's day. This, however, is revoked, as relates to the rich man, by a subsequent provision. We have then a penalty of not less than fifty, nor more than one hundred pounds, upon any person participating in the control, or having the command of any vessel which shall commence her voyage on the Lord's day, should the wind prove favourable. The next time this bill is brought forward (which will no doubt be at an early period of the next session of Parliament) perhaps it will be better to amend this clause by declaring, that from and after the passing of the act, it shall be deemed unlawful for the wind to blow at all upon the Sabbath. It would remove a great deal of temptation from the owners and captains of vessels.

The reader is now in possession of the principal enacting clauses of Sir Andrew Agnew's bill, with the exception of one, for preventing the killing or taking of 'FISH, OR OTHER WILD ANIMALS,' and the ordinary provisions which are inserted for form's sake in all acts of Parliament. I now beg his attention to the clauses of exemption.

They are two in number. The first exempts menial servants from any rest, and all poor men from any recreation: outlaws a milkman after nine o'clock in the morning, and makes eating-houses lawful for only two hours in the afternoon; permits a medical man to use his carriage on Sunday, and declares that a clergyman may either use his own, or hire one.

The second is artful, cunning, and designing; shielding the rich man from the possibility of being entrapped, and affecting at the same time, to have a tender and scrupulous regard, for the interests of the whole community. It declares, 'that nothing in this act contained, shall extend to works of piety, charity, or necessity.'

What is meant by the word 'necessity' in this clause? Simply this- -that the rich man shall be at liberty to make use of all the splendid luxuries he has collected around him, on any day in the week, because habit and custom have rendered them 'necessary' to his easy existence; but that the poor man who saves his money to provide some little pleasure for himself and family at lengthened intervals, shall not be permitted to enjoy it. It is not 'necessary' to him:- Heaven knows, he very often goes long enough without it. This is the plain English of the clause. The carriage and pair of horses, the coachman, the footman, the helper, and the groom, are 'necessary' on Sundays, as on other days, to the bishop and the nobleman; but the hackney-coach, the hired gig, or the taxed cart, cannot possibly be 'necessary' to the working-man on Sunday, for he has it not at other times. The sumptuous dinner and the rich wines, are 'necessaries' to a great man in his own mansion: but the pint of beer and the plate of meat, degrade the national character in an eating-house.

Such is the bill for promoting the true and sincere worship of God according to his Holy Will, and for protecting every class of society against being required to sacrifice their health and comfort on the Sabbath. Instances in which its operation would be as unjust as it would be absurd, might be multiplied to an endless amount; but it is sufficient to place its leading provisions before the reader. In doing so, I have purposely abstained from drawing upon the imagination for possible cases; the provisions to which I have referred, stand in so many words upon the bill as printed by order of the House of Commons; and they can neither be disowned, nor explained away.

Let us suppose such a bill as this, to have actually passed both branches of the legislature; to have received the royal assent; and to have come into operation. Imagine its effect in a great city like London.

Sunday comes, and brings with it a day of general gloom and austerity. The man who has been toiling hard all the week, has been looking towards the Sabbath, not as to a day of rest from labour, and healthy recreation, but as one of grievous tyranny and grinding oppression. The day which his Maker intended as a blessing, man has converted into a curse. Instead of being hailed by him as his period of relaxation, he finds it remarkable only as depriving him of every comfort and enjoyment. He has many children about him, all sent into the world at an early age, to struggle for a livelihood; one is kept in a warehouse all day, with an interval of rest too short to enable him to reach home, another walks four or five miles to his employment at the docks, a third earns a few shillings weekly, as an errand boy, or office messenger; and the employment of the man himself, detains him at some distance from his home from morning till night. Sunday is the only day on which they could all meet together, and enjoy a homely meal in social comfort; and now they sit down to a cold and cheerless dinner: the pious guardians of the man's salvation having, in their regard for the welfare of his precious soul, shut up the bakers' shops. The fire blazes high in the kitchen chimney of these well-fed hypocrites, and the rich steams of the savoury dinner scent the air. What care they to be told that this class of men have neither a place to cook in--nor means to bear the expense, if they had?

Look into your churches--diminished congregations, and scanty attendance. People have grown sullen and obstinate, and are becoming disgusted with the faith which condemns them to such a day as this, once in every seven. And as you cannot make people religious by Act of Parliament, or force them to church by constables, they display their feeling by staying away.

Turn into the streets, and mark the rigid gloom that reigns over everything around. The roads are empty, the fields are deserted, the houses of entertainment are closed. Groups of filthy and discontented-looking men, are idling about at the street corners, or sleeping in the sun; but there are no decently-dressed people of the poorer class, passing to and fro. Where should they walk to? It would take them an hour, at least, to get into the fields, and when they reached them, they could procure neither bite nor sup, without the informer and the penalty. Now and then, a carriage rolls smoothly on, or a well-mounted horseman, followed by a liveried attendant, canters by; but with these exceptions, all is as melancholy and quiet as if a pestilence had fallen on the city.

Bend your steps through the narrow and thickly-inhabited streets, and observe the sallow faces of the men and women who are lounging at the doors, or lolling from the windows. Regard well the closeness of these crowded rooms, and the noisome exhalations that rise from the drains and kennels; and then laud the triumph of religion and morality, which condemns people to drag their lives out in such stews as these, and makes it criminal for them to eat or drink in the fresh air, or under the clear sky. Here and there, from some half-opened window, the loud shout of drunken revelry strikes upon the ear, and the noise of oaths and quarrelling--the effect of the close and heated atmosphere--is heard on all sides. See how the men all rush to join the crowd that are making their way down the street, and how loud the execrations of the mob become as they draw nearer. They have assembled round a little knot of constables, who have seized the stock-in-trade, heinously exposed on Sunday, of some miserable walking-stick seller, who follows clamouring for his property. The dispute grows warmer and fiercer, until at last some of the more furious among the crowd, rush forward to restore the goods to their owner. A general conflict takes place; the sticks of the constables are exercised in all directions; fresh assistance is procured; and half a dozen of the assailants are conveyed to the station-house, struggling, bleeding, and cursing. The case is taken to the police-office on the following morning; and after a frightful amount of perjury on both sides, the men are sent to prison for resisting the officers, their families to the workhouse to keep them from starving: and there they both remain for a month afterwards, glorious trophies of the sanctified enforcement of the Christian Sabbath. Add to such scenes as these, the profligacy, idleness, drunkenness, and vice, that will be committed to an extent which no man can foresee, on Monday, as an atonement for the restraint of the preceding day; and you have a very faint and imperfect picture of the religious effects of this Sunday legislation, supposing it could ever be forced upon the people.

But let those who advocate the cause of fanaticism, reflect well upon the probable issue of their endeavours. They may by perseverance, succeed with Parliament. Let them ponder on the probability of succeeding with the people. You may deny the concession of a political question for a time, and a nation will bear it patiently. Strike home to the comforts of every man's fireside--tamper with every man's freedom and liberty--and one month, one week, may rouse a feeling abroad, which a king would gladly yield his crown to quell, and a peer would resign his coronet to allay.

It is the custom to affect a deference for the motives of those who advocate these measures, and a respect for the feelings by which they are actuated. They do not deserve it. If they legislate in ignorance, they are criminal and dishonest; if they do so with their eyes open, they commit wilful injustice; in either case, they bring religion into contempt. But they do NOT legislate in ignorance. Public prints, and public men, have pointed out to them again and again, the consequences of their proceedings. If they persist in thrusting themselves forward, let those consequences rest upon their own heads, and let them be content to stand upon their own merits.

It may be asked, what motives can actuate a man who has so little regard for the comfort of his fellow-beings, so little respect for their wants and necessities, and so distorted a notion of the beneficence of his Creator. I reply, an envious, heartless, ill- conditioned dislike to seeing those whom fortune has placed below him, cheerful and happy--an intolerant confidence in his own high worthiness before God, and a lofty impression of the demerits of others--pride, selfish pride, as inconsistent with the spirit of Christianity itself, as opposed to the example of its Founder upon earth.

To these may be added another class of men--the stern and gloomy enthusiasts, who would make earth a hell, and religion a torment: men who, having wasted the earlier part of their lives in dissipation and depravity, find themselves when scarcely past its meridian, steeped to the neck in vice, and shunned like a loathsome disease. Abandoned by the world, having nothing to fall back upon, nothing to remember but time mis-spent, and energies misdirected, they turn their eyes and not their thoughts to Heaven, and delude themselves into the impious belief, that in denouncing the lightness of heart of which they cannot partake, and the rational pleasures from which they never derived enjoyment, they are more than remedying the sins of their old career, and--like the founders of monasteries and builders of churches, in ruder days-- establishing a good set claim upon their Maker.

CHAPTER III

AS IT MIGHT BE MADE

The supporters of Sabbath Bills, and more especially the extreme class of

Dissenters, lay great stress upon the declarations occasionally made by criminals from the condemned cell or the scaffold, that to Sabbath-breaking they attribute their first deviation from the path of rectitude; and they point to these statements, as an incontestable proof of the evil consequences which await a departure from that strict and rigid observance of the Sabbath, which they uphold. I cannot help thinking that in this, as in almost every other respect connected with the subject, there is a considerable degree of cant, and a very great deal of wilful blindness. If a man be viciously disposed--and with very few exceptions, not a man dies by the executioner's hands, who has not been in one way or other a most abandoned and profligate character for many years--if a man be viciously disposed, there is no doubt that he will turn his Sunday to bad account, that he will take advantage of it, to dissipate with other bad characters as vile as himself; and that in this way, he may trace his first yielding to temptation, possibly his first commission of crime, to an infringement of the Sabbath. But this would be an argument against any holiday at all. If his holiday had been Wednesday instead of Sunday, and he had devoted it to the same improper uses, it would have been productive of the same results. It is too much to judge of the character of a whole people, by the confessions of the very worst members of society. It is not fair, to cry down things which are harmless in themselves, because evil-disposed men may turn them to bad account. Who ever thought of deprecating the teaching poor people to write, because some porter in a warehouse had committed forgery? Or into what man's head did it ever enter, to prevent the crowding of churches, because it afforded a temptation for the picking of pockets?

When the Book of Sports, for allowing the peasantry of England to divert themselves with certain games in the open air, on Sundays, after evening service, was published by Charles the First, it is needless to say the English people were comparatively rude and uncivilised. And yet it is extraordinary to how few excesses it gave rise, even in that day, when men's minds were not enlightened, or their passions moderated, by the influence of education and refinement. That some excesses were committed through its means, in the remoter parts of the country, and that it was discontinued in those places, in consequence, cannot be denied: but generally speaking, there is no proof whatever on record, of its having had any tendency to increase crime, or to lower the character of the people.

The Puritans of that time, were as much opposed to harmless recreations and healthful amusements as those of the present day, and it is amusing to observe that each in their generation, advance precisely the same description of arguments. In the British Museum, there is a curious pamphlet got up by the Agnews of Charles's time, entitled 'A Divine Tragedie lately acted, or a Collection of sundry memorable examples of God's Judgements upon Sabbath Breakers, and other like Libertines in their unlawful Sports, happening within the realme of England, in the compass only of two yeares last past, since the Booke (of Sports) was published, worthy to be knowne and considered of all men, especially such who are guilty of the sinne, or archpatrons thereof.' This amusing document, contains some fifty or sixty veritable accounts of balls of fire that fell into churchyards and upset the sporters, and sporters that quarrelled, and upset one another, and so forth: and among them is one anecdote containing an example of a rather different kind, which I cannot resist the temptation of quoting, as strongly illustrative of the fact, that this blinking of the question has not even the recommendation of novelty.

'A woman about Northampton, the same day that she heard the booke for sports read, went immediately, and having 3. pence in her purse, hired a fellow to goe to the next towne to fetch a Minstrell, who coming, she with others fell a dauncing, which continued within night; at which time shee was got with child, which at the birth shee murthering, was detected and apprehended, and being converted before the justice, shee confessed it, and withal told the occasion of it, saying it was her falling to sport on the Sabbath, upon the reading of the Booke, so as for this treble sinfull act, her presumptuous profaning of the Sabbath, wh. brought her adultory and that murther. Shee was according to the Law both of God and man, put to death. Much sinne and misery followeth upon Sabbath-breaking.'

It is needless to say, that if the young lady near Northampton had 'fallen to sport' of such a dangerous description, on any other day but Sunday, the first result would probably have been the same: it never having been distinctly shown that Sunday is more favourable to the propagation of the human race than any other day in the week. The second result--the murder of the child-- does not speak very highly for the amiability of her natural disposition; and the whole story, supposing it to have had any foundation at all, is about as much chargeable upon the Book of Sports, as upon the Book of Kings. Such 'sports' have taken place in Dissenting Chapels before now; but religion has never been blamed in consequence; nor has it been proposed to shut up the chapels on that account.

The question, then, very fairly arises, whether we have any reason to suppose that allowing games in the open air on Sundays, or even providing the means of amusement for the humbler classes of society on that day, would be hurtful and injurious to the character and morals of the people.

I was travelling in the west of England a summer or two back, and was induced by the beauty of the scenery, and the seclusion of the spot, to remain for the night in a small village, distant about seventy miles from London. The next morning was Sunday; and I walked out, towards the church. Groups of people--the whole population of the little hamlet apparently--were hastening in the same direction. Cheerful and good-humoured congratulations were heard on all sides, as neighbours overtook each other, and walked on in company. Occasionally I passed an aged couple, whose married daughter and her husband were loitering by the side of the old people, accommodating their rate of walking to their feeble pace, while a little knot of children hurried on before; stout young labourers in clean round frocks; and buxom girls with healthy, laughing faces, were plentifully sprinkled about in couples, and the whole scene was one of quiet and tranquil contentment, irresistibly captivating. The morning was bright and pleasant, the hedges were green and blooming, and a thousand delicious scents were wafted on the air, from the wild flowers which blossomed on either side of the footpath. The little church was one of those venerable simple buildings which abound in the English counties; half overgrown with moss and ivy, and standing in the centre of a little plot of ground, which, but for the green mounds with which it was studded, might have passed for a lovely meadow. I fancied that the old clanking bell which was now summoning the congregation together, would seem less terrible when it rung out the knell of a departed soul, than I had ever deemed possible before--that the sound would tell only of a welcome to calmness and rest, amidst the most peaceful and tranquil scene in nature.

I followed into the church--a low-roofed building with small arched windows, through which the sun's rays streamed upon a plain tablet on the opposite wall, which had once recorded names, now as undistinguishable on its worn surface, as were the bones beneath, from the dust into which they had resolved. The impressive service of the Church of England was spoken--not merely READ--by a grey- headed minister, and the responses delivered by his auditors, with an air of sincere devotion as far removed from affectation or display, as from coldness or indifference. The psalms were accompanied by a few instrumental performers, who were stationed in a small gallery extending across the church at the lower end, over the door: and the voices were led by the clerk, who, it was evident, derived no slight pride and gratification from this portion of the service. The discourse was plain, unpretending, and well adapted to the comprehension of the hearers. At the conclusion of the service, the villagers waited in the churchyard, to salute the clergyman as he passed; and two or three, I observed, stepped aside, as if communicating some little difficulty, and asking his advice. This, to guess from the homely bows, and other rustic expressions of gratitude, the old gentleman readily conceded. He seemed intimately acquainted with the circumstances of all his parishioners; for I heard him inquire after one man's youngest child, another man's wife, and so forth; and that he was fond of his joke, I discovered from overhearing him ask a stout, fresh-coloured young fellow, with a very pretty bashful-looking girl on his arm, 'when those banns were to be put up?'--an inquiry which made the young fellow more fresh-coloured, and the girl more bashful, and which, strange to say, caused a great many other girls who were standing round, to colour up also, and look anywhere but in the faces of their male companions.

As I approached this spot in the evening about half an hour before sunset, I was surprised to hear the hum of voices, and occasionally a shout of merriment from the meadow beyond the churchyard; which I found, when I reached the stile, to be occasioned by a very animated game of cricket, in which the boys and young men of the place were engaged, while the females and old people were scattered about: some seated on the grass watching the progress of the game, and others sauntering about in groups of two or three, gathering little nosegays of wild roses and hedge flowers. I could not but take notice of one old man in particular, with a bright-eyed grand- daughter by his side, who was giving a sunburnt young fellow some instructions in the game, which he received with an air of profound deference, but with an occasional glance at the girl, which induced me to think that his attention was rather distracted from the old gentleman's narration of the fruits of his experience. When it was his turn at the wicket, too, there was a glance towards the pair every now and then, which the old grandfather very complacently considered as an appeal to his judgment of a particular hit, but which a certain blush in the girl's face, and a downcast look of the bright eye, led me to believe was intended for somebody else than the old man,--and understood by somebody else, too, or I am much mistaken.

I was in the very height of the pleasure which the contemplation of this scene afforded me, when I saw the old clergyman making his way towards us. I trembled for an angry interruption to the sport, and was almost on the point of crying out, to warn the cricketers of his approach; he was so close upon me, however, that I could do nothing but remain still, and anticipate the reproof that was preparing. What was my agreeable surprise to see the old gentleman standing at the stile, with his hands in his pockets, surveying the whole scene with evident satisfaction! And how dull I must have been, not to have known till my friend the grandfather (who, by- the-bye, said he had been a wonderful cricketer in his time) told me, that it was the clergyman himself who had established the whole thing: that it was his field they played in; and that it was he who had purchased stumps, bats, ball, and all!

It is such scenes as this, I would see near London, on a Sunday evening. It is such men as this, who would do more in one year to make people properly religious, cheerful, and contented, than all the legislation of a century could ever accomplish.

It will be said--it has been very often--that it would be matter of perfect impossibility to make amusements and exercises succeed in large towns, which may be very well adapted to a country population. Here, again, we are called upon to yield to bare assertions on matters of belief and opinion, as if they were established and undoubted facts. That there is a wide difference between the two cases, no one will be prepared to dispute; that the difference is such as to prevent the application of the same principle to both, no reasonable man, I think, will be disposed to maintain. The great majority of the people who make holiday on Sunday now, are industrious, orderly, and well-behaved persons. It is not unreasonable to suppose that they would be no more inclined to an abuse of pleasures provided for them, than they are to an abuse of the pleasures they provide for themselves; and if any people, for want of something better to do, resort to criminal practices on the Sabbath as at present observed, no better remedy for the evil can be imagined, than giving them the opportunity of doing something which will amuse them, and hurt nobody else.

The propriety of opening the British Museum to respectable people on Sunday, has lately been the subject of some discussion. I think it would puzzle the most austere of the Sunday legislators to assign any valid reason for opposing so sensible a proposition. The Museum contains rich specimens from all the vast museums and repositories of Nature, and rare and curious fragments of the mighty works of art, in bygone ages: all calculated to awaken contemplation and inquiry, and to tend to the enlightenment and improvement of the people. But attendants would be necessary, and a few men would be employed upon the Sabbath. They certainly would; but how many? Why, if the British Museum, and the National Gallery, and the Gallery of Practical Science, and every other exhibition in London, from which knowledge is to be derived and information gained, were to be thrown open on a Sunday afternoon, not fifty people would be required to preside over the whole: and it would take treble the number to enforce a Sabbath bill in any three populous parishes.

I should like to see some large field, or open piece of ground, in every outskirt of London, exhibiting each Sunday evening on a larger scale, the scene of the little country meadow. I should like to see the time arrive, when a man's attendance to his religious duties might be left to that religious feeling which most men possess in a greater or less degree, but which was never forced into the breast of any man by menace or restraint. I should like to see the time when Sunday might be looked forward to, as a recognised day of relaxation and enjoyment, and when every man might feel, what few men do now, that religion is not incompatible with rational pleasure and needful recreation.

How different a picture would the streets and public places then present! The museums, and repositories of scientific and useful inventions, would be crowded with ingenious mechanics and industrious artisans, all anxious for information, and all unable to procure it at any other time. The spacious saloons would be swarming with practical men: humble in appearance, but destined, perhaps, to become the greatest inventors and philosophers of their age. The labourers who now lounge away the day in idleness and intoxication, would be seen hurrying along, with cheerful faces and clean attire, not to the close and smoky atmosphere of the public- house but to the fresh and airy fields. Fancy the pleasant scene. Throngs of people, pouring out from the lanes and alleys of the metropolis, to various places of common resort at some short distance from the town, to join in the refreshing sports and exercises of the day--the children gambolling in crowds upon the grass, the mothers looking on, and enjoying themselves the little game they seem only to direct; other parties strolling along some pleasant walks, or reposing in the shade of the stately trees; others again intent upon their different amusements. Nothing should be heard on all sides, but the sharp stroke of the bat as it sent the ball skimming along the ground, the clear ring of the quoit, as it struck upon the iron peg: the noisy murmur of many voices, and the loud shout of mirth and delight, which would awaken the echoes far and wide, till the fields rung with it. The day would pass away, in a series of enjoyments which would awaken no painful reflections when night arrived; for they would be calculated to bring with them, only health and contentment. The young would lose that dread of religion, which the sour austerity of its professors too often inculcates in youthful bosoms; and the old would find less difficulty in persuading them to respect its observances. The drunken and dissipated, deprived of any excuse for their misconduct, would no longer excite pity but disgust. Above all, the more ignorant and humble class of men, who now partake of many of the bitters of life, and taste but few of its sweets, would naturally feel attachment and respect for that code of morality, which, regarding the many hardships of their station, strove to alleviate its rigours, and endeavoured to soften its asperity.

This is what Sunday might be made, and what it might be made without impiety or profanation. The wise and beneficent Creator who places men upon earth, requires that they shall perform the duties of that station of life to which they are called, and He can never intend that the more a man strives to discharge those duties, the more he shall be debarred from happiness and enjoyment. Let those who have six days in the week for all the world's pleasures, appropriate the seventh to fasting and gloom, either for their own sins or those of other people, if they like to bewail them; but let those who employ their six days in a worthier manner, devote their seventh to a different purpose. Let divines set the example of true morality: preach it to their flocks in the morning, and dismiss them to enjoy true rest in the afternoon; and let them select for their text, and let Sunday legislators take for their motto, the words which fell from the lips of that Master, whose precepts they misconstrue, and whose lessons they pervert--'The Sabbath was made for man, and not man to serve the Sabbath.'

The Magic Fishbone

by Charles Dickens

FOREWORD

The story contained herein was written by Charles Dickens in 1867. It is the second of four stories entitled "Holiday Romance" and was published originally in a children's magazine in America. It purports to be written by a child aged seven. It was republished in England in "All the Year Round" in 1868. For this and four other Christmas pieces Dickens received ?,000.

"Holiday Romance" was published in book form by Messrs Chapman & Hall in 1874, with "Edwin Drood" and other stories.

For this reprint the text of the story as it appeared in "All the Year Round" has been followed.

* * * * *

There was once a King, and he had a Queen; and he was the manliest of his sex, and she was the loveliest of hers. The King was, in his private profession, Under Government. The Queen's father had been a medical man out of town.

They had nineteen children, and were always having more. Seventeen of these children took care of the baby; and Alicia, the eldest, took care of them all. Their ages varied from seven years to seven months.

Let us now resume our story.

One day the King was going to the office, when he stopped at the fishmonger's to buy a pound and a half of salmon not too near the tail, which the Queen (who was a careful housekeeper) had requested him to send home. Mr Pickles, the fishmonger, said, "Certainly, sir, is there any other article, Good-morning."

The King went on towards the office in a melancholy mood, for quarter day was such a long way off, and several of the dear children were growing out of their clothes. He had not proceeded far, when Mr Pickles's errand-boy came running after him, and said, "Sir, you didn't notice the old lady in our shop."

"What old lady?" enquired the King. "I saw none."

Now, the King had not seen any old lady, because this old lady had been invisible to him, though visible to Mr Pickles's boy. Probably because he messed and splashed the water about to that degree, and flopped the pairs of soles down in that violent manner, that, if she had not been visible to him, he would have spoilt her clothes.

Just then the old lady came trotting up. She was dressed in shot-silk of the richest quality, smelling of dried lavender.

"King Watkins the First, I believe?" said the old lady.

"Watkins," replied the King, "is my name."

"Papa, if I am not mistaken, of the beautiful Princess Alicia?" said the old lady.

"And of eighteen other darlings," replied the King.

"Listen. You are going to the office," said the old lady.

It instantly flashed upon the King that she must be a Fairy, or how could she know that?

"You are right," said the old lady, answering his thoughts, "I am the Good Fairy Grandmarina. Attend. When you return home to dinner, politely invite the Princess Alicia to have some of the salmon you bought just now."

"It may disagree with her," said the King.

The old lady became so very angry at this absurd idea, that the King was quite alarmed, and humbly begged her pardon.

"We hear a great deal too much about this thing disagreeing, and that thing disagreeing," said the old lady, with the greatest contempt it was possible to express. "Don't be greedy. I think you want it all yourself."

The King hung his head under this reproof, and said he wouldn't talk about things disagreeing, any more.

"Be good, then," said the Fairy Grandmarina, "and don't! When the beautiful Princess Alicia consents to partake of the salmon--as I think she will--you will find she will leave a fish-bone on her plate. Tell her to dry it, and to rub it, and to polish it till it shines like mother-of-pearl, and to take care of it as a present from me."

"Is that all?" asked the King.

"Don't be impatient, sir," returned the Fairy Grandmarina, scolding him severely. "Don't catch people short, before they have done speaking. Just the way with you grown-up persons. You are always doing it."

The King again hung his head, and said he wouldn't do so any more.

"Be good then," said the Fairy Grandmarina, "and don't! Tell the Princess Alicia, with my love, that the fish-bone is a magic present which can only be used once; but that it will bring her, that once, whatever she wishes for, PROVIDED SHE WISHES FOR IT AT THE RIGHT TIME. That is the message. Take care of it."

The King was beginning, "Might I ask the reason--?" when the Fairy became absolutely furious.

"Will you be good, sir?" she exclaimed, stamping her foot on the ground. "The reason for this, and the reason for that, indeed! You are always wanting the reason. No reason. There! Hoity toity me! I am sick of your grown-up reasons."

The King was extremely frightened by the old lady's flying into such a passion, and said he was very sorry to have offended her, and he wouldn't ask for reasons any more.

"Be good then," said the old lady, "and don't!"

With those words, Grandmarina vanished, and the King went on and on and on, till he came to the office. There he wrote and wrote and wrote, till it was time to go home again. Then he politely invited the Princess Alicia, as the Fairy had directed him, to partake of the salmon. And when she had enjoyed it very much, he saw the fish-bone on her plate, as the Fairy had told him he would, and he delivered the Fairy's message, and the Princess Alicia took care to dry the bone, and to rub it, and to polish it till it shone like mother-of-pearl.

And so when the Queen was going to get up in the morning, she said, "O, dear me, dear me; my head, my head!" and then she fainted away.

The Princess Alicia, who happened to be looking in at the chamber-door, asking about breakfast, was very much alarmed when she saw her Royal Mamma in this state, and she rang the bell for Peggy, which was the name of the Lord Chamberlain. But remembering where the smelling-bottle was, she climbed on a chair and got it, and after that she climbed on another chair by the bedside and held the smelling-bottle to the Queen's nose, and after that she jumped down and got some water, and after that she jumped up again and wetted the Queen's forehead, and, in short, when the Lord Chamberlain came in, that dear old woman said to the little Princess, "What a Trot you are! I couldn't have done it better myself!"

But that was not the worst of the good Queen's illness. O, no! She was very ill indeed, for a long time. The Princess Alicia kept the seventeen young Princes and Princesses quiet, and dressed and undressed and danced the baby, and made the kettle boil, and heated the soup, and swept the hearth, and poured out the medicine, and nursed the Queen, and did all that ever she could, and was as busy busy busy, as busy could be. For there were not many servants at that Palace, for three reasons; because the King was short of money, because a rise in his office never seemed to come, and because quarter day was so far off that it looked almost as far off and as little as one of the stars.

But on the morning when the Queen fainted away, where was the magic fish-bone? Why, there it was in the Princess Alicia's pocket. She had almost taken it out to bring the Queen to life again, when she put it back, and looked for the smelling-bottle.

After the Queen had come out of her swoon that morning, and was dozing, the Princess Alicia hurried up-stairs to tell a most particular secret to a most particularly confidential friend of hers, who was a Duchess. People did suppose her to be a Doll; but she was really a Duchess, though nobody knew it except the Princess.

This most particular secret was a secret about the magic fish-bone, the history of which was well known to the Duchess, because the Princess told her everything. The Princess kneeled down by the bed on which the Duchess was lying, full-dressed and wide awake, and whispered the secret to her. The Duchess smiled and nodded. People might have supposed that she never smiled and nodded, but she often did, though nobody knew it except the Princess.

Then the Princess Alicia hurried downstairs again, to keep watch in the Queen's room. She often kept watch by herself in the Queen's room; but every evening, while the illness lasted, she sat there watching with the King. And every evening the King sat looking at her with a cross look, wondering why she never brought out the magic fish-bone. As often as she noticed this, she ran up-stairs, whispered the secret to the Duchess over again, and said to the Duchess besides, "They think we children never have a reason or a meaning!" And the Duchess, though the most fashionable Duchess that ever was heard of, winked her eye.

"Alicia," said the King, one evening when she wished him Good Night.

"Yes, Papa."

"What is become of the magic fish-bone?"

"In my pocket, Papa."

"I thought you had lost it?"

"O, no, Papa."

"Or forgotten it?"

"No, indeed, Papa."

And so another time the dreadful little snapping pug-dog next door made a rush at one of the young Princes as he stood on the steps coming home from school, and terrified him out of his wits and he put his hand through a pane of glass, and bled bled bled. When the seventeen other young Princes and Princesses saw him bleed bleed bleed, they were terrified out of their wits too, and screamed themselves black in their seventeen faces all at once. But the Princess Alicia put her hands over all their seventeen mouths, one after another, and persuaded them to be quiet because of the sick Queen. And then she put the wounded Prince's hand in a basin of fresh cold water, while they stared with their twice seventeen are thirty-four put down four and carry three eyes, and then she looked in the hand for bits of glass, and there were fortunately no bits of glass there. And then she said to two chubby-legged Princes who were sturdy though small, "Bring me in the Royal rag-bag; I must snip and stitch and cut and contrive." So those two young Princes tugged at the Royal rag-bag and lugged it in, and the Princess Alicia sat down on the floor with a large pair of scissors and a needle and thread, and snipped and stitched and cut and contrived, and made a bandage and put it on, and it fitted beautifully, and so when it was all done she saw the King her Papa looking on by the door.

"Alicia."

"Yes, Papa."

"What have you been doing?"

"Snipping stitching cutting and contriving, Papa."

"Where is the magic fish-bone?"

"In my pocket, Papa."

"I thought you had lost it?"

"O, no, Papa."

"Or forgotten it?"

"No, indeed, Papa."

After that, she ran up-stairs to the Duchess and told her what had passed, and told her the secret over again, and the Duchess shook her flaxen curls and laughed with her rosy lips.

Well! and so another time the baby fell under the grate. The seventeen young Princes and Princesses were used to it, for they were almost always falling under the grate or down the stairs, but the baby was not used to it yet, and it gave him a swelled face and a black eye. The way the poor little darling came to tumble was, that he slid out of the Princess Alicia's lap just as she was sitting in a great coarse apron that quite smothered her, in front of the kitchen-fire, beginning to peel the turnips for the broth for dinner; and the way she came to be doing that was, that the King's cook had run away that morning with her own true love who was a very tall but very tipsy soldier. Then, the seventeen young Princes and Princesses, who cried at everything that happened, cried and roared. But the Princess Alicia (who couldn't help crying a little herself) quietly called to them to be still, on account of not throwing back the Queen up-stairs, who was fast getting well, and said, "Hold your tongues, you wicked little monkeys, every one of you, while I examine baby!" Then she examined baby, and found that he hadn't broken anything, and she held cold iron to his poor dear eye, and smoothed his poor dear face, and he presently fell asleep in her arms. Then, she said to the seventeen Princes and Princesses, "I am afraid to lay him down yet, lest he should wake and feel pain, be good, and you shall all be cooks." They jumped for joy when they heard that, and began making themselves cooks' caps out of old newspapers. So to one she gave the salt-box, and to one she gave the barley, and to one she gave the herbs, and to one she gave the turnips, and to one she gave the carrots, and to one she gave the onions, and to one she gave the spice-box, till they were all cooks, and all running about at work, she sitting in the middle smothered in the great coarse apron, nursing baby. By and by the broth was done, and the baby woke up smiling like an angel, and was trusted to the sedatest Princess to hold, while the other Princes and Princesses were squeezed into a far-off corner to look at the Princess Alicia turning out the saucepan-full of broth, for fear (as they were always getting into trouble) they should get splashed and scalded. When the broth came tumbling out, steaming beautifully, and smelling like a nosegay good to eat, they clapped their hands. That made the baby clap his hands; and that, and his looking as if he had a comic toothache, made all the Princes and Princesses laugh. So the Princess Alicia said, "Laugh and be good, and after dinner we will make him a nest on the floor in a corner, and he shall sit in his nest and see a dance of eighteen cooks." That delighted the young Princes and Princesses, and they ate up all the broth, and washed up all the plates and dishes, and cleared away, and pushed the table into a corner, and then they in their cooks' caps, and the Princess Alicia in the smothering coarse apron that belonged to the cook that had run away with her own true love that was the very tall but very tipsy soldier, danced a dance of eighteen cooks before the angelic baby, who forgot his swelled face and his black eye, and crowed with joy.

And so then, once more the Princess Alicia saw King Watkins the First, her father, standing in the doorway looking on, and he said: "What have you been doing, Alicia?"

"Cooking and contriving, Papa."

"What else have you been doing, Alicia?"

"Keeping the children light-hearted, Papa."

"Where is the magic fish-bone, Alicia?"

"In my pocket, Papa."

"I thought you had lost it?"

"O, no, Papa."

"Or forgotten it?"

"No, indeed, Papa."

The King then sighed so heavily, and seemed so low-spirited, and sat down so miserably, leaning his head upon his hand, and his elbow upon the kitchen table pushed away in the corner, that the seventeen Princes and Princesses crept softly out of the kitchen, and left him alone with the Princess Alicia and the angelic baby.

"What is the matter, Papa?"

"I am dreadfully poor, my child."

"Have you no money at all, Papa?"

[Illustration: "What is the matter, Papa?"]

"None my child."

"Is there no way left of getting any, Papa?"

"No way," said the King. "I have tried very hard, and I have tried all ways."

When she heard those last words, the Princess Alicia began to put her hand into the pocket where she kept the magic fish-bone.

"Papa," said she, "when we have tried very hard, and tried all ways, we must have done our very very best?"

"No doubt, Alicia."

"When we have done our very very best, Papa, and that is not enough, then I think the right time must have come for asking help of others." This was the very secret connected with the magic fish-bone, which she had found out for herself from the good fairy Grandmarina's words, and which she had so often whispered to her beautiful and fashionable friend the Duchess.

So she took out of her pocket the magic fish-bone that had been dried and rubbed and polished till it shone like mother-of-pearl; and she gave it one little kiss and wished it was quarter day. And immediately it was quarter day; and the King's quarter's salary came rattling down the chimney, and bounced into the middle of the floor.

But this was not half of what happened, no not a quarter, for immediately afterwards the good fairy Grandmarina came riding in, in a carriage and four (Peacocks), with Mr Pickles's boy up behind, dressed in silver and gold, with a cocked hat, powdered hair, pink silk stockings, a jewelled cane, and a nosegay. Down jumped Mr Pickles's boy with his cocked hat in his hand and wonderfully polite (being entirely changed by enchantment), and handed Grandmarina out, and there she stood in her rich shot silk smelling of dried lavender, fanning herself with a sparkling fan.

"Alicia, my dear," said this charming old Fairy, "how do you do, I hope I see you pretty well, give me a kiss."

The Princess Alicia embraced her, and then Grandmarina turned to the King, and said rather sharply:--"Are you good?"

[Illustration: "Alicia, my dear ... how do you do?"]

The King said he hoped so.

"I suppose you know the reason, now, why my god-Daughter here," kissing the Princess again, "did not apply to the fish-bone sooner?" said the Fairy.

The King made her a shy bow.

"Ah! but you didn't then!" said the Fairy.

The King made her a shyer bow.

"Any more reasons to ask for?" said the Fairy.

The King said no, and he was very sorry.

"Be good then," said the Fairy, "and live happy ever afterwards."

Then, Grandmarina waved her fan, and the Queen came in most splendidly dressed, and the seventeen young Princes and Princesses, no longer grown out of their clothes, came in newly fitted out from top to toe, with tucks in everything to admit of its being let out. After that, the Fairy tapped the Princess Alicia with her fan, and the smothering coarse apron flew away, and she appeared exquisitely dressed, like a little Bride, with a wreath of orange-flowers and a silver veil. After that, the kitchen dresser changed of itself into a wardrobe, made of beautiful woods and gold and looking glass, which was full of dresses of all sorts, all for her and all exactly fitting her. After that, the angelic baby came in, running alone, with his face and eye not a bit the worse but much the better. Then, Grandmarina begged to be introduced to the Duchess, and, when the Duchess was brought down many compliments passed between them.

A little whispering took place between the Fairy and the Duchess, and then the Fairy said out loud, "Yes. I thought she would have told you." Grandmarina then turned to the King and Queen, and said, "We are going in search of Prince Certainpersonio. The pleasure of your company is requested at church in half an hour precisely." So she and the Princess Alicia got into the carriage, and Mr Pickles's boy handed in the Duchess who sat by herself on the opposite seat, and then Mr Pickles's boy put up the steps and got up behind, and the Peacocks flew away with their tails spread.

Prince Certainpersonio was sitting by himself, eating barley-sugar and waiting to be ninety. When he saw the Peacocks followed by the carriage, coming in at the window, it immediately occurred to him that something uncommon was going to happen.

"Prince," said Grandmarina, "I bring you your Bride."

The moment the Fairy said those words, Prince Certainpersonio's face left off being stickey, and his jacket and corduroys changed to peach-bloom velvet, and his hair curled, and a cap and feather flew in like a bird and settled on his head. He got into the carriage by the Fairy's invitation, and there he renewed his acquaintance with the Duchess, whom he had seen before.

In the church were the Prince's relations and friends, and the Princess

Alicia's relations and friends, and the seventeen Princes and Princesses, and the baby, and a crowd of the neighbours. The marriage was beautiful beyond expression. The Duchess was bridesmaid, and beheld the ceremony from the pulpit where she was supported by the cushion of the desk.

Grandmarina gave a magnificent wedding feast afterwards, in which there was everything and more to eat, and everything and more to drink. The wedding cake was delicately ornamented with white satin ribbons, frosted silver and white lilies, and was forty-two yards round.

When Grandmarina had drunk her love to the young couple, and Prince Certainpersonio had made a speech, and everybody had cried Hip hip hip hurrah! Grandmarina announced to the King and Queen that in future there would be eight quarter days in every year, except in leap year, when there would be ten. She then turned to Certainpersonio and Alicia, and said, "My dears, you will have thirty-five children, and they will all be good and beautiful. Seventeen of your children will be boys, and eighteen will be girls. The hair of the whole of your children will curl naturally. They will never have the measles, and will have recovered from the whooping-cough before being born."

On hearing such good news, everybody cried out "Hip hip hip hurrah!" again.

"It only remains," said Grandmarina in conclusion, "to make an end of the fish-bone."

So she took it from the hand of the Princess Alicia, and it instantly flew down the throat of the dreadful little snapping pug-dog next door and choked him, and he expired in convulsions.

THE END

The Wreck of the Golden Mary

by Charles Dickens

THE WRECK

I was apprenticed to the Sea when I was twelve years old, and I have encountered a great deal of rough weather, both literal and metaphorical. It has always been my opinion since I first possessed such a thing as an opinion, that the man who knows only one subject is next tiresome to the man who knows no subject. Therefore, in the course of my life I have taught myself whatever I could, and although I am not an educated man, I am able, I am thankful to say, to have an intelligent interest in most things.

A person might suppose, from reading the above, that I am in the habit of holding forth about number one. That is not the case. Just as if I was to come into a room among strangers, and must either be introduced or introduce myself, so I have taken the liberty of passing these few remarks, simply and plainly that it may be known who and what I am. I will add no more of the sort than that my name is William George Ravender, that I was born at Penrith half a year after my own father was drowned, and that I am on the second day of this present blessed Christmas week of one thousand eight hundred and fifty-six, fifty-six years of age.

When the rumour first went flying up and down that there was gold in California--which, as most people know, was before it was discovered in the British colony of Australia--I was in the West Indies, trading among the Islands. Being in command and likewise part-owner of a smart schooner, I had my work cut out for me, and I was doing it. Consequently, gold in California was no business of mine.

But, by the time when I came home to England again, the thing was as clear as your hand held up before you at noon-day. There was Californian gold in the museums and in the goldsmiths' shops, and the very first time I went upon 'Change, I met a friend of mine (a seafaring man like myself), with a Californian nugget hanging to his watch-chain. I handled it. It was as like a peeled walnut with bits unevenly broken off here and there, and then electrotyped all over, as ever I saw anything in my life.

I am a single man (she was too good for this world and for me, and she died six weeks before our marriage-day), so when I am ashore, I live in my house at Poplar. My house at Poplar is taken care of and kept ship-shape by an old lady who was my mother's maid before I was born. She is as handsome and as upright as any old lady in the world. She is as fond of me as if she had ever had an only son, and I was he. Well do I know wherever I sail that she never lays down her head at night without having said, "Merciful Lord! bless and preserve William George Ravender, and send him safe home, through Christ our Saviour!" I have thought of it in many a dangerous moment, when it has done me no harm, I am sure.

In my house at Poplar, along with this old lady, I lived quiet for best part of a year: having had a long spell of it among the Islands, and having (which was very uncommon in me) taken the fever rather badly. At last, being strong and hearty, and having read every book I could lay hold of, right out, I was walking down Leadenhall Street in the City of London, thinking of turning-to again, when I met what I call Smithick and Watersby of Liverpool. I chanced to lift up my eyes from looking in at a ship's chronometer in a window, and I saw him bearing down upon me, head on.

It is, personally, neither Smithick, nor Watersby, that I here mention, nor was I ever acquainted with any man of either of those names, nor do I think that there has been any one of either of those names in that Liverpool House for years back. But, it is in reality the House itself that I refer to; and a wiser merchant or a truer gentleman never stepped.

"My dear Captain Ravender," says he. "Of all the men on earth, I wanted to see you most. I was on my way to you."

"Well!" says I. "That looks as if you WERE to see me, don't it?" With that I put my arm in his, and we walked on towards the Royal Exchange, and when we got there, walked up and down at the back of it where the Clock-Tower is. We walked an hour and more, for he had much to say to me. He had a scheme for chartering a new ship of their own to take out cargo to the diggers and emigrants in California, and to buy and bring back gold. Into the particulars of that scheme I will not enter, and I have no right to enter. All I say of it is, that it was a very original one, a very fine one, a very sound one, and a very lucrative one beyond doubt.

He imparted it to me as freely as if I had been a part of himself. After doing so, he made me the handsomest sharing offer that ever was made to me, boy or man--or I believe to any other captain in the Merchant Navy--and he took this round turn to finish with:

"Ravender, you are well aware that the lawlessness of that coast and country at present, is as special as the circumstances in which it is placed. Crews of vessels outward-bound, desert as soon as they make the land; crews of vessels homeward-bound, ship at enormous wages, with the express intention of murdering the captain and seizing the gold freight; no man can trust another, and the devil seems let loose. Now," says he, "you know my opinion of you, and you know I am only expressing it, and with no singularity, when I tell you that you are almost the only man on whose integrity, discretion, and energy--" &c., &c. For, I don't want to repeat what he said, though I was and am sensible of it.

Notwithstanding my being, as I have mentioned, quite ready for a voyage, still I had some doubts of this voyage. Of course I knew, without being told, that there were peculiar difficulties and dangers in it, a long way over and above those which attend all voyages. It must not be supposed that I was afraid to face them; but, in my opinion a man has no manly motive or sustainment in his own breast for facing dangers, unless he has well considered what they are, and is able quietly to say to himself, "None of these perils can now take me by surprise; I shall know what to do for the best in any of them; all the rest lies in the higher and greater hands to which I humbly commit myself." On this principle I have so attentively considered (regarding it as my duty) all the hazards I have ever been able to think of, in the ordinary way of storm, shipwreck, and fire at sea, that I hope I should be prepared to do, in any of those cases, whatever could be done, to save the lives intrusted to my charge.

As I was thoughtful, my good friend proposed that he should leave me to walk there as long as I liked, and that I should dine with him by-and-by at his club in Pall Mall. I accepted the invitation and I walked up and down there, quarter-deck fashion, a matter of a couple of hours; now and then looking up at the weathercock as I might have looked up aloft; and now and then taking a look into Cornhill, as I might have taken a look over the side.

All dinner-time, and all after dinner-time, we talked it over again. I gave him my views of his plan, and he very much approved of the same. I told him I had nearly decided, but not quite. "Well, well," says he, "come down to Liverpool to-morrow with me, and see the Golden Mary." I liked the name (her name was Mary, and she was golden, if golden stands for good), so I began to feel that it was almost done when I said I would go to Liverpool. On the next morning but one we were on board the Golden Mary. I might have known, from his asking me to come down and see her, what she was. I declare her to have been the completest and most exquisite Beauty that ever I set my eyes upon.

We had inspected every timber in her, and had come back to the gangway to go ashore from the dock-basin, when I put out my hand to my friend. "Touch upon it," says I, "and touch heartily. I take command of this ship, and I am hers and yours, if I can get John Steadiman for my chief mate."

John Steadiman had sailed with me four voyages. The first voyage John was third mate out to China, and came home second. The other three voyages he was my first officer. At this time of chartering the Golden Mary, he was aged thirty-two. A brisk, bright, blue-eyed fellow, a very neat figure and rather under the middle size, never out of the way and never in it, a face that pleased everybody and that all children took to, a habit of going about singing as cheerily as a blackbird, and a perfect sailor.

We were in one of those Liverpool hackney-coaches in less than a minute, and we cruised about in her upwards of three hours, looking for John. John had come home from Van Diemen's Land barely a month before, and I had heard of him as taking a frisk in Liverpool. We asked after him, among many other places, at the two boarding-houses he was fondest of, and we found he had had a week's spell at each of them; but, he had gone here and gone there, and had set off "to lay out on the main-to'-gallant-yard of the highest Welsh mountain" (so he had told the people of the house), and where he might be then, or when he might come back, nobody could tell us. But it was surprising, to be sure, to see how every face brightened the moment there was mention made of the name of Mr. Steadiman.

We were taken aback at meeting with no better luck, and we had wore ship and put her head for my friends, when as we were jogging through the streets, I clap my eyes on John himself coming out of a toyshop! He was carrying a little boy, and conducting two uncommon pretty women to their coach, and he told me afterwards that he had never in his life seen one of the three before, but that he was so taken with them on looking in at the toyshop while they were buying the child a cranky Noah's Ark, very much down by the head, that he had gone in and asked the ladies' permission to treat him to a tolerably correct Cutter there was in the window, in order that such a handsome boy might not grow up with a lubberly idea of naval architecture.

We stood off and on until the ladies' coachman began to give way, and then we hailed John. On his coming aboard of us, I told him, very gravely, what I had said to my friend. It struck him, as he said himself, amidships. He was quite shaken by it. "Captain Ravender," were John Steadiman's words, "such an opinion from you is true commendation, and I'll sail round the world with you for twenty years if you hoist the signal, and stand by you for ever!" And now indeed I felt that it was done, and that the Golden Mary was afloat.

Grass never grew yet under the feet of Smithick and Watersby. The riggers were out of that ship in a fortnight's time, and we had begun taking in cargo. John was always aboard, seeing everything stowed with his own eyes; and whenever I went aboard myself early or late, whether he was below in the hold, or on deck at the hatchway, or overhauling his cabin, nailing up pictures in it of the Blush Roses of England, the Blue Belles of Scotland, and the female Shamrock of Ireland: of a certainty I heard John singing like a blackbird.

We had room for twenty passengers. Our sailing advertisement was no sooner out, than we might have taken these twenty times over. In entering our men, I and John (both together) picked them, and we entered none but good hands--as good as were to be found in that port. And so, in a good ship of the best build, well owned, well arranged, well officered, well manned, well found in all respects, we parted with our pilot at a quarter past four o'clock in the afternoon of the seventh of March, one thousand eight hundred and fifty-one, and stood with a fair wind out to sea.

It may be easily believed that up to that time I had had no leisure to be intimate with my passengers. The most of them were then in their berths sea-sick; however, in going among them, telling them what was good for them, persuading them not to be there, but to come up on deck and feel the breeze, and in rousing them with a joke, or a comfortable word, I made acquaintance with them, perhaps, in a more friendly and confidential way from the first, than I might have done at the cabin table.

Of my passengers, I need only particularise, just at present, a bright-eyed blooming young wife who was going out to join her husband in California, taking with her their only child, a little girl of three years old, whom he had never seen; a sedate young woman in black, some five years older (about thirty as I should say), who was going out to join a brother; and an old gentleman, a good deal like a hawk if his eyes had been better and not so red, who was always talking, morning, noon, and night, about the gold discovery. But, whether he was making the voyage, thinking his old arms could dig for gold, or whether his speculation was to buy it, or to barter for it, or to cheat for it, or to snatch it anyhow from other people, was his secret. He kept his secret.

These three and the child were the soonest well. The child was a most engaging child, to be sure, and very fond of me: though I am bound to admit that John Steadiman and I were borne on her pretty little books in reverse order, and that he was captain there, and I was mate. It was beautiful to watch her with John, and it was beautiful to watch John with her. Few would have thought it possible, to see John playing at bo-peep round the mast, that he was the man who had caught up an iron bar and struck a Malay and a Maltese dead, as they were gliding with their knives down the cabin stair aboard the barque Old England, when the captain lay ill in his cot, off Saugar Point. But he was; and give him his back against a bulwark, he would have done the same by half a dozen of them. The name of the young mother was Mrs. Atherfield, the name of the young lady in black was Miss Coleshaw, and the name of the old gentleman was Mr. Rarx.

As the child had a quantity of shining fair hair, clustering in curls all about her face, and as her name was Lucy, Steadiman gave her the name of the Golden Lucy. So, we had the Golden Lucy and the Golden Mary; and John kept up the idea to that extent as he and the child went playing about the decks, that I believe she used to think the ship was alive somehow--a sister or companion, going to the same place as herself. She liked to be by the wheel, and in fine weather, I have often stood by the man whose trick it was at the wheel, only to hear her, sitting near my feet, talking to the ship. Never had a child such a doll before, I suppose; but she made a doll of the Golden Mary, and used to dress her up by tying ribbons and little bits of finery to the belaying-pins; and nobody ever moved them, unless it was to save them from being blown away.

Of course I took charge of the two young women, and I called them "my dear," and they never minded, knowing that whatever I said was said in a fatherly and protecting spirit. I gave them their places on each side of me at dinner, Mrs. Atherfield on my right and Miss Coleshaw on my left; and I directed the unmarried lady to serve out the breakfast, and the married lady to serve out the tea. Likewise I said to my black steward in their presence, "Tom Snow, these two ladies are equally the mistresses of this house, and do you obey their orders equally;" at which Tom laughed, and they all laughed.

Old Mr. Rarx was not a pleasant man to look at, nor yet to talk to, or to be with, for no one could help seeing that he was a sordid and selfish character, and that he had warped further and further out of the straight with time. Not but what he was on his best behaviour with us, as everybody was; for we had no bickering among us, for'ard or aft. I only mean to say, he was not the man one would have chosen for a messmate. If choice there had been, one might even have gone a few points out of one's course, to say, "No! Not him!" But, there was one curious inconsistency in Mr. Rarx. That was, that he took an astonishing interest in the child. He looked, and I may add, he was, one of the last of men to care at all for a child, or to care much for any human creature. Still, he went so far as to be habitually uneasy, if the child was long on deck, out of his sight. He was always afraid of her falling overboard, or falling down a hatchway, or of a block or what not coming down upon her from the rigging in the working of the ship, or of her getting some hurt or other. He used to look at her and touch her, as if she was something precious to him. He was always solicitous about her not injuring her health, and constantly entreated her mother to be careful of it. This was so much the more curious, because the child did not like him, but used to shrink away from him, and would not even put out her hand to him without coaxing from others. I believe that every soul on board frequently noticed this, and not one of us understood it. However, it was such a plain fact, that John Steadiman said more than once when old Mr. Rarx was not within earshot, that if the Golden Mary felt a tenderness for the dear old gentleman she carried in her lap, she must be bitterly jealous of the Golden Lucy.

Before I go any further with this narrative, I will state that our ship was a barque of three hundred tons, carrying a crew of eighteen men, a second mate in addition to John, a carpenter, an armourer or smith, and two apprentices (one a Scotch boy, poor little fellow). We had three boats; the Long-boat, capable of carrying twenty-five men; the Cutter, capable of carrying fifteen; and the Surf-boat, capable of carrying ten. I put down the capacity of these boats according to the numbers they were really meant to hold.

We had tastes of bad weather and head-winds, of course; but, on the whole we had as fine a run as any reasonable man could expect, for sixty days. I then began to enter two remarks in the ship's Log and in my Journal; first, that there was an unusual and amazing quantity of ice; second, that the nights were most wonderfully dark, in spite of the ice.

For five days and a half, it seemed quite useless and hopeless to alter the ship's course so as to stand out of the way of this ice. I made what southing I could; but, all that time, we were beset by it. Mrs. Atherfield after standing by me on deck once, looking for some time in an awed manner at the great bergs that surrounded us, said in a whisper, "O! Captain Ravender, it looks as if the whole solid earth had changed into ice, and broken up!" I said to her, laughing, "I don't wonder that it does, to your inexperienced eyes, my dear." But I had never seen a twentieth part of the quantity, and, in reality, I was pretty much of her opinion.

However, at two p.m. on the afternoon of the sixth day, that is to say, when we were sixty-six days out, John Steadiman who had gone aloft, sang out from the top, that the sea was clear ahead. Before four p.m. a strong breeze springing up right astern, we were in open water at sunset. The breeze then freshening into half a gale of wind, and the Golden Mary being a very fast sailer, we went before the wind merrily, all night.

I had thought it impossible that it could be darker than it had been, until the sun, moon, and stars should fall out of the Heavens, and Time should be destroyed; but, it had been next to light, in comparison with what it was now. The darkness was so profound, that looking into it was painful and oppressive--like looking, without a ray of light, into a dense black bandage put as close before the eyes as it could be, without touching them. I doubled the look-out, and John and I stood in the bow side-by-side, never leaving it all night. Yet I should no more have known that he was near me when he was silent, without putting out my arm and touching him, than I should if he had turned in and been fast asleep below. We were not so much looking out, all of us, as listening to the utmost, both with our eyes and ears.

Next day, I found that the mercury in the barometer, which had risen steadily since we cleared the ice, remained steady. I had had very good observations, with now and then the interruption of a day or so, since our departure. I got the sun at noon, and found that we were in Lat. 58 degrees S., Long. 60 degrees W., off New South Shetland; in the neighbourhood of Cape Horn. We were sixty-seven days out, that day. The ship's reckoning was accurately worked and made up. The ship did her duty admirably, all on board were well, and all hands were as smart, efficient, and contented, as it was possible to be.

When the night came on again as dark as before, it was the eighth night I had been on deck. Nor had I taken more than a very little sleep in the day-time, my station being always near the helm, and often at it, while we were among the ice. Few but those who have tried it can imagine the difficulty and pain of only keeping the eyes open--physically open--under such circumstances, in such darkness. They get struck by the darkness, and blinded by the darkness. They make patterns in it, and they flash in it, as if they had gone out of your head to look at you. On the turn of midnight, John Steadiman, who was alert and fresh (for I had always made him turn in by day), said to me, "Captain Ravender, I entreat of you to go below. I am sure you can hardly stand, and your voice is getting weak, sir. Go below, and take a little rest. I'll call you if a block chafes." I said to John in answer, "Well, well, John! Let us wait till the turn of one o'clock, before we talk about that." I had just had one of the ship's lanterns held up, that I might see how the night went by my watch, and it was then twenty minutes after twelve.

At five minutes before one, John sang out to the boy to bring the lantern again, and when I told him once more what the time was, entreated and prayed of me to go below. "Captain Ravender," says he, "all's well; we can't afford to have you laid up for a single hour; and I respectfully and earnestly beg of you to go below." The end of it was, that I agreed to do so, on the understanding that if I failed to come up of my own accord within three hours, I was to be punctually called. Having settled that, I left John in charge. But I called him to me once afterwards, to ask him a question. I had been to look at the barometer, and had seen the mercury still perfectly steady, and had come up the companion again to take a last look about me--if I can use such a word in reference to such darkness--when I thought that the waves, as the Golden Mary parted them and shook them off, had a hollow sound in them; something that I fancied was a rather unusual reverberation. I was standing by the quarter-deck rail on the starboard side, when I called John aft to me, and bade him listen. He did so with the greatest attention. Turning to me he then said, "Rely upon it, Captain Ravender, you have been without rest too long, and the novelty is only in the state of your sense of hearing." I thought so too by that time, and I think so now, though I can never know for absolute certain in this world, whether it was or not.

When I left John Steadiman in charge, the ship was still going at a great rate through the water. The wind still blew right astern. Though she was making great way, she was under shortened sail, and had no more than she could easily carry. All was snug, and nothing complained. There was a pretty sea running, but not a very high sea neither, nor at all a confused one.

I turned in, as we seamen say, all standing. The meaning of that is, I did not pull my clothes off--no, not even so much as my coat: though I did my shoes, for my feet were badly swelled with the deck. There was a little swing-lamp alight in my cabin. I thought, as I looked at it before shutting my eyes, that I was so tired of darkness, and troubled by darkness, that I could have gone to sleep best in the midst of a million of flaming gas-lights. That was the last thought I had before I went off, except the prevailing thought that I should not be able to get to sleep at all.

I dreamed that I was back at Penrith again, and was trying to get round the church, which had altered its shape very much since I last saw it, and was cloven all down the middle of the steeple in a most singular manner. Why I wanted to get round the church I don't know; but I was as anxious to do it as if my life depended on it. Indeed, I believe it did in the dream. For all that, I could not get round the church. I was still trying, when I came against it with a violent shock, and was flung out of my cot against the ship's side. Shrieks and a terrific outcry struck me far harder than the bruising timbers, and amidst sounds of grinding and crashing, and a heavy rushing and breaking of water--sounds I understood too well--I made my way on deck. It was not an easy thing to do, for the ship heeled over frightfully, and was beating in a furious manner.

I could not see the men as I went forward, but I could hear that they were hauling in sail, in disorder. I had my trumpet in my hand, and, after directing and encouraging them in this till it was done, I hailed first John Steadiman, and then my second mate, Mr. William Rames. Both answered clearly and steadily. Now, I had practised them and all my crew, as I have ever made it a custom to practise all who sail with me, to take certain stations and wait my orders, in case of any unexpected crisis. When my voice was heard hailing, and their voices were heard answering, I was aware, through all the noises of the ship and sea, and all the crying of the passengers below, that there was a pause. "Are you ready, Rames?"-- "Ay, ay, sir!"--"Then light up, for God's sake!" In a moment he and another were burning blue-lights, and the ship and all on board seemed to be enclosed in a mist of light, under a great black dome.

The light shone up so high that I could see the huge Iceberg upon which we had struck, cloven at the top and down the middle, exactly like Penrith Church in my dream. At the same moment I could see the watch last relieved, crowding up and down on deck; I could see Mrs. Atherfield and Miss Coleshaw thrown about on the top of the companion as they struggled to bring the child up from below; I could see that the masts were going with the shock and the beating of the ship; I could see the frightful breach stove in on the starboard side, half the length of the vessel, and the sheathing and timbers spirting up; I could see that the Cutter was disabled, in a wreck of broken fragments; and I could see every eye turned upon me. It is my belief that if there had been ten thousand eyes there, I should have seen them all, with their different looks. And all this in a moment. But you must consider what a moment.

I saw the men, as they looked at me, fall towards their appointed stations, like good men and true. If she had not righted, they could have done very little there or anywhere but die--not that it is little for a man to die at his post--I mean they could have done nothing to save the passengers and themselves. Happily, however, the violence of the shock with which we had so determinedly borne down direct on that fatal Iceberg, as if it had been our destination instead of our destruction, had so smashed and pounded the ship that she got off in this same instant and righted. I did not want the carpenter to tell me she was filling and going down; I could see and hear that. I gave

Rames the word to lower the Long-boat and the Surf-boat, and I myself told off the men for each duty. Not one hung back, or came before the other. I now whispered to John Steadiman, "John, I stand at the gangway here, to see every soul on board safe over the side. You shall have the next post of honour, and shall be the last but one to leave the ship. Bring up the passengers, and range them behind me; and put what provision and water you can got at, in the boats. Cast your eye for'ard, John, and you'll see you have not a moment to lose."

My noble fellows got the boats over the side as orderly as I ever saw boats lowered with any sea running, and, when they were launched, two or three of the nearest men in them as they held on, rising and falling with the swell, called out, looking up at me, "Captain Ravender, if anything goes wrong with us, and you are saved, remember we stood by you!"--"We'll all stand by one another ashore, yet, please God, my lads!" says I. "Hold on bravely, and be tender with the women."

The women were an example to us. They trembled very much, but they were quiet and perfectly collected. "Kiss me, Captain Ravender," says Mrs. Atherfield, "and God in heaven bless you, you good man!" "My dear," says I, "those words are better for me than a life-boat." I held her child in my arms till she was in the boat, and then kissed the child and handed her safe down. I now said to the people in her, "You have got your freight, my lads, all but me, and I am not coming yet awhile. Pull away from the ship, and keep off!"

That was the Long-boat. Old Mr. Rarx was one of her complement, and he was the only passenger who had greatly misbehaved since the ship struck. Others had been a little wild, which was not to be wondered at, and not very blamable; but, he had made a lamentation and uproar which it was dangerous for the people to hear, as there is always contagion in weakness and selfishness. His incessant cry had been that he must not be separated from the child, that he couldn't see the child, and that he and the child must go together. He had even tried to wrest the child out of my arms, that he might keep her in his. "Mr. Rarx," said I to him when it came to that, "I have a loaded pistol in my pocket; and if you don't stand out of the gang- way, and keep perfectly quiet, I shall shoot you through the heart, if you have got one." Says he, "You won't do murder, Captain Ravender!" "No, sir," says I, "I won't murder forty-four people to humour you, but I'll shoot you to save them."

After that he was quiet, and stood shivering a little way off, until I named him to go over the side.

The Long-boat being cast off, the Surf-boat was soon filled. There only remained aboard the Golden Mary, John Mullion the man who had kept on burning the blue-lights (and who had lighted every new one at every old one before it went out, as quietly as if he had been at an illumination); John Steadiman; and myself. I hurried those two into the Surf-boat, called to them to keep off, and waited with a grateful and relieved heart for the Long-boat to come and take me in, if she could. I looked at my watch, and it showed me, by the blue-light, ten minutes past two. They lost no time. As soon as she was near enough, I swung myself into her, and called to the men, "With a will, lads! She's reeling!" We were not an inch too far out of the inner vortex of her going down, when, by the blue-light which John Mullion still burnt in the bow of the Surf-boat, we saw her lurch, and plunge to the bottom head-foremost. The child cried, weeping wildly, "O the dear Golden Mary! O look at her! Save her! Save the poor Golden Mary!" And then the light burnt out, and the black dome seemed to come down upon us.

I suppose if we had all stood a-top of a mountain, and seen the whole remainder of the world sink away from under us, we could hardly have felt more shocked and solitary than we did when we knew we were alone on the wide ocean, and that the beautiful ship in which most of us had been securely asleep within half an hour was gone for ever. There was an awful silence in our boat, and such a kind of palsy on the rowers and the man at the rudder, that I felt they were scarcely keeping her before the sea. I spoke out then, and said, "Let every one here thank the Lord for our preservation!" All the voices answered (even the child's), "We thank the Lord!" I then said the Lord's Prayer, and all hands said it after me with a solemn murmuring. Then I gave the word "Cheerily, O men, Cheerily!" and I felt that they were handling the boat again as a boat ought to be handled.

The Surf-boat now burnt another blue-light to show us where they were, and we made for her, and laid ourselves as nearly alongside of her as we dared. I had always kept my boats with a coil or two of good stout stuff in each of them, so both boats had a rope at hand. We made a shift, with much labour and trouble, to got near enough to one another to divide the blue-lights (they were no use after that night, for the sea-water soon got at them), and to get a tow-rope out between us. All night long we kept together, sometimes obliged to cast off the rope, and sometimes getting it out again, and all of us wearying for the morning--which appeared so long in coming that old Mr. Rarx screamed out, in spite of his fears of me, "The world is drawing to an end, and the sun will never rise any more!"

When the day broke, I found that we were all huddled together in a miserable manner. We were deep in the water; being, as I found on mustering, thirty-one in number, or at least six too many. In the Surf-boat they were fourteen in number, being at least four too many. The first thing I did, was to get myself passed to the rudder--which I took from that time--and to get Mrs. Atherfield, her child, and Miss Coleshaw, passed on to sit next me. As to old Mr. Rarx, I put him in the bow, as far from us as I could. And I put some of the best men near us in order that if I should drop there might be a skilful hand ready to take the helm.

The sea moderating as the sun came up, though the sky was cloudy and wild, we spoke the other boat, to know what stores they had, and to overhaul what we had. I had a compass in my pocket, a small telescope, a double-barrelled pistol, a knife, and a fire-box and matches. Most of my men had knives, and some had a little tobacco: some, a pipe as well. We had a mug among us, and an iron spoon. As to provisions, there were in my boat two bags of biscuit, one piece of raw beef, one piece of raw pork, a bag of coffee, roasted but not ground (thrown in, I imagine, by mistake, for something else), two small casks of water, and about half-a-gallon of rum in a keg. The Surf-boat, having rather more rum than we, and fewer to drink it, gave us, as I estimated, another quart into our keg. In return, we gave them three double handfuls of coffee, tied up in a piece of a handkerchief; they reported that they had aboard besides, a bag of biscuit, a piece of beef, a small cask of water, a small box of lemons, and a Dutch cheese. It took a long time to make these exchanges, and they were not made without risk to both parties; the sea running quite high enough to make our approaching near to one another very hazardous. In the bundle with the coffee, I conveyed to John Steadiman (who had a ship's compass with him), a paper written in pencil, and torn from my pocket-book, containing the course I meant to steer, in the hope of making land, or being picked up by some vessel--I say in the hope, though I had little hope of either deliverance. I then sang out to him, so as all might hear, that if we two boats could live or die together, we would; but, that if we should be parted by the weather, and join company no more, they should have our prayers and blessings, and we asked for theirs. We then gave them three cheers, which they returned, and I saw the men's heads droop in both boats as they fell to their oars again.

These arrangements had occupied the general attention advantageously for all, though (as I expressed in the last sentence) they ended in a sorrowful feeling. I now said a few words to my fellow-voyagers on the subject of the small stock of food on which our lives depended if they were preserved from the great deep, and on the rigid necessity of our eking it out in the most frugal manner. One and all replied that whatever allowance I thought best to lay down should be strictly kept to. We made a pair of scales out of a thin scrap of iron-plating and some twine, and I got together for weights such of the heaviest buttons among us as I calculated made up some fraction over two ounces. This was the allowance of solid food served out once a-day to each, from that time to the end; with the addition of a coffee-berry, or sometimes half a one, when the weather was very fair, for breakfast. We had nothing else whatever, but half a pint of water each per day, and sometimes, when we were coldest and weakest, a teaspoonful of rum each, served out as a dram. I know how learnedly it can be shown that rum is poison, but I also know that in this case, as in all similar cases I have ever read of--which are numerous--no words can express the comfort and support derived from it. Nor have I the least doubt that it saved the lives of far more than half our number. Having mentioned half a pint of water as our daily allowance, I ought to observe that sometimes we had less, and sometimes we had more; for much rain fell, and we caught it in a canvas stretched for the purpose.

Thus, at that tempestuous time of the year, and in that tempestuous part of the world, we shipwrecked people rose and fell with the waves. It is not my intention to relate (if I can avoid it) such circumstances appertaining to our doleful condition as have been better told in many other narratives of the kind than I can be expected to tell them. I will only note, in so many passing words, that day after day and night after night, we received the sea upon our backs to prevent it from swamping the boat; that one party was always kept baling, and that every hat and cap among us soon got worn out, though patched up fifty times, as the only vessels we had for that service; that another party lay down in the bottom of the boat, while a third rowed; and that we were soon all in boils and blisters and rags.

The other boat was a source of such anxious interest to all of us that I used to wonder whether, if we were saved, the time could ever come when the survivors in this boat of ours could be at all indifferent to the fortunes of the survivors in that. We got out a tow-rope whenever the weather permitted, but that did not often happen, and how we two parties kept within the same horizon, as we did, He, who mercifully permitted it to be so for our consolation, only knows. I never shall forget the looks with which, when the morning light came, we used to gaze about us over the stormy waters, for the other boat. We once parted company for seventy-two hours, and we believed them to have gone down, as they did us. The joy on both sides when we came within view of one another again, had something in a manner Divine in it; each was so forgetful of individual suffering, in tears of delight and sympathy for the people in the other boat.

I have been wanting to get round to the individual or personal part of my subject, as I call it, and the foregoing incident puts me in the right way. The patience and good disposition aboard of us, was wonderful. I was not surprised by it in the women; for all men born of women know what great qualities they will show when men will fail; but, I own I was a little surprised by it in some of the men. Among one-and-thirty people assembled at the best of times, there will usually, I should say, be two or three uncertain tempers. I knew that I had more than one rough temper with me among my own people, for I had chosen those for the Long-boat that I might have them under my eye. But, they softened under their misery, and were as considerate of the ladies, and as compassionate of the child, as the best among us, or among men--they could not have been more so. I heard scarcely any complaining. The party lying down would moan a good deal in their sleep, and I would often notice a man--not always the same man, it is to be understood, but nearly all of them at one time or other--sitting moaning at his oar, or in his place, as he looked mistily over the sea. When it happened to be long before I could catch his eye, he would go on moaning all the time in the dismallest manner; but, when our looks met, he would brighten and leave off. I almost always got the impression that he did not know what sound he had been making, but that he thought he had been humming a tune.

Our sufferings from cold and wet were far greater than our sufferings from hunger. We managed to keep the child warm; but, I doubt if any one else among us ever was warm for five minutes together; and the shivering, and the chattering of teeth, were sad to hear. The child cried a little at first for her lost playfellow, the Golden Mary; but hardly ever whimpered afterwards; and when the state of the weather made it possible, she used now and then to be held up in the arms of some of us, to look over the sea for John Steadiman's boat. I see the golden hair and the innocent face now, between me and the driving clouds, like an angel going to fly away.

It had happened on the second day, towards night, that Mrs. Atherfield, in getting Little Lucy to sleep, sang her a song. She had a soft, melodious voice, and, when she had finished it, our people up and begged for another. She sang them another, and after it had fallen dark ended with the Evening Hymn. From that time, whenever anything could be heard above the sea and wind, and while she had any voice left, nothing would serve the people but that she should sing at sunset. She always did, and always ended with the Evening Hymn. We mostly took up the last line, and shed tears when it was done, but not miserably. We had a prayer night and morning, also, when the weather allowed of it.

Twelve nights and eleven days we had been driving in the boat, when old Mr. Rarx began to be delirious, and to cry out to me to throw the gold overboard or it would sink us, and we should all be lost. For days past the child had been declining, and that was the great cause of his wildness. He had been over and over again shrieking out to me to give her all the remaining meat, to give her all the remaining rum, to save her at any cost, or we should all be ruined. At this time, she lay in her mother's arms at my feet. One of her little hands was almost always creeping about her mother's neck or chin. I had watched the wasting of the little hand, and I knew it was nearly over.

The old man's cries were so discordant with the mother's love and submission, that I called out to him in an angry voice, unless he held his peace on the instant, I would order him to be knocked on the head and thrown overboard. He was mute then, until the child died, very peacefully, an hour afterwards: which was known to all in the boat by the mother's breaking out into lamentations for the first time since the wreck--for, she had great fortitude and constancy, though she was a little gentle woman. Old Mr. Rarx then became quite ungovernable, tearing what rags he had on him, raging in imprecations, and calling to me that if I had thrown the gold overboard (always the gold with him!) I might have saved the child. "And now," says he, in a terrible voice, "we shall founder, and all go to the Devil, for our sins will sink us, when we have no innocent child to bear us up!" We so discovered with amazement, that this old wretch had only cared for the life of the pretty little creature dear to all of us, because of the influence he superstitiously hoped she might have in preserving him! Altogether it was too much for the smith or armourer, who was sitting next the old man, to bear. He took him by the throat and rolled him under the thwarts, where he lay still enough for hours afterwards.

All that thirteenth night, Miss Coleshaw, lying across my knees as I kept the helm, comforted and supported the poor mother. Her child, covered with a pea-jacket of mine, lay in her lap. It troubled me all night to think that there was no Prayer-Book among us, and that I could remember but very few of the exact words of the burial service. When I stood up at broad day, all knew what was going to be done, and I noticed that my poor fellows made the motion of uncovering their heads, though their heads had been stark bare to the sky and sea for many a weary hour. There was a long heavy swell on, but otherwise it was a fair morning, and there were broad fields of sunlight on the waves in the east. I said no more than this: "I am the Resurrection and the Life, saith the Lord. He raised the daughter of Jairus the ruler, and said she was not dead but slept. He raised the widow's son. He arose Himself, and was seen of many. He loved little children, saying, Suffer them to come unto Me and rebuke them not, for of such is the kingdom of heaven. In His name, my friends, and committed to His merciful goodness!" With those words I laid my rough face softly on the placid little forehead, and buried the Golden Lucy in the grave of the Golden Mary.

Having had it on my mind to relate the end of this dear little child, I have omitted something from its exact place, which I will supply here. It will come quite as well here as anywhere else.

Foreseeing that if the boat lived through the stormy weather, the time must come, and soon come, when we should have absolutely no morsel to eat, I had one momentous point often in my thoughts. Although I had, years before that, fully satisfied myself that the instances in which human beings in the last distress have fed upon each other, are exceedingly few, and have very seldom indeed (if ever) occurred when the people in distress, however dreadful their extremity, have been accustomed to moderate forbearance and restraint; I say, though I had long before quite satisfied my mind on this topic, I felt doubtful whether there might not have been in former cases some harm and danger from keeping it out of sight and pretending not to think of it. I felt doubtful whether some minds, growing weak with fasting and exposure and having such a terrific idea to dwell upon in secret, might not magnify it until it got to have an awful attraction about it. This was not a new thought of mine, for it had grown out of my reading. However, it came over me stronger than it had ever done before--as it had reason for doing-- in the boat, and on the fourth day I decided that I would bring out into the light that unformed fear which must have been more or less darkly in every brain among us. Therefore, as a means of beguiling the time and inspiring hope, I gave them the best summary in my power of Bligh's voyage of more than three thousand miles, in an open boat, after the Mutiny of the Bounty, and of the wonderful preservation of that boat's crew. They listened throughout with great interest, and I concluded by telling them, that, in my opinion, the happiest circumstance in the whole narrative was, that Bligh, who was no delicate man either, had solemnly placed it on record therein that he was sure and certain that under no conceivable circumstances whatever would that emaciated party, who had gone through all the pains of famine, have preyed on one another. I cannot describe the visible relief which this spread through the boat, and how the tears stood in every eye. From that time I was as well convinced as Bligh himself that there was no danger, and that this phantom, at any rate, did not haunt us.

Now, it was a part of Bligh's experience that when the people in his boat were most cast down, nothing did them so much good as hearing a story told by one of their number. When I mentioned that, I saw that it struck the general attention as much as it did my own, for I had not thought of it until I came to it in my summary. This was on the day after Mrs. Atherfield first sang to us. I proposed that, whenever the weather would permit, we should have a story two hours after dinner (I always issued the allowance I have mentioned at one o'clock, and called it by that name), as well as our song at sunset. The proposal was received with a cheerful satisfaction that warmed my heart within me; and I do not say too much when I say that those two periods in the four-and-twenty hours were expected with positive pleasure, and were really enjoyed by all hands. Spectres as we soon were in our bodily wasting, our imaginations did not perish like the gross flesh upon our bones.

Music and Adventure, two of the great gifts of Providence to mankind, could charm us long after that was lost.

The wind was almost always against us after the second day; and for many days together we could not nearly hold our own. We had all varieties of bad weather. We had rain, hail, snow, wind, mist, thunder and lightning. Still the boats lived through the heavy seas, and still we perishing people rose and fell with the great waves.

Sixteen nights and fifteen days, twenty nights and nineteen days, twenty-four nights and twenty-three days. So the time went on. Disheartening as I knew that our progress, or want of progress, must be, I never deceived them as to my calculations of it. In the first place, I felt that we were all too near eternity for deceit; in the second place, I knew that if I failed, or died, the man who followed me must have a knowledge of the true state of things to begin upon. When I told them at noon, what I reckoned we had made or lost, they generally received what I said in a tranquil and resigned manner, and always gratefully towards me. It was not unusual at any time of the day for some one to burst out weeping loudly without any new cause; and, when the burst was over, to calm down a little better than before. I had seen exactly the same thing in a house of mourning.

During the whole of this time, old Mr. Rarx had had his fits of calling out to me to throw the gold (always the gold!) overboard, and of heaping violent reproaches upon me for not having saved the child; but now, the food being all gone, and I having nothing left to serve out but a bit of coffee-berry now and then, he began to be too weak to do this, and consequently fell silent. Mrs. Atherfield and Miss Coleshaw generally lay, each with an arm across one of my knees, and her head upon it. They never complained at all. Up to the time of her child's death, Mrs. Atherfield had bound up her own beautiful hair every day; and I took particular notice that this was always before she sang her song at night, when everyone looked at her. But she never did it after the loss of her darling; and it would have been now all tangled with dirt and wet, but that Miss Coleshaw was careful of it long after she was herself, and would sometimes smooth it down with her weak thin hands.

We were past mustering a story now; but one day, at about this period, I reverted to the superstition of old Mr. Rarx, concerning the Golden Lucy, and told them that nothing vanished from the eye of God, though much might pass away from the eyes of men. "We were all of us," says I, "children once; and our baby feet have strolled in green woods ashore; and our baby hands have gathered flowers in gardens, where the birds were singing. The children that we were, are not lost to the great knowledge of our Creator. Those innocent creatures will appear with us before Him, and plead for us. What we were in the best time of our generous youth will arise and go with us too. The purest part of our lives will not desert us at the pass to which all of us here present are gliding. What we were then, will be as much in existence before Him, as what we are now." They were no less comforted by this consideration, than I was myself; and Miss Coleshaw, drawing my ear nearer to her lips, said, "Captain Ravender, I was on my way to marry a disgraced and broken man, whom I dearly loved when he was honourable and good. Your words seem to have come out of my own poor heart." She pressed my hand upon it, smiling.

Twenty-seven nights and twenty-six days. We were in no want of rain-water, but we had nothing else. And yet, even now, I never turned my eyes upon a waking face but it tried to brighten before mine. O, what a thing it is, in a time of danger and in the presence of death, the shining of a face upon a face! I have heard it broached that orders should be given in great new ships by electric telegraph. I admire machinery as much is any man, and am as thankful to it as any man can be for what it does for us. But it will never be a substitute for the face of a man, with his soul in it, encouraging another man to be brave and true. Never try it for that. It will break down like a straw.

I now began to remark certain changes in myself which I did not like. They caused me much disquiet. I often saw the Golden Lucy in the air above the boat. I often saw her I have spoken of before, sitting beside me. I saw the Golden Mary go down, as she really had gone down, twenty times in a day. And yet the sea was mostly, to my thinking, not sea neither, but moving country and extraordinary mountainous regions, the like of which have never been beheld. I felt it time to leave my last words regarding John Steadiman, in case any lips should last out to repeat them to any living ears. I said that John had told me (as he had on deck) that he had sung out "Breakers ahead!" the instant they were audible, and had tried to wear ship, but she struck before it could be done. (His cry, I dare say, had made my dream.) I said that the circumstances were altogether without warning, and out of any course that could have been guarded against; that the same loss would have happened if

I had been in charge; and that John was not to blame, but from first to last had done his duty nobly, like the man he was. I tried to write it down in my pocket-book, but could make no words, though I knew what the words were that I wanted to make. When it had come to that, her hands--though she was dead so long--laid me down gently in the bottom of the boat, and she and the Golden Lucy swung me to sleep.

ALL THAT FOLLOWS, WAS WRITTEN BY JOHN STEADIMAN, CHIEF MATE,

On the twenty-sixth day after the foundering of the Golden Mary at sea, I, John Steadiman, was sitting in my place in the stern-sheets of the Surf-boat, with just sense enough left in me to steer--that is to say, with my eyes strained, wide-awake, over the bows of the boat, and my brains fast asleep and dreaming--when I was roused upon a sudden by our second mate, Mr. William Rames.

"Let me take a spell in your place," says he. "And look you out for the Long-boat astern. The last time she rose on the crest of a wave, I thought I made out a signal flying aboard her."

We shifted our places, clumsily and slowly enough, for we were both of us weak and dazed with wet, cold, and hunger. I waited some time, watching the heavy rollers astern, before the Long-boat rose a-top of one of them at the same time with us. At last, she was heaved up for a moment well in view, and there, sure enough, was the signal flying aboard of her--a strip of rag of some sort, rigged to an oar, and hoisted in her bows.

"What does it mean?" says Rames to me in a quavering, trembling sort of voice. "Do they signal a sail in sight?"

"Hush, for God's sake!" says I, clapping my hand over his mouth. "Don't let the people hear you. They'll all go mad together if we mislead them about that signal. Wait a bit, till I have another look at it."

I held on by him, for he had set me all of a tremble with his notion of a sail in sight, and watched for the Long-boat again. Up she rose on the top of another roller. I made out the signal clearly, that second time, and saw that it was rigged half-mast high.

"Rames," says I, "it's a signal of distress. Pass the word forward to keep her before the sea, and no more. We must get the Long-boat within hailing distance of us, as soon as possible."

I dropped down into my old place at the tiller without another word- -for the thought went through me like a knife that something had happened to Captain Ravender. I should consider myself unworthy to write another line of this statement, if I had not made up my mind to speak the truth, the whole truth, and nothing but the truth--and I must, therefore, confess plainly that now, for the first time, my heart sank within me. This weakness on my part was produced in some degree, as I take it, by the exhausting effects of previous anxiety and grief.

Our provisions--if I may give that name to what we had left--were reduced to the rind of one lemon and about a couple of handsfull of coffee-berries. Besides these great distresses, caused by the death, the danger, and the suffering among my crew and passengers, I had had a little distress of my own to shake me still more, in the death of the child whom I had got to be very fond of on the voyage out--so fond that I was secretly a little jealous of her being taken in the Long-boat instead of mine when the ship foundered. It used to be a great comfort to me, and I think to those with me also, after we had seen the last of the Golden Mary, to see the Golden Lucy, held up by the men in the Long-boat, when the weather allowed it, as the best and brightest sight they had to show. She looked, at the distance we saw her from, almost like a little white bird in the air. To miss her for the first time, when the weather lulled a little again, and we all looked out for our white bird and looked in vain, was a sore disappointment. To see the men's heads bowed down and the captain's hand pointing into the sea when we hailed the Long-boat, a few days after, gave me as heavy a shock and as sharp a pang of heartache to bear as ever I remember suffering in all my life. I only mention these things to show that if I did give way a little at first, under the dread that our captain was lost to us, it was not without having been a good deal shaken beforehand by more trials of one sort or another than often fall to one man's share.

I had got over the choking in my throat with the help of a drop of water, and had steadied my mind again so as to be prepared against the worst, when I heard the hail (Lord help the poor fellows, how weak it sounded!) -

"Surf-boat, ahoy!"

I looked up, and there were our companions in misfortune tossing abreast of us; not so near that we could make out the features of any of them, but near enough, with some exertion for people in our condition, to make their voices heard in the intervals when the wind was weakest.

I answered the hail, and waited a bit, and heard nothing, and then sung out the captain's name. The voice that replied did not sound like his; the words that reached us were:

"Chief-mate wanted on board!"

Every man of my crew knew what that meant as well as I did. As second officer in command, there could be but one reason for wanting me on board the Long-boat. A groan went all round us, and my men looked darkly in each other's faces, and whispered under their breaths:

"The captain is dead!"

I commanded them to be silent, and not to make too sure of bad news, at such a pass as things had now come to with us. Then, hailing the Long-boat, I signified that I was ready to go on board when the weather would let me-- stopped a bit to draw a good long breath--and then called out as loud as I could the dreadful question:

"Is the captain dead?"

The black figures of three or four men in the after-part of the Long-boat all stooped down together as my voice reached them. They were lost to view for about a minute; then appeared again--one man among them was held up on his feet by the rest, and he hailed back the blessed words (a very faint hope went a very long way with people in our desperate situation): "Not yet!"

The relief felt by me, and by all with me, when we knew that our captain, though unfitted for duty, was not lost to us, it is not in words--at least, not in such words as a man like me can command--to express. I did my best to cheer the men by telling them what a good sign it was that we were not as badly off yet as we had feared; and then communicated what instructions I had to give, to William Rames, who was to be left in command in my place when I took charge of the Long-boat. After that, there was nothing to be done, but to wait for the chance of the wind dropping at sunset, and the sea going down afterwards, so as to enable our weak crews to lay the two boats alongside of each other, without undue risk--or, to put it plainer, without saddling ourselves with the necessity for any extraordinary exertion of strength or skill. Both the one and the other had now been starved out of us for days and days together.

At sunset the wind suddenly dropped, but the sea, which had been running high for so long a time past, took hours after that before it showed any signs of getting to rest. The moon was shining, the sky was wonderfully clear, and it could not have been, according to my calculations, far off midnight, when the long, slow, regular swell of the calming ocean fairly set in, and I took the responsibility of lessening the distance between the Long-boat and ourselves.

It was, I dare say, a delusion of mine; but I thought I had never seen the moon shine so white and ghastly anywhere, either on sea or on land, as she shone that night while we were approaching our companions in misery. When there was not much more than a boat's length between us, and the white light streamed cold and clear over all our faces, both crews rested on their oars with one great shudder, and stared over the gunwale of either boat, panic-stricken at the first sight of each other.

"Any lives lost among you?" I asked, in the midst of that frightful silence.

The men in the Long-bout huddled together like sheep at the sound of my voice.

"None yet, but the child, thanks be to God!" answered one among them.

And at the sound of his voice, all my men shrank together like the men in the Long-boat. I was afraid to let the horror produced by our first meeting at close quarters after the dreadful changes that wet, cold, and famine had produced, last one moment longer than could be helped; so, without giving time for any more questions and answers, I commanded the men to lay the two boats close alongside of each other. When I rose up and committed the tiller to the hands of Rames, all my poor follows raised their white faces imploringly to mine. "Don't leave us, sir," they said, "don't leave us." "I leave you," says I, "under the command and the guidance of Mr. William Rames, as good a sailor as I am, and as trusty and kind a man as ever stepped. Do your duty by him, as you have done it by me; and remember to the last, that while there is life there is hope. God bless and help you all!" With those words I collected what strength I had left, and caught at two arms that were held out to me, and so got from the stern-sheets of one boat into the stern-sheets of the other.

"Mind where you step, sir," whispered one of the men who had helped me into the Long-boat. I looked down as he spoke. Three figures were huddled up below me, with the moonshine falling on them in ragged streaks through the gaps between the men standing or sitting above them. The first face I made out was the face of Miss Coleshaw, her eyes were wide open and fixed on me. She seemed still to keep her senses, and, by the alternate parting and closing of her lips, to be trying to speak, but I could not hear that she uttered a single word. On her shoulder rested the head of Mrs. Atherfield. The mother of our poor little Golden Lucy must, I think, have been dreaming of the child she had lost; for there was a faint smile just ruffling the white stillness of her face, when I first saw it turned upward, with peaceful closed eyes towards the heavens. From her, I looked down a little, and there, with his head on her lap, and with one of her hands resting tenderly on his cheek-- there lay the Captain, to whose help and guidance, up to this miserable time, we had never looked in vain,--there, worn out at last in our service, and for our sakes, lay the best and bravest man of all our company. I stole my hand in gently through his clothes and laid it on his heart, and felt a little feeble warmth over it, though my cold dulled touch could not detect even the faintest beating. The two men in the stern-sheets with me, noticing what I was doing--knowing I loved him like a brother--and seeing, I suppose, more distress in my face than I myself was conscious of its showing, lost command over themselves altogether, and burst into a piteous moaning, sobbing lamentation over him. One of the two drew aside a jacket from his feet, and showed me that they were bare, except where a wet, ragged strip of stocking still clung to one of them. When the ship struck the Iceberg, he had run on deck leaving his shoes in his cabin. All through the voyage in the boat his feet had been unprotected; and not a soul had discovered it until he dropped! As long as he could keep his eyes open, the very look of them had cheered the men, and comforted and upheld the women. Not one living creature in the boat, with any sense about him, but had felt the good influence of that brave man in one way or another. Not one but had heard him, over and over again, give the credit to others which was due only to himself; praising this man for patience, and thanking that man for help, when the patience and the help had really and truly, as to the best part of both, come only from him. All this, and much more, I heard pouring confusedly from the men's lips while they crouched down, sobbing and crying over their commander, and wrapping the jacket as warmly and tenderly as they could over is cold feet. It went to my heart to check them; but I knew that if this lamenting spirit spread any further, all chance of keeping alight any last sparks of hope and resolution among the boat's company would be lost for ever. Accordingly I sent them to their places, spoke a few encouraging words to the men forward, promising to serve out, when the morning came, as much as I dared, of any eatable thing left in the lockers; called to Rames, in my old boat, to keep as near us as he safely could; drew the garments and coverings of the two poor suffering women more closely about them; and, with a secret prayer to be directed for the best in bearing the awful responsibility now laid on my shoulders, took my Captain's vacant place at the helm of the Long-boat.

This, as well as I can tell it, is the full and true account of how I came to be placed in charge of the lost passengers and crew of the Golden Mary, on the morning of the twenty-seventh day after the ship struck the Iceberg, and foundered at sea.

To Be Read At Dusk

by Charles Dickens

One, two, three, four, five. There were five of them.

Five couriers, sitting on a bench outside the convent on the summit of the Great St. Bernard in Switzerland, looking at the remote heights, stained by the setting sun as if a mighty quantity of red wine had been broached upon the mountain top, and had not yet had time to sink into the snow.

This is not my simile. It was made for the occasion by the stoutest courier, who was a German. None of the others took any more notice of it than they took of me, sitting on another bench on the other side of the convent door, smoking my cigar, like them, and - also like them - looking at the reddened snow, and at the lonely shed hard by, where the bodies of belated travellers, dug out of it, slowly wither away, knowing no corruption in that cold region.

The wine upon the mountain top soaked in as we looked; the mountain became white; the sky, a very dark blue; the wind rose; and the air turned piercing cold. The five couriers buttoned their rough coats. There being no safer man to imitate in all such proceedings than a courier, I buttoned mine.

The mountain in the sunset had stopped the five couriers in a conversation. It is a sublime sight, likely to stop conversation. The mountain being now out of the sunset, they resumed. Not that I had heard any part of their previous discourse; for indeed, I had not then broken away from the American gentleman, in the travellers' parlour of the convent, who, sitting with his face to the fire, had undertaken to realise to me the whole progress of events which had led to the accumulation by the Honourable Ananias Dodger of one of the largest acquisitions of dollars ever made in our country.

'My God!' said the Swiss courier, speaking in French, which I do not hold (as some authors appear to do) to be such an all- sufficient excuse for a naughty word, that I have only to write it in that language to make it innocent; 'if you talk of ghosts - '

'But I DON'T talk of ghosts,' said the German.

'Of what then?' asked the Swiss.

'If I knew of what then,' said the German, 'I should probably know a great deal more.'

It was a good answer, I thought, and it made me curious. So, I moved my position to that corner of my bench which was nearest to them, and leaning my back against the convent wall, heard perfectly, without appearing to attend.

'Thunder and lightning!' said the German, warming, 'when a certain man is coming to see you, unexpectedly; and, without his own knowledge, sends some invisible messenger, to put the idea of him into your head all day, what do you call that? When you walk along a crowded street - at Frankfort, Milan, London, Paris - and think that a passing stranger is like your friend Heinrich, and then that another passing stranger is like your friend Heinrich, and so begin to have a strange foreknowledge that presently you'll meet your friend Heinrich - which you do, though you believed him at Trieste - what do you call THAT?'

'It's not uncommon, either,' murmured the Swiss and the other three.

'Uncommon!' said the German. 'It's as common as cherries in the Black Forest. It's as common as maccaroni at Naples. And Naples reminds me! When the old Marchesa Senzanima shrieks at a card- party on the Chiaja - as I heard and saw her, for it happened in a Bavarian family of mine, and I was overlooking the service that evening - I say, when the old Marchesa starts up at the card-table, white through her rouge, and cries, "My sister in Spain is dead! I felt her cold touch on my back!" - and when that sister IS dead at the moment - what do you call that?'

'Or when the blood of San Gennaro liquefies at the request of the clergy - as all the world knows that it does regularly once a-year, in my native city,' said the Neapolitan courier after a pause, with a comical look, 'what do you call that?'

'THAT!' cried the German. 'Well, I think I know a name for that.'

'Miracle?' said the Neapolitan, with the same sly face.

The German merely smoked and laughed; and they all smoked and laughed.

'Bah!' said the German, presently. 'I speak of things that really do happen. When I want to see the conjurer, I pay to see a professed one, and have my money's worth. Very strange things do happen without ghosts. Ghosts! Giovanni Baptista, tell your story of the English bride. There's no ghost in that, but something full as strange. Will any man tell me what?'

As there was a silence among them, I glanced around. He whom I took to be Baptista was lighting a fresh cigar. He presently went on to speak. He was a Genoese, as I judged.

'The story of the English bride?' said he. 'Basta! one ought not to call so slight a thing a story. Well, it's all one. But it's true. Observe me well, gentlemen, it's true. That which glitters is not always gold; but what I am going to tell, is true.'

He repeated this more than once.

Ten years ago, I took my credentials to an English gentleman at Long's Hotel, in Bond Street, London, who was about to travel - it might be for one year, it might be for two. He approved of them; likewise of me. He was pleased to make inquiry. The testimony that he received was favourable. He engaged me by the six months, and my entertainment was generous.

He was young, handsome, very happy. He was enamoured of a fair young English lady, with a sufficient fortune, and they were going to be married. It was the wedding-trip, in short, that we were going to take. For three months' rest in the hot weather (it was early summer then) he had hired an old place on the Riviera, at an easy distance from my city, Genoa, on the road to Nice. Did I know that place? Yes; I told him I knew it well. It was an old palace with great gardens. It was a little bare, and it was a little dark and gloomy, being close surrounded by trees; but it was spacious, ancient, grand, and on the seashore. He said it had been so described to him exactly, and he was well pleased that I knew it. For its being a little bare of furniture, all such places were. For its being a little gloomy, he had hired it principally for the gardens, and he and my mistress would pass the summer weather in their shade.

'So all goes well, Baptista?' said he.

'Indubitably, signore; very well.'

We had a travelling chariot for our journey, newly built for us, and in all respects complete. All we had was complete; we wanted for nothing. The marriage took place. They were happy. I was happy, seeing all so bright, being so well situated, going to my own city, teaching my language in the rumble to the maid, la bella Carolina, whose heart was gay with laughter: who was young and rosy.

The time flew. But I observed - listen to this, I pray! (and here the courier dropped his voice) - I observed my mistress sometimes brooding in a manner very strange; in a frightened manner; in an unhappy manner; with a cloudy, uncertain alarm upon her. I think that I began to notice this when I was walking up hills by the carriage side, and master had gone on in front. At any rate, I remember that it impressed itself upon my mind one evening in the South of France, when she called to me to call master back; and when he came back, and walked for a long way, talking encouragingly and affectionately to her, with his hand upon the open window, and hers in it. Now and then, he laughed in a merry way, as if he were bantering her out of something. By-and-by, she laughed, and then all went well again.

It was curious. I asked la bella Carolina, the pretty little one, Was mistress unwell? - No. - Out of spirits? - No. - Fearful of bad roads, or brigands? - No. And what made it more mysterious was, the pretty little one would not look at me in giving answer, but WOULD look at the view.

But, one day she told me the secret.

'If you must know,' said Carolina, 'I find, from what I have overheard, that mistress is haunted.'

'How haunted?'

'By a dream.'

'What dream?'

'By a dream of a face. For three nights before her marriage, she saw a face in a dream - always the same face, and only One.'

'A terrible face?'

'No. The face of a dark, remarkable-looking man, in black, with black hair and a grey moustache - a handsome man except for a reserved and secret air.

Not a face she ever saw, or at all like a face she ever saw. Doing nothing in the dream but looking at her fixedly, out of darkness.'

'Does the dream come back?'

'Never. The recollection of it is all her trouble.'

'And why does it trouble her?'

Carolina shook her head.

'That's master's question,' said la bella. 'She don't know. She wonders why, herself. But I heard her tell him, only last night, that if she was to find a picture of that face in our Italian house (which she is afraid she will) she did not know how she could ever bear it.'

Upon my word I was fearful after this (said the Genoese courier) of our coming to the old palazzo, lest some such ill-starred picture should happen to be there. I knew there were many there; and, as we got nearer and nearer to the place, I wished the whole gallery in the crater of Vesuvius. To mend the matter, it was a stormy dismal evening when we, at last, approached that part of the Riviera. It thundered; and the thunder of my city and its environs, rolling among the high hills, is very loud. The lizards ran in and out of the chinks in the broken stone wall of the garden, as if they were frightened; the frogs bubbled and croaked their loudest; the sea-wind moaned, and the wet trees dripped; and the lightning - body of San Lorenzo, how it lightened!

We all know what an old palace in or near Genoa is - how time and the sea air have blotted it - how the drapery painted on the outer walls has peeled off in great flakes of plaster - how the lower windows are darkened with rusty bars of iron - how the courtyard is overgrown with grass - how the outer buildings are dilapidated - how the whole pile seems devoted to ruin. Our palazzo was one of the true kind. It had been shut up close for months. Months? - years! - it had an earthy smell, like a tomb. The scent of the orange trees on the broad back terrace, and of the lemons ripening on the wall, and of some shrubs that grew around a broken fountain, had got into the house somehow, and had never been able to get out again. There was, in every room, an aged smell, grown faint with confinement. It pined in all the cupboards and drawers. In the little rooms of communication between great rooms, it was stifling. If you turned a picture - to come back to the pictures - there it still was, clinging to the wall behind the frame, like a sort of bat.

The lattice-blinds were close shut, all over the house. There were two ugly, grey old women in the house, to take care of it; one of them with a spindle, who stood winding and mumbling in the doorway, and who would as soon have let in the devil as the air. Master, mistress, la bella Carolina, and I, went all through the palazzo. I went first, though I have named myself last, opening the windows and the lattice-blinds, and shaking down on myself splashes of rain, and scraps of mortar, and now and then a dozing mosquito, or a monstrous, fat, blotchy, Genoese spider.

When I had let the evening light into a room, master, mistress, and la bella Carolina, entered. Then, we looked round at all the pictures, and I went forward again into another room. Mistress secretly had great fear of meeting with the likeness of that face - we all had; but there was no such thing. The Madonna and Bambino, San Francisco, San Sebastiano, Venus, Santa Caterina, Angels, Brigands, Friars, Temples at Sunset, Battles, White Horses, Forests, Apostles, Doges, all my old acquaintances many times repeated? - yes. Dark, handsome man in black, reserved and secret, with black hair and grey moustache, looking fixedly at mistress out of darkness? - no.

At last we got through all the rooms and all the pictures, and came out into the gardens. They were pretty well kept, being rented by a gardener, and were large and shady. In one place there was a rustic theatre, open to the sky; the stage a green slope; the coulisses, three entrances upon a side, sweet-smelling leafy screens. Mistress moved her bright eyes, even there, as if she looked to see the face come in upon the scene; but all was well.

'Now, Clara,' master said, in a low voice, 'you see that it is nothing? You are happy.'

Mistress was much encouraged. She soon accustomed herself to that grim palazzo, and would sing, and play the harp, and copy the old pictures, and stroll with master under the green trees and vines all day. She was beautiful. He was happy. He would laugh and say to me, mounting his horse for his morning ride before the heat:

'All goes well, Baptista!'

'Yes, signore, thank God, very well.'

We kept no company. I took la bella to the Duomo and Annunciata, to the Cafe, to the Opera, to the village Festa, to the Public Garden, to the Day Theatre, to the Marionetti. The pretty little one was charmed with all she saw. She learnt Italian - heavens! miraculously! Was mistress quite forgetful of that dream? I asked Carolina sometimes. Nearly, said la bella - almost. It was wearing out.

One day master received a letter, and called me.

'Baptista!'

'Signore!'

'A gentleman who is presented to me will dine here to-day. He is called the Signor Dellombra. Let me dine like a prince.'

It was an odd name. I did not know that name. But, there had been many noblemen and gentlemen pursued by Austria on political suspicions, lately, and some names had changed. Perhaps this was one. Altro! Dellombra was as good a name to me as another.

When the Signor Dellombra came to dinner (said the Genoese courier in the low voice, into which he had subsided once before), I showed him into the reception-room, the great sala of the old palazzo. Master received him with cordiality, and presented him to mistress. As she rose, her face changed, she gave a cry, and fell upon the marble floor.

Then, I turned my head to the Signor Dellombra, and saw that he was dressed in black, and had a reserved and secret air, and was a dark, remarkable-looking man, with black hair and a grey moustache.

Master raised mistress in his arms, and carried her to her own room, where I sent la bella Carolina straight. La bella told me afterwards that mistress was nearly terrified to death, and that she wandered in her mind about her dream, all night.

Master was vexed and anxious - almost angry, and yet full of solicitude. The Signor Dellombra was a courtly gentleman, and spoke with great respect and sympathy of mistress's being so ill. The African wind had been blowing for some days (they had told him at his hotel of the Maltese Cross), and he knew that it was often hurtful. He hoped the beautiful lady would recover soon. He begged permission to retire, and to renew his visit when he should have the happiness of hearing that she was better. Master would not allow of this, and they dined alone.

He withdrew early. Next day he called at the gate, on horse-back, to inquire for mistress. He did so two or three times in that week.

What I observed myself, and what la bella Carolina told me, united to explain to me that master had now set his mind on curing mistress of her fanciful terror. He was all kindness, but he was sensible and firm. He reasoned with her, that to encourage such fancies was to invite melancholy, if not madness. That it rested with herself to be herself. That if she once resisted her strange weakness, so successfully as to receive the Signor Dellombra as an English lady would receive any other guest, it was for ever conquered. To make an end, the signore came again, and mistress received him without marked distress (though with constraint and apprehension still), and the evening passed serenely. Master was so delighted with this change, and so anxious to confirm it, that the Signor Dellombra became a constant guest. He was accomplished in pictures, books, and music; and his society, in any grim palazzo, would have been welcome.

I used to notice, many times, that mistress was not quite recovered. She would cast down her eyes and droop her head, before the Signor Dellombra, or would look at him with a terrified and fascinated glance, as if his presence had some evil influence or power upon her. Turning from her to him, I used to see him in the shaded gardens, or the large half-lighted sala, looking, as I might say, 'fixedly upon her out of darkness.' But, truly, I had not forgotten la bella Carolina's words describing the face in the dream.

After his second visit I heard master say:

'Now, see, my dear Clara, it's over! Dellombra has come and gone, and your apprehension is broken like glass.'

'Will he - will he ever come again?' asked mistress.

'Again? Why, surely, over and over again! Are you cold?' (she shivered).

'No, dear - but - he terrifies me: are you sure that he need come again?'

'The surer for the question, Clara!' replied master, cheerfully.

But, he was very hopeful of her complete recovery now, and grew more and more so every day. She was beautiful. He was happy.

'All goes well, Baptista?' he would say to me again.

'Yes, signore, thank God; very well.'

We were all (said the Genoese courier, constraining himself to speak a little louder), we were all at Rome for the Carnival. I had been out, all day, with a Sicilian, a friend of mine, and a courier, who was there with an English family. As I returned at night to our hotel, I met the little Carolina, who never stirred from home alone, running distractedly along the Corso.

'Carolina! What's the matter?'

'O Baptista! O, for the Lord's sake! where is my mistress?'

'Mistress, Carolina?'

'Gone since morning - told me, when master went out on his day's journey, not to call her, for she was tired with not resting in the night (having been in pain), and would lie in bed until the evening; then get up refreshed. She is gone! - she is gone! Master has come back, broken down the door, and she is gone! My beautiful, my good, my innocent mistress!'

The pretty little one so cried, and raved, and tore herself that I could not have held her, but for her swooning on my arm as if she had been shot. Master came up - in manner, face, or voice, no more the master that I knew, than I was he. He took me (I laid the little one upon her bed in the hotel, and left her with the chamber-women), in a carriage, furiously through the darkness, across the desolate Campagna. When it was day, and we stopped at a miserable post-house, all the horses had been hired twelve hours ago, and sent away in different directions. Mark me! by the Signor Dellombra, who had passed there in a carriage, with a frightened English lady crouching in one corner.

I never heard (said the Genoese courier, drawing a long breath) that she was ever traced beyond that spot. All I know is, that she vanished into infamous oblivion, with the dreaded face beside her that she had seen in her dream.

'What do you call THAT?' said the German courier, triumphantly. 'Ghosts! There are no ghosts THERE! What do you call this, that I am going to tell you? Ghosts! There are no ghosts HERE!'

I took an engagement once (pursued the German courier) with an English gentleman, elderly and a bachelor, to travel through my country, my Fatherland. He was a merchant who traded with my country and knew the language, but who had never been there since he was a boy - as I judge, some sixty years before.

His name was James, and he had a twin-brother John, also a bachelor. Between these brothers there was a great affection. They were in business together, at Goodman's Fields, but they did not live together. Mr. James dwelt in Poland Street, turning out of Oxford Street, London; Mr. John resided by Epping Forest.

Mr. James and I were to start for Germany in about a week. The exact day depended on business. Mr. John came to Poland Street (where I was staying in the house), to pass that week with Mr. James. But, he said to his brother on the second day, 'I don't feel very well, James. There's not much the matter with me; but I think I am a little gouty. I'll go home and put myself under the care of my old housekeeper, who understands my ways. If I get quite better, I'll come back and see you before you go. If I don't feel well enough to resume my visit where I leave it off, why YOU will come and see me before you go.' Mr. James, of course, said he would, and they shook hands - both hands, as they always did - and Mr. John ordered out his old-fashioned chariot and rumbled home.

It was on the second night after that - that is to say, the fourth in the week - when I was awoke out of my sound sleep by Mr. James coming into my bedroom in his flannel-gown, with a lighted candle. He sat upon the side of my bed, and looking at me, said:

'Wilhelm, I have reason to think I have got some strange illness upon me.'

I then perceived that there was a very unusual expression in his face.

'Wilhelm,' said he, 'I am not afraid or ashamed to tell you what I might be afraid or ashamed to tell another man. You come from a sensible country, where mysterious things are inquired into and are not settled to have been weighed and measured - or to have been unweighable and unmeasurable - or in either case to have been completely disposed of, for all time - ever so many years ago. I have just now seen the phantom of my brother.'

I confess (said the German courier) that it gave me a little tingling of the blood to hear it.

'I have just now seen,' Mr. James repeated, looking full at me, that I might see how collected he was, 'the phantom of my brother John. I was sitting up in bed, unable to sleep, when it came into my room, in a white dress, and regarding me earnestly, passed up to the end of the room, glanced at some papers on my writing-desk, turned, and, still looking earnestly at me as it passed the bed, went out at the door. Now, I am not in the least mad, and am not in the least disposed to invest that phantom with any external existence out of myself. I think it is a warning to me that I am ill; and I think I had better be bled.'

I got out of bed directly (said the German courier) and began to get on my clothes, begging him not to be alarmed, and telling him that I would go myself to the doctor. I was just ready, when we heard a loud knocking and ringing at the street door. My room being an attic at the back, and Mr. James's being the second-floor room in the front, we went down to his room, and put up the window, to see what was the matter.

'Is that Mr. James?' said a man below, falling back to the opposite side of the way to look up.

'It is,' said Mr. James, 'and you are my brother's man, Robert.'

'Yes, Sir. I am sorry to say, Sir, that Mr. John is ill. He is very bad, Sir. It is even feared that he may be lying at the point of death. He wants to see you, Sir. I have a chaise here. Pray come to him. Pray lose no time.'

Mr. James and I looked at one another. 'Wilhelm,' said he, 'this is strange. I wish you to come with me!' I helped him to dress, partly there and partly in the chaise; and no grass grew under the horses' iron shoes between Poland Street and the Forest.

Now, mind! (said the German courier) I went with Mr. James into his brother's room, and I saw and heard myself what follows.

His brother lay upon his bed, at the upper end of a long bed- chamber. His old housekeeper was there, and others were there: I think three others were there, if not four, and they had been with him since early in the afternoon. He was in white, like the figure - necessarily so, because he had his night-dress on. He looked like the figure - necessarily so, because he looked earnestly at his brother when he saw him come into the room.

But, when his brother reached the bed-side, he slowly raised himself in bed, and looking full upon him, said these words:

'JAMES, YOU HAVE SEEN ME BEFORE, TO-NIGHT - AND YOU KNOW IT!'

And so died!

I waited, when the German courier ceased, to hear something said of this strange story. The silence was unbroken. I looked round, and the five couriers were gone: so noiselessly that the ghostly mountain might have absorbed them into its eternal snows. By this time, I was by no means in a mood to sit alone in that awful scene, with the chill air coming solemnly upon me - or, if I may tell the truth, to sit alone anywhere. So I went back into the convent-parlour, and, finding the American gentleman still disposed to relate the biography of the Honourable Ananias Dodger, heard it all out.

Tom Tiddler's Ground

by Charles Dickens

CHAPTER I

PICKING UP SOOT AND CINDERS

"And why Tom Tiddler's ground?" said the Traveller.

"Because he scatters halfpence to Tramps and such-like," returned the Landlord, "and of course they pick 'em up. And this being done on his own land (which it IS his own land, you observe, and were his family's before him), why it is but regarding the halfpence as gold and silver, and turning the ownership of the property a bit round your finger, and there you have the name of the children's game complete. And it's appropriate too," said the Landlord, with his favourite action of stooping a little, to look across the table out of window at vacancy, under the window-blind which was half drawn down. "Leastwise it has been so considered by many gentlemen which have partook of chops and tea in the present humble parlour."

The Traveller was partaking of chops and tea in the present humble parlour, and the Landlord's shot was fired obliquely at him.

"And you call him a Hermit?" said the Traveller.

"They call him such," returned the Landlord, evading personal responsibility; "he is in general so considered."

"What IS a Hermit?" asked the Traveller.

"What is it?" repeated the Landlord, drawing his hand across his chin.

"Yes, what is it?"

The Landlord stooped again, to get a more comprehensive view of vacancy under the window-blind, and--with an asphyxiated appearance on him as one unaccustomed to definition--made no answer.

"I'll tell you what I suppose it to be," said the Traveller. "An abominably dirty thing."

"Mr. Mopes is dirty, it cannot be denied," said the Landlord.

"Intolerably conceited."

"Mr. Mopes is vain of the life he leads, some do say," replied the Landlord, as another concession.

"A slothful, unsavoury, nasty reversal of the laws of human mature," said the Traveller; "and for the sake of GOD'S working world and its wholesomeness, both moral and physical, I would put the thing on the treadmill (if I had my way) wherever I found it; whether on a pillar, or in a hole; whether on Tom Tiddler's ground, or the Pope of Rome's ground, or a Hindoo fakeer's ground, or any other ground."

"I don't know about putting Mr. Mopes on the treadmill," said the Landlord, shaking his head very seriously. "There ain't a doubt but what he has got landed property."

"How far may it be to this said Tom Tiddler's ground?" asked the Traveller.

"Put it at five mile," returned the Landlord.

"Well! When I have done my breakfast," said the Traveller, "I'll go there. I came over here this morning, to find it out and see it."

"Many does," observed the Landlord.

The conversation passed, in the Midsummer weather of no remote year of grace, down among the pleasant dales and trout-streams of a green English county. No matter what county. Enough that you may hunt there, shoot there, fish there, traverse long grass-grown Roman roads there, open ancient barrows there, see many a square mile of richly cultivated land there, and hold Arcadian talk with a bold peasantry, their country's pride, who will tell you (if you want to know) how pastoral housekeeping is done on nine shillings a week.

Mr. Traveller sat at his breakfast in the little sanded parlour of the Peal of Bells village alehouse, with the dew and dust of an early walk upon his shoes--an early walk by road and meadow and coppice, that had sprinkled him bountifully with little blades of grass, and scraps of new hay, and with leaves both young and old, and with other such fragrant tokens of the freshness and wealth of summer. The window through which the landlord had concentrated his gaze upon vacancy was shaded, because the morning sun was hot and bright on the village street. The village street was like most other village streets: wide for its height, silent for its size, and drowsy in the dullest degree. The quietest little dwellings with the largest of window-shutters (to shut up Nothing as carefully as if it were the Mint, or the Bank of England) had called in the Doctor's house so suddenly, that his brass door-plate and three stories stood among them as conspicuous and different as the doctor himself in his broadcloth, among the smock-frocks of his patients. The village residences seemed to have gone to law with a similar absence of consideration, for a score of weak little lath-and- plaster cabins clung in confusion about the Attorney's red-brick house, which, with glaring door-steps and a most terrific scraper, seemed to serve all manner of ejectments upon them. They were as various as labourers--high-shouldered, wry-necked, one-eyed, goggle- eyed, squinting, bow-legged, knock-knee'd, rheumatic, crazy. Some of the small tradesmen's houses, such as the crockery-shop and the harness-maker, had a Cyclops window in the middle of the gable, within an inch or two of its apex, suggesting that some forlorn rural Prentice must wriggle himself into that apartment horizontally, when he retired to rest, after the manner of the worm. So bountiful in its abundance was the surrounding country, and so lean and scant the village, that one might have thought the village had sown and planted everything it once possessed, to convert the same into crops. This would account for the bareness of the little shops, the bareness of the few boards and trestles designed for market purposes in a corner of the street, the bareness of the obsolete Inn and Inn Yard, with the ominous inscription "Excise Office" not yet faded out from the gateway, as indicating the very last thing that poverty could get rid of. This would also account for the determined abandonment of the village by one stray dog, fast lessening in the perspective where the white posts and the pond were, and would explain his conduct on the hypothesis that he was going (through the act of suicide) to convert himself into manure, and become a part proprietor in turnips or mangold-wurzel.

Mr. Traveller having finished his breakfast and paid his moderate score, walked out to the threshold of the Peal of Bells, and, thence directed by the pointing finger of his host, betook himself towards the ruined hermitage of Mr. Mopes the hermit.

For, Mr. Mopes, by suffering everything about him to go to ruin, and by dressing himself in a blanket and skewer, and by steeping himself in soot and grease and other nastiness, had acquired great renown in all that country-side--far greater renown than he could ever have won for himself, if his career had been that of any ordinary Christian, or decent Hottentot. He had even blanketed and skewered and sooted and greased himself, into the London papers. And it was curious to find, as Mr. Traveller found by stopping for a new direction at this farm-house or at that cottage as he went along, with how much accuracy the morbid Mopes had counted on the weakness of his neighbours to embellish him. A mist of home-brewed marvel and romance surrounded Mopes, in which (as in all fogs) the real proportions of the real object were extravagantly heightened. He had murdered his beautiful beloved in a fit of jealousy and was doing penance; he had made a vow under the influence of grief; he had made a vow under the influence of a fatal accident; he had made a vow under the influence of religion; he had made a vow under the influence of drink; he had made a vow under the influence of disappointment; he had never made any vow, but "had got led into it" by the possession of a mighty and most awful secret; he was enormously rich, he was stupendously charitable, he was profoundly learned, he saw spectres, he knew and could do all kinds of wonders. Some said he went out every night, and was met by terrified wayfarers stalking along dark roads, others said he never went out, some knew his penance to be nearly expired, others had positive information that his seclusion was not a penance at all, and would never expire but with himself. Even, as to the easy facts of how old he was, or how long he had held verminous occupation of his blanket and skewer, no consistent information was to be got, from those who must know if they would. He was represented as being all the ages between five-and-twenty and sixty, and as having been a hermit seven years, twelve, twenty, thirty,-- though twenty, on the whole, appeared the favourite term.

"Well, well!" said Mr. Traveller. "At any rate, let us see what a real live Hermit looks like."

So, Mr. Traveller went on, and on, and on, until he came to Tom Tiddler's Ground.

It was a nook in a rustic by-road, which the genius of Mopes had laid waste as completely, as if he had been born an Emperor and a Conqueror. Its centre object was a dwelling-house, sufficiently substantial, all the window-glass of which had been long ago abolished by the surprising genius of Mopes, and all the windows of which were barred across with rough-split logs of trees nailed over them on the outside. A rickyard, hip-high in vegetable rankness and ruin, contained outbuildings from which the thatch had lightly fluttered away, on all the winds of all the seasons of the year, and from which the planks and beams had heavily dropped and rotted. The frosts and damps of winter, and the heats of summer, had warped what wreck remained, so that not a post or a board retained the position it was meant to hold, but everything was twisted from its purpose, like its owner, and degraded and debased. In this homestead of the sluggard, behind the ruined hedge, and sinking away among the ruined grass and the nettles, were the last perishing fragments of certain ricks: which had gradually mildewed and collapsed, until they looked like mounds of rotten honeycomb, or dirty sponge. Tom Tiddler's ground could even show its ruined water; for, there was a slimy pond into which a tree or two had fallen--one soppy trunk and branches lay across it then-- which in its accumulation of stagnant weed, and in its black decomposition, and in all its foulness and filth, was almost comforting, regarded as the only water that could have reflected the shameful place without seeming polluted by that low office.

Mr. Traveller looked all around him on Tom Tiddler's ground, and his glance at last encountered a dusky Tinker lying among the weeds and rank grass, in the shade of the dwelling-house. A rough walking- staff lay on the ground by his side, and his head rested on a small wallet. He met Mr. Traveller's eye without lifting up his head, merely depressing his chin a little (for he was lying on his back) to get a better view of him.

"Good day!" said Mr. Traveller.

"Same to you, if you like it," returned the Tinker.

"Don't YOU like it? It's a very fine day."

"I ain't partickler in weather," returned the Tinker, with a yawn.

Mr. Traveller had walked up to where he lay, and was looking down at him. "This is a curious place," said Mr. Traveller.

"Ay, I suppose so!" returned the Tinker. "Tom Tiddler's ground, they call this."

"Are you well acquainted with it?"

"Never saw it afore to-day," said the Tinker, with another yawn, "and don't care if I never see it again. There was a man here just now, told me what it was called. If you want to see Tom himself, you must go in at that gate." He faintly indicated with his chin a little mean ruin of a wooden gate at the side of the house.

"Have you seen Tom?"

"No, and I ain't partickler to see him. I can see a dirty man anywhere."

"He does not live in the house, then?" said Mr. Traveller, casting his eyes upon the house anew.

"The man said," returned the Tinker, rather irritably,--"him as was here just now, 'this what you're a laying on, mate, is Tom Tiddler's ground. And if you want to see Tom,' he says, 'you must go in at that gate.' The man come out at that gate himself, and he ought to know."

"Certainly," said Mr. Traveller.

"Though, perhaps," exclaimed the Tinker, so struck by the brightness of his own idea, that it had the electric effect upon him of causing him to lift up his head an inch or so, "perhaps he was a liar! He told some rum 'uns--him as was here just now, did about this place of Tom's. He says--him as was here just now--'When Tom shut up the house, mate, to go to rack, the beds was left, all made, like as if somebody was a-going to sleep in every bed. And if you was to walk through the bedrooms now, you'd see the ragged mouldy bedclothes a heaving and a heaving like seas. And a heaving and a heaving with what?' he says. 'Why, with the rats under 'em.'"

"I wish I had seen that man," Mr. Traveller remarked.

"You'd have been welcome to see him instead of me seeing him," growled the Tinker; "for he was a long-winded one."

Not without a sense of injury in the remembrance, the Tinker gloomily closed his eyes. Mr. Traveller, deeming the Tinker a short-winded one, from whom no further breath of information was to be derived, betook himself to the gate.

Swung upon its rusty hinges, it admitted him into a yard in which there was nothing to be seen but an outhouse attached to the ruined building, with a barred window in it. As there were traces of many recent footsteps under this window, and as it was a low window, and unglazed, Mr. Traveller made bold to peep within the bars. And there to be sure he had a real live Hermit before him, and could judge how the real dead Hermits used to look.

He was lying on a bank of soot and cinders, on the floor, in front of a rusty fireplace. There was nothing else in the dark little kitchen, or scullery, or whatever his den had been originally used as, but a table with a litter of old bottles on it. A rat made a clatter among these bottles, jumped down, and ran over the real live Hermit on his way to his hole, or the man in HIS hole would not have been so easily discernible. Tickled in the face by the rat's tail, the owner of Tom Tiddler's ground opened his eyes, saw Mr. Traveller, started up, and sprang to the window.

"Humph!" thought Mr. Traveller, retiring a pace or two from the bars. "A compound of Newgate, Bedlam, a Debtors' Prison in the worst time, a chimney-sweep, a mudlark, and the Noble Savage! A nice old family, the

Hermit family. Hah!"

Mr. Traveller thought this, as he silently confronted the sooty object in the blanket and skewer (in sober truth it wore nothing else), with the matted hair and the staring eyes. Further, Mr. Traveller thought, as the eye surveyed him with a very obvious curiosity in ascertaining the effect they produced, "Vanity, vanity, vanity! Verily, all is vanity!"

"What is your name, sir, and where do you come from?" asked Mr. Mopes the Hermit--with an air of authority, but in the ordinary human speech of one who has been to school.

Mr. Traveller answered the inquiries.

"Did you come here, sir, to see ME?"

"I did. I heard of you, and I came to see you.--I know you like to be seen." Mr. Traveller coolly threw the last words in, as a matter of course, to forestall an affectation of resentment or objection that he saw rising beneath the grease and grime of the face. They had their effect.

"So," said the Hermit, after a momentary silence, unclasping the bars by which he had previously held, and seating himself behind them on the ledge of the window, with his bare legs and feet crouched up, "you know I like to be seen?"

Mr. Traveller looked about him for something to sit on, and, observing a billet of wood in a corner, brought it near the window. Deliberately seating himself upon it, he answered, "Just so."

Each looked at the other, and each appeared to take some pains to get the measure of the other.

"Then you have come to ask me why I lead this life," said the Hermit, frowning in a stormy manner. "I never tell that to any human being. I will not be asked that."

"Certainly you will not be asked that by me," said Mr. Traveller, "for I have not the slightest desire to know."

"You are an uncouth man," said Mr. Mopes the Hermit.

"You are another," said Mr. Traveller.

The Hermit, who was plainly in the habit of overawing his visitors with the novelty of his filth and his blanket and skewer, glared at his present visitor in some discomfiture and surprise: as if he had taken aim at him with a sure gun, and his piece had missed fire.

"Why do you come here at all?" he asked, after a pause.

"Upon my life," said Mr. Traveller, "I was made to ask myself that very question only a few minutes ago--by a Tinker too."

As he glanced towards the gate in saying it, the Hermit glanced in that direction likewise.

"Yes. He is lying on his back in the sunlight outside," said Mr, Traveller, as if he had been asked concerning the man, "and he won't come in; for he says-- and really very reasonably--'What should I come in for? I can see a dirty man anywhere.'"

"You are an insolent person. Go away from my premises. Go!" said the Hermit, in an imperious and angry tone.

"Come, come!" returned Mr. Traveller, quite undisturbed. "This is a little too much. You are not going to call yourself clean? Look at your legs. And as to these being your premises:- they are in far too disgraceful a condition to claim any privilege of ownership, or anything else."

The Hermit bounced down from his window-ledge, and cast himself on his bed of soot and cinders.

"I am not going," said Mr. Traveller, glancing in after him; "you won't get rid of me in that way. You had better come and talk."

"I won't talk," said the Hermit, flouncing round to get his back towards the window.

"Then I will," said Mr. Traveller. "Why should you take it ill that I have no curiosity to know why you live this highly absurd and highly indecent life? When I contemplate a man in a state of disease, surely there is no moral obligation on me to be anxious to know how he took it."

After a short silence, the Hermit bounced up again, and came back to the barred window.

"What? You are not gone?" he said, affecting to have supposed that he was.

"Nor going," Mr. Traveller replied: "I design to pass this summer day here."

"How dare you come, sir, upon my promises--" the Hermit was returning, when his visitor interrupted him.

"Really, you know, you must NOT talk about your premises. I cannot allow such a place as this to be dignified with the name of premises."

"How dare you," said the Hermit, shaking his bars, "come in at my gate, to taunt me with being in a diseased state?"

"Why, Lord bless my soul," returned the other, very composedly, "you have not the face to say that you are in a wholesome state? Do allow me again to call your attention to your legs. Scrape yourself anywhere--with anything-- and then tell me you are in a wholesome state. The fact is, Mr. Mopes, that you are not only a Nuisance--"

"A Nuisance?" repeated the Hermit, fiercely.

"What is a place in this obscene state of dilapidation but a Nuisance? What is a man in your obscene state of dilapidation but a Nuisance? Then, as you very well know, you cannot do without an audience, and your audience is a Nuisance. You attract all the disreputable vagabonds and prowlers within ten miles around, by exhibiting yourself to them in that objectionable blanket, and by throwing copper money among them, and giving them drink out of those very dirty jars and bottles that I see in there (their stomachs need be strong!); and in short," said Mr. Traveller, summing up in a quietly and comfortably settled manner, "you are a Nuisance, and this kennel is a Nuisance, and the audience that you cannot possibly dispense with is a Nuisance, and the Nuisance is not merely a local Nuisance, because it is a general Nuisance to know that there CAN BE such a Nuisance left in civilisation so very long after its time."

"Will you go away? I have a gun in here," said the Hermit.

"Pooh!"

"I HAVE!"

"Now, I put it to you. Did I say you had not? And as to going away, didn't I say I am not going away? You have made me forget where I was. I now remember that I was remarking on your conduct being a Nuisance. Moreover, it is in the last and lowest degree inconsequent foolishness and weakness."

"Weakness?" echoed the Hermit.

"Weakness," said Mr. Traveller, with his former comfortably settled final air.

"I weak, you fool?" cried the Hermit, "I, who have held to my purpose, and my diet, and my only bed there, all these years?"

"The more the years, the weaker you," returned Mr. Traveller. "Though the years are not so many as folks say, and as you willingly take credit for. The crust upon your face is thick and dark, Mr. Mopes, but I can see enough of you through it, to see that you are still a young man."

"Inconsequent foolishness is lunacy, I suppose?" said the Hermit.

"I suppose it is very like it," answered Mr. Traveller.

"Do I converse like a lunatic?"

"One of us two must have a strong presumption against him of being one, whether or no. Either the clean and decorously clad man, or the dirty and indecorously clad man. I don't say which."

"Why, you self-sufficient bear," said the Hermit, "not a day passes but I am justified in my purpose by the conversations I hold here; not a day passes but I am shown, by everything I hear and see here, how right and strong I am in holding my purpose."

Mr. Traveller, lounging easily on his billet of wood, took out a pocket pipe and began to fill it. "Now, that a man," he said, appealing to the summer sky as he did so, "that a man--even behind bars, in a blanket and skewer--should tell me that he can see, from day to day, any orders or conditions of men, women, or children, who can by any possibility teach him that it is anything but the miserablest drivelling for a human creature to quarrel with his social nature--not to go so far as to say, to renounce his common human decency, for that is an extreme case; or who can teach him that he can in any wise separate himself from his kind and the habits of his kind, without becoming a deteriorated spectacle calculated to give the Devil (and perhaps the monkeys) pleasure,--is something wonderful! I repeat," said Mr. Traveller, beginning to smoke, "the unreasoning hardihood of it is something wonderful--even in a man with the dirt upon him an inch or two thick--behind bars-- in a blanket and skewer!"

The Hermit looked at him irresolutely, and retired to his soot and cinders and lay down, and got up again and came to the bars, and again looked at him irresolutely, and finally said with sharpness: "I don't like tobacco."

"I don't like dirt," rejoined Mr. Traveller; "tobacco is an excellent disinfectant. We shall both be the better for my pipe. It is my intention to sit here through this summer day, until that blessed summer sun sinks low in the west, and to show you what a poor creature you are, through the lips of every chance wayfarer who may come in at your gate."

"What do you mean?" inquired the Hermit, with a furious air.

"I mean that yonder is your gate, and there are you, and here am I; I mean that I know it to be a moral impossibility that any person can stray in at that gate from any point of the compass, with any sort of experience, gained at first hand, or derived from another, that can confute me and justify you."

"You are an arrogant and boastful hero," said the Hermit. "You think yourself profoundly wise."

"Bah!" returned Mr. Traveller, quietly smoking. "There is little wisdom in knowing that every man must be up and doing, and that all mankind are made dependent on one another."

"You have companions outside," said the Hermit. "I am not to be imposed upon by your assumed confidence in the people who may enter."

"A depraved distrust," returned the visitor, compassionately raising his eyebrows, "of course belongs to your state, I can't help that."

"Do you mean to tell me you have no confederates?"

"I mean to tell you nothing but what I have told you. What I have told you is, that it is a moral impossibility that any son or daughter of Adam can stand on this ground that I put my foot on, or on any ground that mortal treads, and gainsay the healthy tenure on which we hold our existence."

"Which is," sneered the Hermit, "according to you--"

"Which is," returned the other, "according to Eternal Providence, that we must arise and wash our faces and do our gregarious work and act and re-act on one another, leaving only the idiot and the palsied to sit blinking in the corner. Come!" apostrophising the gate. "Open Sesame! Show his eyes and grieve his heart! I don't care who comes, for I know what must come of it!"

With that, he faced round a little on his billet of wood towards the gate; and Mr. Mopes, the Hermit, after two or three ridiculous bounces of indecision at his bed and back again, submitted to what he could not help himself against, and coiled himself on his window- ledge, holding to his bars and looking out rather anxiously.

CHAPTER VI

--PICKING UP MISS KIMMEENS {1}

The day was by this time waning, when the gate again opened, and, with the brilliant golden light that streamed from the declining sun and touched the very bars of the sooty creature's den, there passed in a little child; a little girl with beautiful bright hair. She wore a plain straw hat, had a door-key in her hand, and tripped towards Mr. Traveller as if she were pleased to see him and were going to repose some childish confidence in him, when she caught sight of the figure behind the bars, and started back in terror.

"Don't be alarmed, darling!" said Mr. Traveller, taking her by the hand.

"Oh, but I don't like it!" urged the shrinking child; "it's dreadful."

"Well! I don't like it either," said Mr. Traveller.

"Who has put it there?" asked the little girl. "Does it bite?"

"No,--only barks. But can't you make up your mind to see it, my dear?" For she was covering her eyes.

"O no no no!" returned the child. "I cannot bear to look at it!"

Mr. Traveller turned his head towards his friend in there, as much as to ask him how he liked that instance of his success, and then took the child out at the still open gate, and stood talking to her for some half an hour in the mellow sunlight. At length he returned, encouraging her as she held his arm with both her hands; and laying his protecting hand upon her head and smoothing her pretty hair, he addressed his friend behind the bars as follows:

Miss Pupford's establishment for six young ladies of tender years, is an establishment of a compact nature, an establishment in miniature, quite a pocket establishment. Miss Pupford, Miss Pupford's assistant with the Parisian accent, Miss Pupford's cook, and Miss Pupford's housemaid, complete what Miss Pupford calls the educational and domestic staff of her Lilliputian College.

Miss Pupford is one of the most amiable of her sex; it necessarily follows that she possesses a sweet temper, and would own to the possession of a great deal of sentiment if she considered it quite reconcilable with her duty to parents. Deeming it not in the bond, Miss Pupford keeps it as far out of sight as she can--which (God bless her!) is not very far.

Miss Pupford's assistant with the Parisian accent, may be regarded as in some sort an inspired lady, for she never conversed with a Parisian, and was never out of England--except once in the pleasure- boat Lively, in the foreign waters that ebb and flow two miles off Margate at high water. Even under those geographically favourable circumstances for the acquisition of the French language in its utmost politeness and purity, Miss Pupford's assistant did not fully profit by the opportunity; for the pleasure-boat, Lively, so strongly asserted its title to its name on that occasion, that she was reduced to the condition of lying in the bottom of the boat pickling in brine--as if she were being salted down for the use of the Navy--undergoing at the same time great mental alarm, corporeal distress, and clear-starching derangement.

When Miss Pupford and her assistant first foregathered, is not known to men, or pupils. But, it was long ago. A belief would have established itself among pupils that the two once went to school together, were it not for the difficulty and audacity of imagining Miss Pupford born without mittens, and without a front, and without a bit of gold wire among her front teeth, and without little dabs of powder on her neat little face and nose. Indeed, whenever Miss Pupford gives a little lecture on the mythology of the misguided heathens (always carefully excluding Cupid from recognition), and tells how Minerva sprang, perfectly equipped, from the brain of Jupiter, she is half supposed to hint, "So I myself came into the world, completely up in Pinnock, Mangnall, Tables, and the use of the Globes."

Howbeit, Miss Pupford and Miss Pupford's assistant are old old friends. And it is thought by pupils that, after pupils are gone to bed, they even call one another by their christian names in the quiet little parlour. For, once upon a time on a thunderous afternoon, when Miss Pupford fainted away without notice, Miss Pupford's assistant (never heard, before or since, to address her otherwise than as Miss Pupford) ran to her, crying out, "My dearest Euphemia!" And Euphemia is Miss Pupford's christian name on the sampler (date picked out) hanging up in the College-hall, where the two peacocks, terrified to death by some German text that is waddling down-hill after them out of a cottage, are scuttling away to hide their profiles in two immense bean-stalks growing out of flower-pots.

Also, there is a notion latent among pupils, that Miss Pupford was once in love, and that the beloved object still moves upon this ball. Also, that he is a public character, and a personage of vast consequence. Also, that Miss Pupford's assistant knows all about it. For, sometimes of an afternoon when Miss Pupford has been reading the paper through her little gold eye-glass (it is necessary to read it on the spot, as the boy calls for it, with ill- conditioned punctuality, in an hour), she has become agitated, and has said to her assistant "G!" Then Miss Pupford's assistant has gone to Miss Pupford, and Miss Pupford has pointed out, with her eye-glass, G in the paper, and then Miss Pupford's assistant has read about G, and has shown sympathy. So stimulated has the pupil- mind been in its time to curiosity on the subject of G, that once, under temporary circumstances favourable to the bold sally, one fearless pupil did actually obtain possession of the paper, and range all over it in search of G, who had been discovered therein by Miss Pupford not ten minutes before. But no G could be identified, except one capital offender who had been executed in a state of great hardihood, and it was not to be supposed that Miss Pupford could ever have loved HIM. Besides, he couldn't be always being executed. Besides, he got into the paper again, alive, within a month.

On the whole, it is suspected by the pupil-mind that G is a short chubby old gentleman, with little black sealing-wax boots up to his knees, whom a sharply observant pupil, Miss Linx, when she once went to Tunbridge Wells with Miss Pupford for the holidays, reported on her return (privately and confidentially) to have seen come capering up to Miss Pupford on the

Promenade, and to have detected in the act of squeezing Miss Pupford's hand, and to have heard pronounce the words, "Cruel Euphemia, ever thine!"--or something like that. Miss Linx hazarded a guess that he might be House of Commons, or Money Market, or Court Circular, or Fashionable Movements; which would account for his getting into the paper so often. But, it was fatally objected by the pupil-mind, that none of those notabilities could possibly be spelt with a G.

There are other occasions, closely watched and perfectly comprehended by the pupil-mind, when Miss Pupford imparts with mystery to her assistant that there is special excitement in the morning paper. These occasions are, when Miss Pupford finds an old pupil coming out under the head of Births, or Marriages. Affectionate tears are invariably seen in Miss Pupford's meek little eyes when this is the case; and the pupil-mind, perceiving that its order has distinguished itself--though the fact is never mentioned by Miss Pupford-- becomes elevated, and feels that it likewise is reserved for greatness.

Miss Pupford's assistant with the Parisian accent has a little more bone than Miss Pupford, but is of the same trim orderly diminutive cast, and, from long contemplation, admiration, and imitation of Miss Pupford, has grown like her. Being entirely devoted to Miss Pupford, and having a pretty talent for pencil-drawing, she once made a portrait of that lady: which was so instantly identified and hailed by the pupils, that it was done on stone at five shillings. Surely the softest and milkiest stone that ever was quarried, received that likeness of Miss Pupford! The lines of her placid little nose are so undecided in it that strangers to the work of art are observed to be exceedingly perplexed as to where the nose goes to, and involuntarily feel their own noses in a disconcerted manner. Miss Pupford being represented in a state of dejection at an open window, ruminating over a bowl of gold fish, the pupil-mind has settled that the bowl was presented by G, and that he wreathed the bowl with flowers of soul, and that Miss Pupford is depicted as waiting for him on a memorable occasion when he was behind his time.

The approach of the last Midsummer holidays had a particular interest for the pupil-mind, by reason of its knowing that Miss Pupford was bidden, on the second day of those holidays, to the nuptials of a former pupil. As it was impossible to conceal the fact--so extensive were the dress-making preparations--Miss Pupford openly announced it. But, she held it due to parents to make the announcement with an air of gentle melancholy, as if marriage were (as indeed it exceptionally has been) rather a calamity. With an air of softened resignation and pity, therefore, Miss Pupford went on with her preparations: and meanwhile no pupil ever went up- stairs, or came down, without peeping in at the door of Miss Pupford's bedroom (when Miss Pupford wasn't there), and bringing back some surprising intelligence concerning the bonnet.

The extensive preparations being completed on the day before the holidays, an unanimous entreaty was preferred to Miss Pupford by the pupil-mind-- finding expression through Miss Pupford's assistant-- that she would deign to appear in all her splendour. Miss Pupford consenting, presented a lovely spectacle. And although the oldest pupil was barely thirteen, every one of the six became in two minutes perfect in the shape, cut, colour, price, and quality, of every article Miss Pupford wore.

Thus delightfully ushered in, the holidays began. Five of the six pupils kissed little Kitty Kimmeens twenty times over (round total, one hundred times, for she was very popular), and so went home. Miss Kitty Kimmeens remained behind, for her relations and friends were all in India, far away. A self-helpful steady little child is Miss Kitty Kimmeens: a dimpled child too, and a loving.

So, the great marriage-day came, and Miss Pupford, quite as much fluttered as any bride could be (G! thought Miss Kitty Kimmeens), went away, splendid to behold, in the carriage that was sent for her. But not Miss Pupford only went away; for Miss Pupford's assistant went away with her, on a dutiful visit to an aged uncle-- though surely the venerable gentleman couldn't live in the gallery of the church where the marriage was to be, thought Miss Kitty Kimmeens--and yet Miss Pupford's assistant had let out that she was going there. Where the cook was going, didn't appear, but she generally conveyed to Miss Kimmeens that she was bound, rather against her will, on a pilgrimage to perform some pious office that rendered new ribbons necessary to her best bonnet, and also sandals to her shoes.

"So you see," said the housemaid, when they were all gone, "there's nobody left in the house but you and me, Miss Kimmeens."

"Nobody else," said Miss Kitty Kimmeens, shaking her curls a little sadly.

"Nobody!"

"And you wouldn't like your Bella to go too; would you, Miss Kimmeens?" said the housemaid. (She being Bella.)

"N-no," answered little Miss Kimmeens.

"Your poor Bella is forced to stay with you, whether she likes it or not; ain't she, Miss Kimmeens?"

"DON'T you like it?" inquired Kitty.

"Why, you're such a darling, Miss, that it would be unkind of your Bella to make objections. Yet my brother-in-law has been took unexpected bad by this morning's post. And your poor Bella is much attached to him, letting alone her favourite sister, Miss Kimmeens."

"Is he very ill?" asked little Kitty.

"Your poor Bella has her fears so, Miss Kimmeens," returned the housemaid, with her apron at her eyes. "It was but his inside, it is true, but it might mount, and the doctor said that if it mounted he wouldn't answer." Here the housemaid was so overcome that Kitty administered the only comfort she had ready: which was a kiss.

"If it hadn't been for disappointing Cook, dear Miss Kimmeens," said the housemaid, "your Bella would have asked her to stay with you. For Cook is sweet company, Miss Kimmeens, much more so than your own poor Bella."

"But you are very nice, Bella."

"Your Bella could wish to be so, Miss Kimmeens," returned the housemaid, "but she knows full well that it do not lay in her power this day."

With which despondent conviction, the housemaid drew a heavy sigh, and shook her head, and dropped it on one side.

"If it had been anyways right to disappoint Cook," she pursued, in a contemplative and abstracted manner, "it might have been so easy done! I could have got to my brother-in-law's, and had the best part of the day there, and got back, long before our ladies come home at night, and neither the one nor the other of them need never have known it. Not that Miss Pupford would at all object, but that it might put her out, being tender-hearted. Hows'ever, your own poor Bella, Miss Kimmeens," said the housemaid, rousing herself, "is forced to stay with you, and you're a precious love, if not a liberty."

"Bella," said little Kitty, after a short silence.

"Call your own poor Bella, your Bella, dear," the housemaid besought her.

"My Bella, then."

"Bless your considerate heart!" said the housemaid.

"If you would not mind leaving me, I should not mind being left. I am not afraid to stay in the house alone. And you need not be uneasy on my account, for I would be very careful to do no harm."

"O! As to harm, you more than sweetest, if not a liberty," exclaimed the housemaid, in a rapture, "your Bella could trust you anywhere, being so steady, and so answerable. The oldest head in this house (me and Cook says), but for its bright hair, is Miss Kimmeens. But no, I will not leave you; for you would think your Bella unkind."

"But if you are my Bella, you MUST go," returned the child.

"Must I?" said the housemaid, rising, on the whole with alacrity. "What must be, must be, Miss Kimmeens. Your own poor Bella acts according, though unwilling. But go or stay, your own poor Bella loves you, Miss Kimmeens."

It was certainly go, and not stay, for within five minutes Miss Kimmeens's own poor Bella--so much improved in point of spirits as to have grown almost sanguine on the subject of her brother-in-law-- went her way, in apparel that seemed to have been expressly prepared for some festive occasion. Such are the changes of this fleeting world, and so short-sighted are we poor mortals!

When the house door closed with a bang and a shake, it seemed to Miss Kimmeens to be a very heavy house door, shutting her up in a wilderness of a house. But, Miss Kimmeens being, as before stated, of a self-reliant and methodical character, presently began to parcel out the long summer-day before her.

And first she thought she would go all over the house, to make quite sure that nobody with a great-coat on and a carving-knife in it, had got under one of the beds or into one of the cupboards. Not that she had ever before been troubled by the image of anybody armed with a great-coat and a carving-knife, but that it seemed to have been shaken into existence by the shake and the bang of the great street- door, reverberating through the solitary house. So, little Miss Kimmeens looked under the five empty beds of the five departed pupils, and looked, under her own bed, and looked under Miss Pupford's bed, and looked under Miss Pupford's assistants bed. And when she had done this, and was making the tour of the cupboards, the disagreeable thought came into her young head, What a very alarming thing it would be to find somebody with a mask on, like Guy Fawkes, hiding bolt upright in a corner and pretending not to be alive! However, Miss Kimmeens having finished her inspection without making any such uncomfortable discovery, sat down in her tidy little manner to needlework, and began stitching away at a great rate.

The silence all about her soon grew very oppressive, and the more so because of the odd inconsistency that the more silent it was, the more noises there were. The noise of her own needle and thread as she stitched, was infinitely louder in her ears than the stitching of all the six pupils, and of Miss Pupford, and of Miss Pupford's assistant, all stitching away at once on a highly emulative afternoon. Then, the schoolroom clock conducted itself in a way in which it had never conducted itself before--fell lame, somehow, and yet persisted in running on as hard and as loud as it could: the consequence of which behaviour was, that it staggered among the minutes in a state of the greatest confusion, and knocked them about in all directions without appearing to get on with its regular work. Perhaps this alarmed the stairs; but be that as it might, they began to creak in a most unusual manner, and then the furniture began to crack, and then poor little Miss Kimmeens, not liking the furtive aspect of things in general, began to sing as she stitched. But, it was not her own voice that she heard--it was somebody else making believe to be Kitty, and singing excessively flat, without any heart--so as that would never mend matters, she left off again.

By-and-by the stitching became so palpable a failure that Miss Kitty Kimmeens folded her work neatly, and put it away in its box, and gave it up. Then the question arose about reading. But no; the book that was so delightful when there was somebody she loved for her eyes to fall on when they rose from the page, had not more heart in it than her own singing now. The book went to its shelf as the needlework had gone to its box, and, since something MUST be done-- thought the child, "I'll go put my room to rights."

She shared her room with her dearest little friend among the other five pupils, and why then should she now conceive a lurking dread of the little friend's bedstead? But she did. There was a stealthy air about its innocent white curtains, and there were even dark hints of a dead girl lying under the coverlet. The great want of human company, the great need of a human face, began now to express itself in the facility with which the furniture put on strange exaggerated resemblances to human looks. A chair with a menacing frown was horribly out of temper in a corner; a most vicious chest of drawers snarled at her from between the windows. It was no relief to escape from those monsters to the looking-glass, for the reflection said, "What? Is that you all alone there? How you stare!" And the background was all a great void stare as well.

The day dragged on, dragging Kitty with it very slowly by the hair of her head, until it was time to eat. There were good provisions in the pantry, but their right flavour and relish had evaporated with the five pupils, and Miss Pupford, and Miss Pupford's assistant, and the cook and housemaid. Where was the use of laying the cloth symmetrically for one small guest, who had gone on ever since the morning growing smaller and smaller, while the empty house had gone on swelling larger and larger? The very Grace came out wrong, for who were "we" who were going to receive and be thankful? So, Miss Kimmeens was NOT thankful, and found herself taking her dinner in very slovenly style--gobbling it up, in short, rather after the manner of the lower animals, not to particularise the pigs.

But, this was by no means the worst of the change wrought out in the naturally loving and cheery little creature as the solitary day wore on. She began to brood and be suspicious. She discovered that she was full of wrongs and injuries. All the people she knew, got tainted by her lonely thoughts and turned bad.

It was all very well for Papa, a widower in India, to send her home to be educated, and to pay a handsome round sum every year for her to Miss Pupford, and to write charming letters to his darling little daughter; but what did he care for her being left by herself, when he was (as no doubt he always was) enjoying himself in company from morning till night? Perhaps he only sent her here, after all, to get her out of the way. It looked like it--looked like it to-day, that is, for she had never dreamed of such a thing before.

And this old pupil who was being married. It was unsupportably conceited and selfish in the old pupil to be married. She was very vain, and very glad to show off; but it was highly probable that she wasn't pretty; and even if she were pretty (which Miss Kimmeens now totally denied), she had no business to be married; and, even if marriage were conceded, she had no business to ask Miss Pupford to her wedding. As to Miss Pupford, she was too old to go to any wedding. She ought to know that. She had much better attend to her business. She had thought she looked nice in the morning, but she didn't look nice. She was a stupid old thing. G was another stupid old thing. Miss Pupford's assistant was another. They were all stupid old things together.

More than that: it began to be obvious that this was a plot. They had said to one another, "Never mind Kitty; you get off, and I'll get off; and we'll leave Kitty to look after herself. Who cares for her?" To be sure they were right in that question; for who DID care for her, a poor little lonely thing against whom they all planned and plotted? Nobody, nobody! Here Kitty sobbed.

At all other times she was the pet of the whole house, and loved her five companions in return with a child's tenderest and most ingenuous attachment; but now, the five companions put on ugly colours, and appeared for the first time under a sullen cloud. There they were, all at their homes that day, being made much of, being taken out, being spoilt and made disagreeable, and caring nothing for her. It was like their artful selfishness always to tell her when they came back, under pretence of confidence and friendship, all those details about where they had been, and what they had done and seen, and how often they had said, "O! If we had only darling little Kitty here!" Here indeed! I dare say! When they came back after the holidays, they were used to being received by Kitty, and to saying that coming to Kitty was like coming to another home. Very well then, why did they go away? If the meant it, why did they go away? Let them answer that. But they didn't mean it, and couldn't answer that, and they didn't tell the truth, and people who didn't tell the truth were hateful. When they came back next time, they should be received in a new manner; they should be avoided and shunned.

And there, the while she sat all alone revolving how ill she was used, and how much better she was than the people who were not alone, the wedding breakfast was going on: no question of it! With a nasty great bride-cake, and with those ridiculous orange-flowers, and with that conceited bride, and that hideous bridegroom, and those heartless bridesmaids, and Miss Pupford stuck up at the table! They thought they were enjoying themselves, but it would come home to them one day to have thought so. They would all be dead in a few years, let them enjoy themselves ever so much. It was a religious comfort to know that.

It was such a comfort to know it, that little Miss Kitty Kimmeens suddenly sprang from the chair in which she had been musing in a corner, and cried out, "O those envious thoughts are not mine, O this wicked creature isn't me! Help me, somebody! I go wrong, alone by my weak self! Help me, anybody!"

"--Miss Kimmeens is not a professed philosopher, sir," said Mr. Traveller, presenting her at the barred window, and smoothing her shining hair, "but I apprehend there was some tincture of philosophy in her words, and in the prompt action with which she followed them. That action was, to emerge from her unnatural solitude, and look abroad for wholesome sympathy, to bestow and to receive. Her footsteps strayed to this gate, bringing her here by chance, as an apposite contrast to you. The child came out, sir. If you have the wisdom to learn from a child (but I doubt it, for that requires more wisdom than one in your condition would seem to possess), you cannot do better than imitate the child, and come out too--from that very demoralising hutch of yours."

CHAPTER VII

PICKING UP THE TINKER

It was now sunset. The Hermit had betaken himself to his bed of cinders half an hour ago, and lying on it in his blanket and skewer with his back to the window, took not the smallest heed of the appeal addressed to him.

All that had been said for the last two hours, had been said to a tinkling accompaniment performed by the Tinker, who had got to work upon some villager's pot or kettle, and was working briskly outside. This music still continuing, seemed to put it into Mr. Traveller's mind to have another word or two with the Tinker. So, holding Miss Kimmeens (with whom he was now on the most friendly terms) by the hand, he went out at the gate to where the Tinker was seated at his work on the patch of grass on the opposite side of the road, with his wallet of tools open before him, and his little fire smoking.

"I am glad to see you employed," said Mr. Traveller.

"I am glad to BE employed," returned the Tinker, looking up as he put the finishing touches to his job. "But why are you glad?"

I thought you were a lazy fellow when I saw you this morning."

"I was only disgusted," said the Tinker.

"Do you mean with the fine weather?"

"With the fine weather?" repeated the Tinker, staring.

"You told me you were not particular as to weather, and I thought--"

"Ha, ha! How should such as me get on, if we WAS particular as to weather? We must take it as it comes, and make the best of it. There's something good in all weathers. If it don't happen to be good for my work to-day, it's good for some other man's to-day, and will come round to me to-morrow. We must all live."

"Pray shake hands," said Mr. Traveller.

"Take care, sir," was the Tinker's caution, as he reached up his hand in surprise; "the black comes off."

"I am glad of it," said Mr. Traveller. "I have been for several hours among other black that does not come off."

"You are speaking of Tom in there?"

"Yes."

"Well now," said the Tinker, blowing the dust off his job: which was finished. "Ain't it enough to disgust a pig, if he could give his mind to it?"

"If he could give his mind to it," returned the other, smiling, "the probability is that he wouldn't be a pig."

"There you clench the nail," returned the Tinker. "Then what's to be said for Tom?"

"Truly, very little."

"Truly nothing you mean, sir," said the Tinker, as he put away his tools.

"A better answer, and (I freely acknowledge) my meaning. I infer that he was the cause of your disgust?"

"Why, look'ee here, sir," said the Tinker, rising to his feet, and wiping his face on the corner of his black apron energetically; "I leave you to judge!--I ask you!--Last night I has a job that needs to be done in the night, and I works all night. Well, there's nothing in that. But this morning I comes along this road here, looking for a sunny and soft spot to sleep in, and I sees this desolation and ruination. I've lived myself in desolation and ruination; I knows many a fellow-creetur that's forced to live life long in desolation and ruination; and I sits me down and takes pity on it, as I casts my eyes about. Then comes up the long-winded one as I told you of, from that gate, and spins himself out like a silkworm concerning the Donkey (if my Donkey at home will excuse me) as has made it all--made it of his own choice! And tells me, if you please, of his likewise choosing to go ragged and naked, and grimy--maskerading, mountebanking, in what is the real hard lot of thousands and thousands! Why, then I say it's a unbearable and nonsensical piece of inconsistency, and I'm disgusted. I'm ashamed and disgusted!"

"I wish you would come and look at him," said Mr. Traveller, clapping the Tinker on the shoulder.

"Not I, sir," he rejoined. "I ain't a going to flatter him up by looking at him!"

"But he is asleep."

"Are you sure he is asleep?" asked the Tinker, with an unwilling air, as he shouldered his wallet.

"Sure."

"Then I'll look at him for a quarter of a minute," said the Tinker, "since you so much wish it; but not a moment longer."

They all three went back across the road; and, through the barred window, by the dying glow of the sunset coming in at the gate--which the child held open for its admission--he could be pretty clearly discerned lying on his bed.

"You see him?" asked Mr. Traveller.

"Yes," returned the Tinker, "and he's worse than I thought him."

Mr. Traveller then whispered in few words what he had done since morning; and asked the Tinker what he thought of that?

"I think," returned the Tinker, as he turned from the window, "that you've wasted a day on him."

"I think so too; though not, I hope, upon myself. Do you happen to be going anywhere near the Peal of Bells?"

"That's my direct way, sir," said the Tinker.

"I invite you to supper there. And as I learn from this young lady that she goes some three-quarters of a mile in the same direction, we will drop her on the road, and we will spare time to keep her company at her garden gate until her own Bella comes home."

So, Mr. Traveller, and the child, and the Tinker, went along very amicably in the sweet-scented evening; and the moral with which the Tinker dismissed the subject was, that he said in his trade that metal that rotted for want of use, had better be left to rot, and couldn't rot too soon, considering how much true metal rotted from over-use and hard service.

Footnotes:

{1} Dickens didn't write chapters 2 to 5 and they are omitted in this edition.

Charles Dickens

Charles John Huffam Dickens (/ˈtʃɑrlz ˈdɪkɪnz/; 7 February 1812 – 9 June 1870) was an English writer and social critic. He created some of the world's best-known fictional characters and is regarded as the greatest novelist of the Victorian era.[1] His works enjoyed unprecedented popularity during his lifetime, and by the twentieth century critics and scholars had recognised him as a literary genius. His novels and short stories enjoy lasting popularity.[2][3]

Born in Portsmouth, Dickens left school to work in a factory when his father was incarcerated in a debtors' prison. Despite his lack of formal education, he edited a weekly journal for 20 years, wrote 15 novels, five novellas, hundreds of short stories and non-fiction articles, lectured and performed extensively, was an indefatigable letter writer, and campaigned vigorously for children's rights, education, and other social reforms.

Dickens's literary success began with the 1836 serial publication of The Pickwick Papers. Within a few years he had become an international literary celebrity, famous for his humour, satire, and keen observation of character and society. His novels, most published in monthly or weekly instalments, pioneered the serial publication of narrative fiction, which became the dominant Victorian mode for novel publication.[4][5] The instalment format allowed Dickens to evaluate his audience's reaction, and he often modified his plot and character development based on such feedback.[5] For example, when his wife's chiropodist expressed distress at the way Miss Mowcher in David Copperfield seemed to reflect her disabilities, Dickens improved the character with positive features.[6] His plots were carefully constructed, and he often wove elements from topical events into his narratives.[7] Masses of the illiterate poor chipped in ha'pennies to have each new monthly episode read to them, opening up and inspiring a new class of readers.[8]

Dickens was regarded as the literary colossus of his age.[9] His 1843 novella, A Christmas Carol, remains popular and continues to inspire adaptations in every artistic genre. Oliver Twist and Great Expectations are also frequently adapted, and, like many of his novels, evoke images of early Victorian London. His 1859 novel, A Tale of Two Cities, set in London and Paris, is his best-known work of historical fiction. Dickens's creative genius has been praised by fellow writers—from Leo Tolstoy to George Orwell and G. K. Chesterton—for its realism, comedy, prose style, unique characterisations, and social criticism. On the other hand, Oscar Wilde, Henry James, and Virginia Woolf complained of a lack of psychological depth, loose writing, and a vein of saccharine sentimentalism. The term Dickensian is used to describe something that is reminiscent of Dickens and his writings, such as poor social conditions or comically repulsive characters.[10]

Early years

Charles John Huffam Dickens was born on 7 February 1812, at 1 Mile End Terrace (now 393 Commercial Road), Landport in Portsea Island (Portsmouth), the second of eight children of John Dickens (1785–1851) and Elizabeth Dickens (née Barrow; 1789–1863). His father was a clerk in the Navy Pay Office and was temporarily stationed in the district. He asked Christopher Huffam,[12] rigger to His Majesty's Navy, gentleman, and head of an established firm, to act as godfather to Charles. Huffam is thought to be the inspiration for Paul Dombey, the owner of a shipping company in Dickens's eponymous Dombey and Son (1848).[12]

In January 1815 John Dickens was called back to London, and the family moved to Norfolk Street, Fitzrovia.[13] When Charles was four, they relocated to Sheerness, and thence to Chatham, Kent, where he spent his formative years until the age of 11. His early life seems to have been idyllic, though he thought himself a "very small and not-over-particularly-taken-care-of boy".[14]

Charles spent time outdoors but also read voraciously, including the picaresque novels of Tobias Smollett and Henry Fielding, as well as Robinson Crusoe and Gil Blas. He read and reread The Arabian Nights and the Collected Farces of Elizabeth Inchbald.[15] He retained poignant memories of childhood, helped by an excellent memory of people and events, which he used in his writing.[16] His father's brief work as a clerk in the Navy Pay Office afforded him a few years of private education, first at a dame school, and then at a school run by William Giles, a dissenter, in Chatham.[17]

This period came to an end in June 1822, when John Dickens was recalled to Navy Pay Office headquarters at Somerset House, and the family—minus Charles, who stayed behind to finish his final term of work—moved to Camden Town in London.[19] The family had left Kent amidst rapidly mounting debts, and, living beyond his means,[20] John Dickens was forced by his creditors into the Marshalsea debtors' prison in Southwark, London in 1824. His wife and youngest children joined him there, as was the practice at the time. Charles, then 12 years old, boarded with Elizabeth Roylance, a family friend, at 112 College Place, Camden Town.[21] Roylance was "a reduced [impoverished] old lady, long known to our family", whom Dickens later immortalised, "with a few alterations and embellishments", as "Mrs. Pipchin" in Dombey and Son. Later, he lived in a back-attic in the house of an agent for the Insolvent Court, Archibald Russell, "a fat, good-natured, kind old gentleman... with a quiet old wife" and lame son, in Lant Street in Southwark.[22] They provided the inspiration for the Garlands in The Old Curiosity Shop.[23]

On Sundays—with his sister Frances, free from her studies at the Royal Academy of Music—he spent the day at the Marshalsea.[24] Dickens later used the prison as a setting in Little Dorrit. To pay for his board and to help his family, Dickens was forced to leave school and work ten-hour days at Warren's Blacking Warehouse, on Hungerford Stairs, near the present Charing Cross railway station, where he earned six shillings a week pasting labels on pots of boot blacking. The strenuous and often harsh working conditions made a lasting impression on Dickens and later influenced his fiction and essays, becoming the foundation of his interest in the reform of socio-economic and labour conditions, the rigours of which he believed were unfairly borne by the poor. He later wrote that he wondered "how I could have been so easily cast away at such an age".[25] As he recalled to John Forster (from The Life of Charles Dickens):

The blacking-warehouse was the last house on the left-hand side of the way, at old Hungerford Stairs. It was a crazy, tumble-down old house, abutting of course on the river, and literally overrun with rats. Its wainscoted rooms, and its rotten floors and staircase, and the old grey rats swarming down in the cellars, and the sound of their squeaking and scuffling coming up the stairs at all times, and the dirt and decay of the place, rise up visibly before me, as if I were there again. The counting-house was on the first floor, looking over the coal-barges and the river. There was a recess in it, in which I was to sit and work. My work was to cover the pots of paste-blacking; first with a piece of oil-paper, and then with a piece of blue paper; to tie them round with a string; and then to clip the paper close and neat, all round, until it looked as smart as a pot of ointment from an apothecary's shop. When a certain number of grosses of pots had attained this pitch of perfection, I was to paste on each a printed label, and then go on again with more pots. Two or three other boys were kept at similar duty down-stairs on similar wages. One of them came up, in a ragged apron and a paper cap, on the first Monday morning, to show me the trick of using the string and tying the knot. His name was Bob Fagin; and I took the liberty of using his name, long afterwards, in Oliver Twist.[25]

When the warehouse was moved to Chandos Street in the smart, busy district of Covent Garden the boys worked in a room in which the window gave onto the street and little audiences gathered and watched them at work—in Dickens biographer Simon Callow's estimation, the public display was "a new refinement added to his misery".[26]

The Marshalsea around 1897, after it had closed
A few months after his imprisonment, John Dickens' paternal grandmother, Elizabeth Dickens, died and bequeathed him £450. On the expectation of this legacy, Dickens was released from prison. Under the Insolvent Debtors Act, Dickens arranged for payment of his creditors, and he and his family left Marshalsea,[27] for the home of Mrs Roylance.

Charles's mother, Elizabeth Dickens, did not immediately support his removal from the boot-blacking warehouse. This influenced Dickens' view that a father should rule the family, and a mother find her proper sphere inside the home: "I never afterwards forgot, I never shall forget, I never can forget, that my mother was warm for my being sent back". His mother's failure to request his return was a factor in his dissatisfied attitude towards women.[28]

Righteous indignation stemming from his own situation and the conditions under which working-class people lived became major themes of his works, and it was this unhappy period in his youth to which he alluded in his favourite, and most autobiographical, novel, David Copperfield:[29] "I had no advice, no counsel, no encouragement, no consolation, no assistance, no support, of any kind, from anyone, that I can call to mind, as I hope to go to heaven!"[30]

Dickens was eventually sent to the Wellington House Academy in Camden Town, where he remained until March 1827, having spent about two years there. He did not consider it to be a good school: "Much of the haphazard, desultory teaching, poor discipline punctuated by the headmaster's sadistic brutality, the seedy ushers and general run-down atmosphere, are embodied in Mr. Creakle's Establishment in David Copperfield."[30]

Dickens worked at the law office of Ellis and Blackmore, attorneys, of Holborn Court, Gray's Inn, as a junior clerk from May 1827 to November 1828. He was a gifted mimic and impersonated those around him: clients, lawyers, and clerks. He went to theatres obsessively—he claimed that for at least three years he went to the theatre every single day. His favourite actor was Charles Mathews, and Dickens learnt his monopolylogues, (farces in which Mathews played every character), by heart.[31] Then, having learned Gurney's system of shorthand in his spare time, he left to become a freelance reporter. A distant relative, Thomas Charlton, was a freelance reporter at Doctors' Commons, and Dickens was able to share his box there to report the legal proceedings for nearly four years.[32][33] This education was to inform works such as Nicholas Nickleby, Dombey and Son, and especially Bleak House—whose vivid portrayal of the machinations and bureaucracy of the legal system did much to enlighten the general public and served as a vehicle for dissemination of Dickens's own views regarding, particularly, the heavy burden on the poor who were forced by circumstances to "go to law".

In 1830, Dickens met his first love, Maria Beadnell, thought to have been the model for the character Dora in David Copperfield. Maria's parents disapproved of the courtship and ended the relationship by sending her to school in Paris.[34]

Journalism and early novels

In 1832, at age 20, Dickens was energetic and increasingly self-confident.[35] He enjoyed mimicry and popular entertainment, lacked a clear, specific sense of what he wanted to become, and yet knew he wanted fame. Drawn to the theatre—he became an early member of the Garrick[36]—he landed an acting audition at Covent Garden, where the manager George Bartley and the actor Charles Kemble were to see him. Dickens prepared meticulously and decided to imitate the comedian Charles Mathews, but ultimately he missed the audition because of a cold. Before another opportunity arose, he had set out on his career as a writer.[37] In 1833 he submitted his first story, "A Dinner at Poplar Walk", to the London periodical Monthly Magazine.[38] William Barrow, a brother of his mother, offered him a job on The Mirror of Parliament and he worked in the House of Commons for the first time early in 1832. He rented rooms at Furnival's Inn and worked as a political journalist, reporting on Parliamentary debates, and he travelled across Britain to cover election campaigns for the Morning Chronicle. His journalism, in the form of sketches in periodicals, formed his first collection of pieces, published in 1836: Sketches by Boz—Boz being a family nickname he employed as a pseudonym for some years.[39][40] Dickens apparently adopted it from the nickname "Moses", which he had given to his youngest brother Augustus Dickens, after a character in Oliver Goldsmith's The Vicar of Wakefield. When pronounced by anyone with a head cold, "Moses" became "Boses"—later shortened to Boz.[40][41] Dickens's own name was considered "queer" by a contemporary critic, who wrote in 1849: "Mr Dickens, as if in revenge for his own queer name, does bestow still queerer ones upon his fictitious creations." He contributed to and edited journals throughout his literary career.[38] In January 1835 the Morning Chronicle launched an evening edition, under the editorship of the Chronicle's music critic, George Hogarth. Hogarth invited Dickens to contribute Street Sketches and Dickens became a regular visitor to his Fulham house, excited by Hogarth's friendship with a hero of his, Walter

Scott, and enjoying the company of Hogarth's three daughters—Georgina, Mary, and nineteen-year-old Catherine.[42]

Catherine Hogarth Dickens by Samuel Lawrence (1838)
Dickens made rapid progress both professionally and socially. He began a friendship with William Harrison Ainsworth, the author of the highwayman novel Rookwood (1834), whose bachelor salon in Harrow Road had become the meeting place for a set that included Daniel Maclise, Benjamin Disraeli, Edward Bulwer-Lytton, and George Cruikshank. All these became his friends and collaborators, with the exception of Disraeli, and he met his first publisher, John Macrone, at the house.[43] The success of Sketches by Boz led to a proposal from publishers Chapman and Hall for Dickens to supply text to match Robert Seymour's engraved illustrations in a monthly letterpress. Seymour committed suicide after the second instalment, and Dickens, who wanted to write a connected series of sketches, hired "Phiz" to provide the engravings (which were reduced from four to two per instalment) for the story. The resulting story became The Pickwick Papers, and though the first few episodes were not successful, the introduction of the Cockney character Sam Weller in the fourth episode (the first to be illustrated by Phiz) marked a sharp climb in its popularity.[44] The final instalment sold 40,000 copies.[38]

In November 1836 Dickens accepted the position of editor of Bentley's Miscellany, a position he held for three years, until he fell out with the owner.[45] In 1836 as he finished the last instalments of The Pickwick Papers, he began writing the beginning instalments of Oliver Twist—writing as many as 90 pages a month—while continuing work on Bentley's and also writing four plays, the production of which he oversaw. Oliver Twist, published in 1838, became one of Dickens's better known stories, and was the first Victorian novel with a child protagonist.[46]

Young Charles Dickens by Daniel Maclise (1839)
On 2 April 1836, after a one-year engagement, and between episodes two and three of The Pickwick Papers, Dickens married Catherine Thomson Hogarth (1816–1879), the daughter of George Hogarth, editor of the Evening Chronicle.[47] After a brief honeymoon in Chalk in Kent the couple returned to lodgings at Furnival's Inn.[48] The first of their ten children, Charley, was born in January 1837, and a few months later the family set up home in Bloomsbury at 48 Doughty Street, London, (on which Charles had a three-

year lease at £80 a year) from 25 March 1837 until December 1839.[47][49] Dickens's younger brother Frederick and Catherine's 17-year-old sister Mary, moved in with them. Dickens became very attached to Mary, and she died in his arms after a brief illness in 1837. Unusually for Dickens, as a consequence of his shock, he stopped working, and he and Kate stayed at a little farm on Hampstead Heath for a fortnight. Dickens idealised Mary,- the character he fashioned after her, Rose Maylie, he found he could not now kill, as he had planned, in his fiction[50] and according to Ackroyd he drew on memories of her for his later descriptions of Little Nell and Florence Dombey.[51] His grief was so great that he was unable to meet the deadline for the June instalment of Pickwick Papers and had to cancel the Oliver Twist instalment that month as well.[46] The time in Hampstead was the occasion for a growing bond between Dickens and John Forster to develop and Forster soon became his unofficial business manager, and the first to read his work.[52]

Barnaby Rudge was Dickens's first popular failure—but the character of Dolly Varden, "pretty, witty, sexy, became central to numerous theatrical adaptations"[53]
His success as a novelist continued. The young Queen Victoria read both Oliver Twist and Pickwick, staying up until midnight to discuss them.[54] Nicholas Nickleby (1838–39), The Old Curiosity Shop and, finally, his first historical novel, Barnaby Rudge: A Tale of the Riots of 'Eighty, as part of the Master Humphrey's Clock series (1840–41), were all published in monthly instalments before being made into books.[55]

In the midst of all his activity during this period there was discontent with his publishers and John Macrone was bought off, while Richard Bentley signed over all his rights in Oliver Twist. Other illustrations of a certain restlessness and discontent emerge—in Broadstairs he flirted with Eleanor Picken, the young fiancée of his solicitor's best friend, and one night grabbed her and ran with her down to the sea. He declared they were both to drown there in the "sad sea waves". She finally got free but afterwards kept her distance. In June 1841 he precipitately set out on a two-month tour of Scotland and then, in September 1841, telegraphed Forster that he had decided to go to America.[56] Master Humphrey's Clock was shut down, though Dickens was still keen on the idea of the weekly magazine, a form he liked, a liking that had begun with his childhood reading of the eighteenth-century magazines Tatler and The Spectator.

First visit to the United States

In 1842, Dickens and his wife made their first trip to the United States and Canada. At this time Georgina Hogarth, another sister of Catherine, joined the Dickens household, now living at Devonshire Terrace, Marylebone, to care for the young family they had left behind.[57] She remained with them as housekeeper, organiser, adviser, and friend until Dickens's death in 1870.[58]

Sketch of Dickens in 1842 during American Tour. Sketch of Dickens's sister Fanny, bottom left
He described his impressions in a travelogue, American Notes for General Circulation. Dickens includes in Notes a powerful condemnation of slavery, which he had attacked as early as The Pickwick Papers, correlating the emancipation of the poor in England with the abolition of slavery abroad[59] citing newspaper accounts of runaway slaves disfigured by their masters. From Richmond, Virginia Dickens returned to Washington, D.C. and started a trek westward to St. Louis. While there, he expressed a desire to see an American prairie before returning east. A group of 13 men then set out with Dickens to visit Looking Glass Prairie, a trip 30 miles into Illinois.

During his visit, Dickens spent a month in New York City, giving lectures, raising the question of international copyright laws and the pirating of his work in America.[60][61] He persuaded a group of twenty-five writers, headed by Washington Irving, to sign a petition for him to take to Congress, but the press were generally hostile to this, saying that he should be grateful for his popularity and that it was mercenary to complain about his work being pirated.[62]

The popularity he gained caused a shift in his self-perception according to critic Kate Flint, who writes the he "found himself a cultural commodity, and its circulation had passed out his control", causing him to become interested in and delve into themes of public and personal personas in the next novels.[63] She writes that he assumed a role of "influential commentator", publicly and in his fiction, evident in his next few books.[63]

Soon after his return to England, Dickens began work on the first of his Christmas stories, A Christmas Carol, written in 1843, which was followed by

The Chimes in 1844 and The Cricket on the Hearth in 1845. Of these, A Christmas Carol was most popular and, tapping into an old tradition, did much to promote a renewed enthusiasm for the joys of Christmas in Britain and America.[64] The seeds for the story became planted in Dickens's mind during a trip to Manchester to witness the conditions of the manufacturing workers there. This, along with scenes he had recently witnessed at the Field Lane Ragged School, caused Dickens to resolve to "strike a sledge hammer blow" for the poor. As the idea for the story took shape and the writing began in earnest, Dickens became engrossed in the book. He later wrote that as the tale unfolded he "wept and laughed, and wept again" as he "walked about the black streets of London fifteen or twenty miles many a night when all sober folks had gone to bed."[65]

After living briefly in Italy (1844), Dickens travelled to Switzerland (1846), where he began work on Dombey and Son (1846–48). This and David Copperfield (1849–50) mark a significant artistic break in Dickens's career as his novels became more serious in theme and more carefully planned than his early works.

Philanthropy

In May 1846 Angela Burdett Coutts, heir to the Coutts banking fortune, approached Dickens about setting up a home for the redemption of fallen women of the working class. Coutts envisioned a home that would replace the punitive regimes of existing institutions with a reformative environment conducive to education and proficiency in domestic household chores. After initially resisting, Dickens eventually founded the home, named "Urania Cottage", in the Lime Grove section of Shepherds Bush, which he managed for ten years,[66] setting the house rules, reviewing the accounts and interviewing prospective residents.[67] Emigration and marriage were central to Dickens's agenda for the women on leaving Urania Cottage, from which it is estimated that about 100 women graduated between 1847 and 1859.[68]

Religious views

As a young man Dickens expressed a distaste for certain aspects of organized religion. In 1836, in a pamphlet titled Sunday Under Three Heads, he defended the people's right to pleasure, opposing a plan to prohibit games on

Sundays. "Look into your churches- diminished congregations and scanty attendance. People have grown sullen and obstinate, and are becoming disgusted with the faith which condemns them to such a day as this, once in every seven. They display their feeling by staying away [from church]. Turn into the streets [on a Sunday] and mark the rigid gloom that reigns over everything around"[69]

Dickens honoured the figure of Christ —though he denied his divinity.[70] Notwithstanding, Dickens has been characterized as a professing Christian.[71] His son Henry Fielding Dickens described Dickens as someone who "possessed deep religious convictions". Though in the early 1840s Dickens had showed an interest in Unitarian Christianity, the writer Gary Colledge has asserted that he 'never strayed from his attachment to popular lay Anglicanism.'[72] He also wrote a religious work called The Life of Our Lord (1849), which was a short book about the life of Jesus Christ, written with the purpose of inculcating his faith to his children and family.[73][74]

Dickens disapproved of Roman Catholicism and 19th-century evangelicalism, and was critical of what he saw as the hypocrisy of religious institutions and philosophies like spiritualism, all of which he considered deviations from the true spirit of Christianity.[75] Leo Tolstoy and Fyodor Dostoyevsky referred to Dickens as "that great Christian writer".[76][77]

Middle years

"Little Dorrit" 1856
In late November 1851, Dickens moved into Tavistock House where he wrote Bleak House (1852–53), Hard Times (1854) and Little Dorrit (1856).[78] It was here that he indulged in the amateur theatricals described in Forster's "Life".[79] During this period he worked closely with the novelist and playwright Wilkie Collins. In 1856, his income from writing allowed him to buy Gad's Hill Place in Higham, Kent. As a child, Dickens had walked past the house and dreamed of living in it. The area was also the scene of some of the events of Shakespeare's Henry IV, Part 1, and this literary connection pleased him.[80]

Ellen Ternan, 1858
In 1857, Dickens hired professional actresses for the play The Frozen Deep,

written by him and his protégé, Wilkie Collins. Dickens fell deeply in love with one of the actresses, Ellen Ternan, and this passion was to last the rest of his life.[81] Dickens was 45 and Ternan 18 when he made the decision, which went strongly against Victorian convention, to separate from his wife, Catherine, in 1858—divorce was still unthinkable for someone as famous as he was. When Catherine left, never to see her husband again, she took with her one child, leaving the other children to be raised by her sister Georgina who chose to stay at Gad's Hill.[58]

During this period, whilst pondering a project to give public readings for his own profit, Dickens was approached through a charitable appeal by Great Ormond Street Hospital, to help it survive its first major financial crisis. His 'Drooping Buds' essay in Household Words earlier in 3 April 1852 was considered by the hospital's founders to have been the catalyst for the hospital's success.[82] Dickens, whose philanthropy was well-known, was asked by his friend, the hospital's founder Charles West, to preside over the appeal, and he threw himself into the task, heart and soul.[83] Dickens's public readings secured sufficient funds for an endowment to put the hospital on a sound financial footing—one reading on 9 February 1858 alone raised £3,000.[84][85][86]

After separating from Catherine,[87] Dickens undertook a series of hugely popular and remunerative reading tours which, together with his journalism, were to absorb most of his creative energies for the next decade, in which he was to write only two more novels.[88] His first reading tour, lasting from April 1858 to February 1859, consisted of 129 appearances in 49 different towns throughout England, Scotland and Ireland.[89] Dickens's continued fascination with the theatrical world was written into the theatre scenes in Nicholas Nickleby, but more importantly he found an outlet in public readings. In 1866, he undertook a series of public readings in England and Scotland, with more the following year in England and Ireland.

At his desk in 1858
Major works soon followed, including A Tale of Two Cities (1859) and Great Expectations (1861), which were resounding successes. During this time he was also the publisher, editor, and a major contributor to the journals Household Words (1850–1859) and All the Year Round (1858–1870).[90]

In early September 1860, in a field behind Gad's Hill, Dickens made a bonfire of most of his correspondence—only those letters on business matters were spared. Since Ellen Ternan also destroyed all of his letters to her,[91] the extent of the affair between the two remains speculative.[92] In the 1930s, Thomas Wright recounted that Ternan had unburdened herself with a Canon Benham, and gave currency to rumours they had been lovers.[93] That the two had a son who died in infancy was alleged by Dickens's daughter, Kate Perugini, whom Gladys Storey had interviewed before her death in 1929. Storey published her account in Dickens and Daughter,[94][95] but no contemporary evidence exists. On his death, Dickens settled an annuity on Ternan which made her a financially independent woman. Claire Tomalin's book, The Invisible Woman, argues that Ternan lived with Dickens secretly for the last 13 years of his life. The book was subsequently turned into a play, Little Nell, by Simon Gray, and a 2013 film.

In the same period, Dickens furthered his interest in the paranormal, becoming one of the early members of The Ghost Club.[96]

In June 1862 he was offered £10,000 for a reading tour of Australia.[97] He was enthusiastic, and even planned a travel book, The Uncommercial Traveller Upside Down, but ultimately decided against the tour.[98] Two of his sons— Alfred D'Orsay Tennyson Dickens and Edward Bulwer Lytton Dickens—migrated to Australia, Edward becoming a member of the Parliament of New South Wales as Member for Wilcannia 1889–94.[99][100]

Last years

After the Staplehurst rail crash
On 9 June 1865, while returning from Paris with Ellen Ternan, Dickens was involved in the Staplehurst rail crash. The train's first seven carriages plunged off a cast iron bridge that was under repair. The only first-class carriage to remain on the track was the one in which Dickens was travelling. Before rescuers arrived, Dickens tended and comforted the wounded and the dying with a flask of brandy and a hat refreshed with water, and saved some lives. Before leaving, he remembered the unfinished manuscript for Our Mutual Friend, and he returned to his carriage to retrieve it.[101] Dickens later used this experience as material for his short ghost story, "The Signal-Man", in which the central character has a premonition of his own death in a rail crash.

He also based the story on several previous rail accidents, such as the Clayton Tunnel rail crash of 1861. Dickens managed to avoid an appearance at the inquest to avoid disclosing that he had been travelling with Ternan and her mother, which would have caused a scandal.[102]

Second visit to the United States

In the late 1850s Dickens began to contemplate a second visit to the United States, tempted by the money that he believed he could make by extending his reading tour there. The outbreak of the Civil War in America in 1861 delayed his plans. Over two years after the war, Dickens set sail from Liverpool on 9 November 1867 for his second American reading tour. Landing at Boston, he devoted the rest of the month to a round of dinners with such notables as Ralph Waldo Emerson, Henry Wadsworth Longfellow and his American publisher James Thomas Fields. In early December, the readings began. He performed 76 readings, netting £19,000, from December 1867 to April 1868.[103] Dickens shuttled between Boston and New York, where he gave 22 readings at Steinway Hall. Although he had started to suffer from what he called the "true American catarrh", he kept to a schedule that would have challenged a much younger man, even managing to squeeze in some sleighing in Central Park.

Poster promoting a reading by Dickens in Nottingham dated 4 February 1869, two months before he suffered a mild stroke
During his travels, he saw a significant change in the people and the circumstances of America. His final appearance was at a banquet the American Press held in his honour at Delmonico's on 18 April, when he promised never to denounce America again. By the end of the tour, the author could hardly manage solid food, subsisting on champagne and eggs beaten in sherry. On 23 April, he boarded his ship to return to Britain, barely escaping a Federal Tax Lien against the proceeds of his lecture tour.[104]

Farewell readings

Between 1868 and 1869, Dickens gave a series of "farewell readings" in England, Scotland, and Ireland, beginning on 6 October. He managed, of a contracted 100 readings, to deliver 75 in the provinces, with a further 12 in London.[103] As he pressed on he was affected by giddiness and fits of paralysis and collapsed on 22 April 1869, at Preston in Lancashire, and on doctor's advice, the tour was cancelled.[105] After further provincial readings were cancelled, he began work on his final novel, The Mystery of Edwin Drood. It was fashionable in the 1860s to 'do the slums' and, in company, Dickens visited opium dens in Shadwell, where he witnessed an elderly addict known as "Laskar Sal", who formed the model for the "Opium Sal" subsequently featured in his mystery novel, Edwin Drood.[106]

After Dickens had regained sufficient strength, he arranged, with medical approval, for a final series of readings to partially make up to his sponsors what they had lost due to his illness. There were to be 12 performances, running between 11 January and 15 March 1870, the last at 8:00 pm at St. James's Hall in London. Although in grave health by this time, he read A Christmas Carol and The Trial from Pickwick. On 2 May, he made his last public appearance at a Royal Academy Banquet in the presence of the Prince and Princess of Wales, paying a special tribute on the death of his friend, the illustrator Daniel Maclise.[107]

Death

Samuel Luke Fildes—The Empty Chair. Fildes was illustrating "Edwin Drood" at the time of Charles Dickens's death. The engraving shows Dickens's empty chair in his study at Gads Hill Place. It appeared in the Christmas 1870 edition of the The Graphic and thousands of prints of it were sold.[108]

21326488R00130

Printed in Great Britain
by Amazon